T0364659

UJJIVAN

UJJIVAN

Transforming with Technology

SUBIR ROY

OXFORD
UNIVERSITY PRESS

OXFORD
UNIVERSITY PRESS

Oxford University Press is a department of the University of Oxford.
It furthers the University's objective of excellence in research, scholarship,
and education by publishing worldwide. Oxford is a registered trademark of
Oxford University Press in the UK and in certain other countries.

Published in India by
Oxford University Press
2/11 Ground Floor, Ansari Road, Daryaganj, New Delhi 110 002, India

© Subir Roy 2018

The moral rights of the author have been asserted.

First Edition published in 2018

All rights reserved. No part of this publication may be reproduced, stored in
a retrieval system, or transmitted, in any form or by any means, without the
prior permission in writing of Oxford University Press, or as expressly permitted
by law, by licence, or under terms agreed with the appropriate reprographics
rights organization. Enquiries concerning reproduction outside the scope of the
above should be sent to the Rights Department, Oxford University Press, at the
address above.

You must not circulate this work in any other form
and you must impose this same condition on any acquirer.

ISBN-13 (print edition): 978-0-19-948298-6
ISBN-10 (print edition): 0-19-948298-5

ISBN-13 (eBook): 978-0-19-909526-1
ISBN-10 (eBook): 0-19-909526-4

All financial data for Ujjivan has been provided by the institution itself.
Photographs courtesy of Ujjivan

Typeset in Arno Pro 10.5/15
by Tranistics Data Technologies, Kolkata 700 091
Printed in India by Replika Press Pvt. Ltd

To Ujjivan's Borrowers

Contents

Abbreviations

AKMI	Association of Karnataka Microfinance Institutions
AUM	Assets under Management
BIC	Business Innovation Centre, Indonesia
BRAC	Building Resources across Communities, Bangladesh
BRI	Bank Rakyat Indonesia
DFID	Department for International Development, UK
EKYC	Electronic Know Your Customer
FWWB	Friends of Women's World Banking, India
IRDP	Integrated Rural Development Programme
Ispirt	Indian Software Product Industry Roundtable
KYC	Know Your Customer
MFI	Microfinance Institution
MFIN	Microfinance Institutions Network
MYRADA	Mysore Rehabilitation and Development Agency
NABARD	National Bank for Agriculture and Rural Development
NBFC	Non-Banking Financial Company
PRADAN	Professional Assistance for Development Action
RBI	Reserve Bank of India
SEBI	Securities and Exchange Board of India
SEWA	Self Employed Women's Association
SFB	Small Finance Bank
SHG	Self-Help Group

SFMC	SIDBI Foundation for Microcredit
SIDBI	Small Industries Development Bank of India
SRO	Self-Regulatory Organization
UPMA	Uttar Pradesh Microfinance Association

Foreword

Organized microfinance in India, and for that matter in the rest of the world, is relatively new. But it has had a stormy history. We all know that finance of any kind, big or small, invariably attracts state and political attention. It is one of those businesses that can never really remain under the radar. Nobel laureate Muhammad Yunus, the eminent guru of microfinance, has had his run-ins with the political establishment in his home country of Bangladesh. The war stories in India are even more abundant and colourful.

While writing the short, but eventful history of Ujjivan, a Bengaluru-headquartered microfinance institution, which has now become a small finance bank, Subir Roy has also woven in the border history of the sector. The evolution of the sector from being a do-good NGO to a profit-making commercially viable sector is well catalogued. The fact that without this change, scaling up and sustainable growth would not have been possible has been analysed and explained lucidly. But commercial profitability can, and should, never be an obsession in any business. It is an important discipline, because in its absence viability and growth are impacted. In other words, while it sets the working boundaries of the organization, it cannot be the driving impetus of any successful human organization. Ujjivan's story is a salutary lesson for all entrepreneurs and businesspersons. It has pursued customer delight and employee satisfaction as primary drivers rather than loan volumes or profits, which have, of course, followed—and guess what, they have been pretty impressive at that. Whether Ujjivan has been lucky or blessed with a consciously wise management, I leave to the reader to judge.

Ujjivan stayed away from Andhra Pradesh, which, at a point in time, had sizzling rates of growth. These seductive growth rates resulted in multiple players making available probably more loan funds than the market could naturally absorb. It also resulted in political and bureaucratic entrepreneurs taking an unusual—and unhealthy—interest in the sector. A mini-crash and a host of strangulating laws and regulations followed. The industry in that state has yet to fully recover from that episode. Ujjivan otherwise has an impressive national footprint. More importantly, in a short time, the organization has managed to create a cadre of employees across a large and diverse physical region who subscribe to similar values and work ethic. Finance has been and always will remain a service industry. It is not about selling products, but about building, developing, nurturing, and occasionally disengaging from customer relationships. While by no means being a technology laggard, Ujjivan's focus has all along been on motivating its employees to develop that special connect with customers and, to paraphrase Abraham Lincoln, creating an organization of customers and for customers.

Jaithirth Rao

Author's Note

The following people have been interviewed during 2015 and 2016 for the purpose of researching this book. Wherever they speak of the present, it should be seen to mean the situation prevailing during 2015 and 2016.

Kumdha

Alagarsamy A.P.

Deepak Ayare

Pradeep B.

Arunava Banerjee

Vibhas Chandra

Ittira Davis

Aloysius Fernandez

Carol Furtado

Premkumar G.

Samit Ghosh

Nipun Goel

Anal Jain

V. Jaya Sankar

Manish Kumar Raj

Vijay Mahajan

Brij Mohan

Partha Mandal

Martin Pampilly

K.R. Ramamoorthy

Hiren Shah

Vikram Shingade

Rajat Singh

M.S. Sriram

S. Subramanian

Sneh Thakur

S. Viswanatha Prasad

Jolly Zachariah

1

Introduction and Overview

In the world of start-ups, a unicorn is a firm which is valued at over USD 1 billion, indicating enormous confidence on the part of investors in the firm well before it has fully arrived. By this token, Ujjivan Financial Services is aspiring to that exalted status and not quite there. Its market capitalization (in late 2017) is well short of the magic figure. But it has a lot going for itself. It embodies many innovative ideas and pursues them with some of the latest available technology. More importantly, a unicorn is a mythical animal, a part of both the worlds of nature and dreams, a symbol of humanity's longings. By that measure, Ujjivan can be considered a unicorn in the world of microfinance—embodying both business and technological innovations in pursuit of a dream that often seems unattainable—ridding India of its poverty.

Microfinance is all about lending small amounts of money to large numbers of poor people, sans security, so that they can raise their income levels, thereby taking that first step out of poverty. In the last decade, from around 2005 to 2006—when leading microfinance institutions (MFIs) of the time converted themselves into non-banking financial companies (NBFCs)—microfinance in India has seen both phenomenal growth and dramatic downs. This is also the story of Ujjivan, which has grown from nothing to an industry leader and—this is the great differentiator—avoided many of the pitfalls affecting most major industry players.

According to the Bharat Microfinance Report 2016, the sector ended FY 2016 with total outstanding credit of Rs 63,853 crore to almost 40 million people. Within this, the MFIs carrying the can for the sector under the supervision of the Reserve Bank of India (RBI), categorized as NBFC–MFIs, account for 88 per cent of the lending.

Where Ujjivan stands can be gauged from its rank among the top ten under various parameters. According to 2015–16 figures, it has the largest reach in terms of geography, being present in 24 states and union territories. Janalakshmi, the MFI that follows Ujjivan, lags way behind, with a presence in 18 states. The big change is that Bandhan, which was running a close second in 2015 with a presence in 22 states, has dropped out of the microfinance league table, having transformed into a universal bank in the meantime. SKS Microfinance (now Bharat Finance Inclusion Limited), which was big in Andhra Pradesh once before being severely bruised in the 2010 crisis that struck the sector there, remains in the third position. But Ujjivan falls to fifth place when it comes to branch network, that is, the total number of branches. SKS leads the pack with 1,191 branches against Ujjivan's 469. In client outreach, Ujjivan is fourth with 3.3 million customers, whereas SKS leads with 4.6 million. In keeping with this, Ujjivan is number three in terms of its gross loan portfolio, at Rs 5,389 crore, with Janalakshmi in the lead with Rs 10,983 crore and SKS second with Rs 7,682 crore. But rankings in the last two years are not really comparable, as on most parameters, the number one company, Bandhan, has exited, allowing SKS Microfinance to take its place.

The year 2015 was, in many ways, a game changer for the microfinance sector, in that it came of age by gaining official acceptance and recognition. During the year, not only did Bandhan secure the universal banking licence, the RBI issued licences for small finance and payments banks. Of the 10 small-finance bank licences issued, eight went to MFIs, Ujjivan being one of them.

To become a small-finance bank (SFB) is going most of the way to become a bank, as this opens the door to becoming eligible to accept deposits. This enables MFI-turned-SFBs to access relatively low-cost deposits which can replace high-cost bank loans—the main source of funding for MFIs. Being able to accept deposits will let MFI-turned-SFBs secure the same regulatory treatment as Mohammad Yunus's Grameen Bank in Bangladesh, that great pioneer on the subcontinent when it comes to lending to the poor. Reflecting the mood while being at the cusp of change, Samit Ghosh, managing director and chief executive officer of Ujjivan, says, 'There are exciting times ahead. Put on your seat belts and enjoy the ride.'

This book is a history of Ujjivan, beginning with the early formative years from late 2004, covering in detail the years from 2006 to 2017—from the end of its pilot phase till the present times. It seeks to capture a story of dramatic growth that did not lose sight of stability. But to understand what has driven Ujjivan, it is necessary to look at it in the right context, and consider the entire microfinance space, both in terms of dry numbers and the remembered stories of the major players. We also look analytically at the factors which made this possible. Thereafter, we recount how Ujjivan prepared to become an SFB. Finally, we gaze a bit into the crystal ball and query—what lies beyond microfinance on the road to the end of poverty? Almost finally, as in the nature of a footnote, there is a chapter describing the tsunami that hit microfinance—demonetization.

SITUATING MICROFINANCE

We first go into a bit of history in Chapter 2. The country has a long history of government loans being given to the poor. Muhammad bin Tughluq, the sultan of Delhi in the early fourteenth century, was the first Indian ruler in recorded history to advance *taccavi* loans to villagers to rehabilitate them following a disastrous famine. The British continued this tradition, as did the Government of India which formed a committee on taccavi loans and cooperative credit in 1962. Globally, in the post-World War II era till the 1970s, donors and governments offered financial services through subsidized credit programmes for the rural poor. But these were often unable to reach them and even when they did, there were high defaults.

The modern global pioneer in microcredit can be said to be ACCION International. It was founded in 1961 by a law student Joseph Blatchford, who, with individual donations, started by building schools and water systems in the shanty towns of Caracas, Venezuela. ACCION turned to microcredit in 1973 and is today a premier microfinance organization with lending partners across Latin America, the United States of America, and Africa.

The terms 'microcredit' and 'microfinance' first began to be widely used from the late 1970s, and Muhammad Yunus and Grameen Bank did more than anyone and anything else to make microfinance both a household term and a part of a widely accepted development strategy to address poverty. In 1976, Yunus realized that the poor in Bangladesh, a country born just five years ago, were trapped in poverty for, among other reasons, lack of affordable finance. He began by lending minuscule sums to women to weave bamboo baskets. The programme's success caused it to grow and in 1983, the Bangladesh government issued an ordinance to create Grameen Bank. It pioneered the group lending joint liability programme, under which a group of women borrowers took the responsibility for one another's loans and ensured very high recovery rates.

In the 1980s, the Grameen Bank and Bank Rakyat Indonesia (BRI) helped shape a critical conceptual and institutional breakthrough. They demonstrated a way to serve small people not just on a large scale but profitably too. The 1990s were marked by an increase in the number and size of microcredit organizations. Microfinance began to be considered as an industry and the decade came to be known as the 'decade of microfinance'. In 2006 Yunus and Grameen Bank were jointly awarded the Nobel Prize for Peace, for their work in fighting poverty.

The India Story

In India, rural poverty and indebtedness have been a concern right since Independence. The Reserve Bank of India undertook the first of its decennial All-India Rural Credit Surveys when the independent nation was barely four years old, in 1951. These surveys, conducted till 1991, indicate some progress. But the next policy initiative, rapid expansion of the banking sector post the 1969 nationalization of banks, touched mostly large farmers. Thus, when microfinance made a significant beginning in the 1990s, it had a huge task laid out in front of it—reaching out to the rural poor.

It was in the 1990s that microfinance through the bank-linked self-help group (SHG) programme took off. Thereafter, MFIs proper, constituted as societies, trusts, or NBFCs came into the picture and have taken the lead in providing credit to the poor since the early 2000s. But long before microfinance took off in a big way, there were a few pioneers. In India, the origin of microfinance can be traced to the establishment of the SEWA Cooperative Bank (1974), MYRADA (1979), and PRADAN (1983).

In the early 1990s, the National Bank for Agriculture and Rural Development (NABARD) took a crucial step and launched the bank–SHG linkage, which involved SHGs taking loans from banks to lend to their members and ensuring recovery and repayment. Critically, this kept the banks out of the individual micro-loan recovery exercise and the bank–SHG model achieved very high repayment rates. In 1996, the RBI included loans to SHGs under the priority sector-lending targets that banks had to meet, giving a major boost to delivery of rural credit under the bank–SHG linked programme. This can be said to be the first large-scale microfinance programme to take off in India.

In the late 1990s, the Small Industries Development Bank (SIDBI) launched a term loan programme to create a national network of large and viable MFIs from the formal and informal sectors. Among those that grew up to size were SHARE, Spandana, and SKS Microfinance. Historically, perhaps the most successful initiative to come out of this programme is the Rs 25 lakh that was given as loan and grant to Bandhan Microfinance in 2002, which got it going.

After a promising start, microfinance experienced a period of tremendous growth in the new millennium. While the overall growth rate has been phenomenal, there have been ups and downs, coinciding with the crises experienced by the industry, notably the developments in Andhra Pradesh around 2010. Microfinance in India has run on two parallel tracks—through MFIs and bank-linked SHGs. The biggest difference between the two groups is the level of non-performing assets (NPAs). For SHGs, in 2016, these stood at 6.5 per cent, whereas for MFIs, the portfolio at risk was a mere 0.29 per cent. This would indicate that till now, the NBFC–MFIs represents the most successful and self-sustaining model for lending to the poor in India.

EXPERTS REMEMBER

In Chapter 3, we look at how experts and players remember the evolution of Indian microfinance. Vijay Mahajan, one of the industry pioneers, recalls, 'Despite bank nationalization and branch expansion, availability of credit to the rural poor remained a huge issue all through.' So NGOs which concern themselves with the poor 'tried to dabble with providing credit themselves', which is how they came into the picture—by trying to fill a bit of the credit gap. In the 1990s, when economic liberalization policies came to India and the Second Narasimham Committee on banking sector reforms effectively told banks that their first concern was their profitability and NPAs, 'the banks took that as a mandate to turn their backs on the poor. So whatever little credit was coming to the poor till 1989–90, just vanished,' says Mahajan. Nature abhors a vacuum and the result of banks—at least in their mindset—winding down their concern for the poor, created a ferment among the NGOs in the microcredit space.

In the early 1990s, three significant policy decisions were taken by the RBI and NABARD:

1. To let banks extend bulk loans to self-help affinity groups (SAGs) and allow the groups to decide on which group member to lend to.
2. To allow banks to lend to even unregistered SAGs so long as they maintained proper books of accounts and records of meetings.
3. And critically, to lend without physical collaterals. This was the basis of the SHG–bank linkage programme launched by NABARD in 1992 in which MYRADA, under the leadership of Aloysius Fernandez, played a path-breaking role.

Fortunately for India, while there were these stirrings of voluntary action at the ground level, things began to happen at the official institutional level, too. SIDBI, which was founded in 1990, realized while working with the poor that nobody was giving them small loans. Brij Mohan, who went on to become executive director of SIDBI, recalls that as a result, they ran a pilot during 1994–98, lending to NGOs to give small loans to the poor. 'Then microfinance had not arrived in India though it was very much there in Bangladesh.' After the pilot, SIDBI found NGOs were getting their money back and clients were benefitting and the business had a future. This represented a conceptual breakthrough.

Thus, SIDBI decided to set up the SIDBI Foundation for Micro Credit (SFMC) in 1999. It would borrow from SIDBI at 10 per cent and on-lend to NGOs at 11 per cent. They would have freedom on pricing as well. During 2000–07, SIDBI ran the National Microfinance Support Project. This was the beginning of the so-called microfinance movement. 'We started with some small institutions in Andhra. Those that grew up included SHARE, Spandana, SKS, and much later, Bandhan in West Bengal,' reminisces Brij Mohan.

Before the SIDBI initiative, few private interests looked at the microfinance market, says M.S. Sriram, long-term academic tracker of microfinance, because there was an unwritten taboo on interest rates. The rhetoric was the exploitative moneylender charging usurious interest rates. 'Because of the taboo on high interest rates, the private sector did not come in and the market remained as it was. All [financial assistance] was government driven, subsidy driven,' he explains.

According to Sriram, the first private phase started with bank-linked SHGs. Those who promoted SHGs declared, in all their wisdom, that interest rates could be up to the discretion of the private players, which legitimized high interest rates. When NGO MFIs were formed, in the second phase—SHARE, SKS, Spandana—they rode on the legitimacy of SHGs but also pointed out that the groups took too long to grow and required a lot of hand-holding. The new debate was more about how to provide access and scale rather than the cost. Ujjivan, Janalakshmi, and Equitas represent what is the third wave of microfinance organizations. They started as NBFCs and since they were centred on earning profits, focused on performance.

When Mahajan launched Basix in 1996, it started off as an NBFC. Basix, in that sense, was the first attempt at delivering commercial microfinance in India. In 1995 the RBI issued a guideline allowing banks to open accounts for unregistered SHGs. It appointed NABARD as the lead agency to take this model all over the country. Tamil Nadu and Andhra Pradesh took to it and supported NABARD in a big way; thus both states had lakhs of SHGs by the late 1990s—and that is where the trouble began. Andhra Pradesh was also where four or five MFIs had come up—including Basix—but more importantly, SHARE, Spandana, and SKS. This troika worked only with women, who were members of SHGs as well as the groups formed by these MFIs.

Till 2005, MFIs—with the exception of Basix—were all NGOs. But a stage came, recalls Samit Ghosh, 'when the balance sheets of NGO MFIs became so big that their lenders started getting nervous as there was no equity in the system and they were not properly regulated. So they were urged and supported by institutions like SIDBI to convert themselves into profit-making NBFCs. However, capital for these institutions could only be raised from national and international development financial institutions and some international private equity players. The microfinance industry was seen to be a close parallel to the mobile telecom industry, which was riding high in the equity markets. Microfinance too caught on as 'flavour of the month' for international private equity without a clear understanding of the risks associated with the business of servicing the most vulnerable sections of society. In order to achieve high valuations, MFIs, especially those whose founders started out as NGOs, were encouraged to ensure very high growth and profitability. This aggressive growth in business with massive customer acquisition was done blindly, without adequate credit information on customers, their debt levels, and their ability to service debt. This started a mad scramble among the MFIs in Andhra Pradesh to lend imprudently. Unfortunately, this was happening in the geography with the highest SHG density. The largest SHG programme was promoted by the government and financed by the World Bank. When the time for repayment arrived, the member women became very distraught trying to decide who to repay from their limited resources. There was pressure for repayment at weekly meetings and they took their problem to their SHG, which took it to the government employee, who amplified their complaints and took it to his bosses. This brought the government department running the programme in direct conflict with the MFIs.

Then, in August 2010, when the SKS IPO was a grand success, oversubscribed 13 times, politicians realized they were being left out. Mahajan recalls the sentiment prevailing at the time: '*Ye log to* "poor, poor" *bolte hain* but they have got thousands of crores; *lekin hamko to kuch nahi diya.* So let's teach these guys a lesson.' So politicians turned against MFIs, with the bureaucrats already put off because of the SHGs members' complaints. In a few cases, borrowers felt so harassed that it led them to commit suicide. 'That completely turned public sentiment against MFIs and the media started painting MFIs as moneylenders and sharks … *India Today* ran my photo in their Telugu edition [with the headline] "Microfinance Mafia of Andhra Pradesh". For 15 years, while one was quietly doing work, nobody came. Then suddenly within two months of the SKS IPO, all of us became villains. The deification [lionizing the microfinance sector for bringing in all the world's money] was not correct; and neither was the demonization.'

The crisis broke in October 2010 when the Andhra Pradesh government issued an ordinance severely restricting the operations of MFIs, and a state law was passed within the year. This sent a signal to borrowers that MFI loans need not be repaid, and collections fell precipitously. The Andhra Pradesh legislation revealed the regulatory gap that existed in microfinance and in late 2010, the RBI appointed a committee under H.Y. Malegam to examine the issue. The committee interacted with all the stakeholders and sought numerous consultations, especially with the MFIs led by Mahajan who had, by then, corralled all the NBFC–MFIs into forming an association—the Microfinance Institutions Network (MFIN). Fortunately for the sector, the eventual RBI circular, which was based on the code of conduct of MFIN, incorporated many changes from what was recommended by the Malegam Committee. On the other hand, the circular initiated a regime of intensive regulation. MFIN also initiated the pioneering work of helping set up High Mark, a credit bureau for the MFI sector.

Sounding like an elder statesman, Brij Mohan says, 'the crisis did a lot of good to the sector. To borrow from genetics, it resulted in mutation which was needed for development of a new gene from the early inbreeding. We felt bad at the time, the sector fell into disrepute. But it emerged stronger, more responsible, more regulated, and more formal. To be fair, whatever we demanded, RBI acceded to over a period of time.'

AN IDEA IS BORN

Chapter 4 brings us to the Ujjivan story. Samit Ghosh, an MBA from Wharton, spent 30 years in the Middle East and India with international banks like Citibank, Arab Bank, Standard Chartered Bank, Bank Muscat, and new-generation Indian start-up HDFC Bank. Not long after the 1991 economic reforms, he was back in the country, setting up a world-class retail banking operation for HDFC. In 1998 he joined Bank Muscat as their India CEO, establishing its operations in the country and making it viable. His base was then Bangalore (as Bengaluru was then called) where, at the personal level, he and his wife also got busy building a home for themselves. But in 2004, at the height of his banking career, he decided to quit Bank Muscat and set out on his own—start a bank for the poor. What made him do this?

Around the time he joined Bank Muscat, India's economic reforms had more or less set in, Ghosh saw how the full range of financial services became available to the Indian middle class, which was quite small at the time. He recalls how the thought struck him—why not make available a full range of financial services to India's 600 million working poor as well, a section that had remained outside the pale of organized financial services. This would transform their lives and create a mass market for financial services—a facility that nationalized banks were unable to provide because of their own constraints.

This was the insight he gained from his working life but there was something more he acquired from his early life and family background. Again, he recalls, 'Our parents' generation was the one that went through the Indian independence movement and the first decades of independent India. They inculcated in us a sort of social objective that we became independent not only to remove the British, but also to eliminate poverty.' Ghosh's father was a government doctor who spent his life in post-Independence India setting up government hospitals in the coalfields of Bihar (now Jharkhand). He died when Ghosh was just 10 years old and 'we had to rebuild our lives from scratch'. Having lived through the tumultuous 1960s and 1970s of revolutionary Calcutta (now Kolkata), his objectives in life, in his own words, became 'very materialistic'. He says: 'I wanted to finish college, university and make a good living so that my children didn't have to go through the kind of insecurity which my family had gone through.'

With that goal, he went through 30 years of banking, and realized he had achieved success 'both professionally as a banker and materially whatever I needed for my family. Then I had a moment of epiphany. I had a discussion in my mind with my father—who was long since dead—asking him, "Are you proud of me, of what I have achieved?" Materially, I had achieved everything. As a banker, I had achieved a lot and was well-regarded, both internationally and in India. And the answer I got was, "So what". What had I achieved? What am I leaving behind? It was then that I started thinking of utilizing my education and experience in the financial sector to make a real societal impact.'

That is how the idea was born, and Ghosh makes his goal clear: 'Ujjivan was set up for a specific purpose—to provide financial services to the various segments of our society who are either excluded or under-served by the organized financial services.' He did not let anything get in the way of serving that purpose.

Ghosh had two assets and a personal philosophy when he set out on this journey. The assets were a retail and a technology vision. The retail vision came from his experience in Citibank and from the couple of years of setting up the retail banking structure in India for HDFC. The technology vision was reinforced by being in Bengaluru, India's tech capital, which made him realize how use of technology could extend the boundaries of what could be achieved with a given level of resources. 'So we built a model where we kept the front end of microfinance intact but brought in technology, disciplines of centralized operations and efficiency, the risk-management process of banks, service quality—to retain our customers—and training, and married all of them together.'

If the Grameen Bank model offered proof of concept for bringing financial services to the poor through a viable business, then there is one area in which Ghosh was a sort of pioneer in India. He applied the Grameen model not to India's rural poor, as several microfinance organizations were already doing, but the urban poor.

A FIRM IS BORN

Chapter 5 takes us through 2004 and 2005, when it all started. To be precise, Ujjivan started functioning from Monday, 2 August 2004. In a communication entitled 'Update 1' to the team dated 22 August, Ghosh announced that the registrar of companies had approved the name of the firm and went on to outline the essential character of the company. 'The company will be branded Ujjivan. We wanted to select a name which reflects the aspirations of our customers and would be understood nationally. "Ujjivan" in Sanskrit means better (or progress) in life.' Ujjivan Financial Services Private Limited was incorporated on 28 December 2004 and the first board meeting was held in the new year, on 25 January 2005.

The immediate task was to put together a business plan that would be necessary to secure equity investment. Also high on priority was to have an impressive enough board of directors. All these were needed to get RBI approval to set up a non-banking financial company (NBFC). Recalls Ghosh, 'As far as the board is concerned, I think, two people were very supportive right from the beginning. One was Sunil Patel, who was my college mate from Wharton. He helped me build the first investor proposals and business plan which enabled me to raise the initial capital. The other was K.R. Ramamoorthy, whom I had known from before as well, who brought his experience as a banker to the table. The two of them formed the core of my support from the board.'

Ghosh reveals: 'actually the most difficult time I faced in the entire existence of Ujjivan was raising the first Rs 2.7 crore of capital.' The ball was set rolling by Ghosh and Ramamoorthy putting in Rs 1.1 lakh in January 2005. Then, 'many of my friends and colleagues—especially from my Citibank days—and alumni from Wharton chipped in. But we were still substantially short. Providentially, S. Viswanatha Prasad was in the process of setting up Bellwether Microfinance Fund, a domestic equity fund to invest primarily in start-up microfinance companies. After our initial discussion in Bangalore, an old colleague from Citibank, Ajit Grewal, and I took an overnight bus to Hyderabad in August 2005 to sign our first institutional investor.'

In August, a critical Rs 2.4 crore came in from Bellwether Microfinance Trust through Caspian Advisers, Jaithirth (Jerry) Rao, and several others. 'With that we were able to raise that initial capital of Rs 2.8 crore, which enabled us to apply for the NBFC licence from RBI.'

Prasad, managing director of Caspian Impact Investment, which is aligned with Bellwether, recalls that by around 2004, the percentage of urban poor in India exceeded the rural level. 'So we said we would invest in entities and business models catering to urban needs. Plus, we decided to back entrepreneurs who would build this on a national scale, that is, scale up their business. Lastly, we wanted to encourage mainstream bankers and entrepreneurs to enter the industry.'

But to get on board, the mainstream people needed to be convinced that this was a viable business model. 'That's when we met Samit Ghosh. Everything I said, he wanted to do. He wanted to put the customer first, like any consumer bank.' The focus for him was to understand the sort of product a customer wanted. 'Ujjivan was the first MFI in those days to be set up like a bank.'

For the first business plan, Ghosh recalls, 'We adopted the Citibank process, but not their culture of competition. We laid great store by employee job satisfaction and customer satisfaction. The idea was to have respect for the customer and grow with the customer. The HR philosophy was to create job satisfaction, rather than the driving force of materialism. We created a lot of internal equity in an open environment, like having the same formula for all increments. That is one of the reasons why we have repeatedly won the best employer rating.'

A lot of the early groundwork was about explaining to the RBI the reason behind setting up Ujjivan. Eventually, it secured RBI approval to become an NBFC in record time, as it was well-structured from day one, with a very wired legal framework. There is palpable excitement in Ghosh's November 2005 update. The first borrowers' group had been formed, the first group recognition test had been done, the first centre meeting had been held, and most importantly, the first batch of officers had been trained. Ujjivan secured the certificate to run as an NBFC on 31 October 2005, 'in a record time of 49 days'. The die was cast and the ball started rolling on a 10-year journey which, in its own way, has been historic.

A PILOT GETS GOING

Chapter 6 begins with the opening of Ujjivan's first branch on 8 November 2005 in the Koramangala area of Bengaluru. Ghosh called this phase of its operations a 'pilot', indicating that it was part of a learning process which would be used to gain insights and validate every aspect of its operations. The first 100 Ujjivan customers who would save for a three-month period before getting a loan, had already been inducted and the first loan was disbursed in January 2006.

Several key learnings emerged during the pilot. Firstly, it was imperative to be able to retain staff in a vibrant job market like Bengaluru where information technology (IT) firms were tirelessly head-hunting. Secondly, there was a need to control quality in operations (selection of borrowers, processing of loans, disbursal, and follow-up) which held the key to survival. Hence, a process of an ongoing audit of field operations was instituted. Thirdly, there was a need to go beyond the 'income generation' single-product model of Grameen Bank and become a multi-product operation which gave education, festival, and housing loans to low-income women. Fourthly, the need to acquire the ability to handle cash, which employees in the early team with a banking background had no experience in.

At the end of the 18-month pilot period in April 2007, Ujjivan had 17 branches in three cities—Bengaluru, Kolkata, and Delhi—and a staff strength of 285. It had also opened its first semi-urban branch in Ramanagara near Bengaluru and had disbursed a total of Rs 13.5 crore in loans to almost 24,000 customers.

The pilot period came to an end with two significant foreign direct investments (FDIs)—by Unitus and the Michael and Susan Dell Foundation (MSDF). Together, they invested Rs 3 crore in equity, taking Ujjivan's equity capital to Rs 5.5 crore. Over the years, MSDF went in for more investment in further rounds of equity funding. When it eventually existed in 2012, the investment had secured a return of 2.2 times. Clearly, the pilot had yielded a successful model.

ON A HIGH GROWTH PATH

Chapter 7 charts the period after the pilot ended in April 2007, when Ujjivan embarked on a rapid growth path over the next four years that would enable it to 'arrive'. The dimensions of the four-year growth phase (2007–11) can be captured by comparing the figures at the beginning and the end of the period. From 19 branches by mid-2007, Ujjivan had grown to 351 by the end of FY 2011. The customer base had grown over 30 times to over 991,000, and total disbursements had gone up by over a hundred times to Rs 2,070 crore. Similarly, staff strength had gone up by over 14 times to just over 4,000. Perhaps, most critically, Ujjivan had established a track record of over 98 per cent repayment.

At the start of the period, Ujjivan looked forward to wiping out all accumulated losses in under three years. In keeping with this, it broke even January 2009 onwards and in the last quarter of the 2008–09 financial year, earned a net profit after tax of Rs 1.7 crore. By the end of the first quarter of the next financial year, two major regions—south and east—turned profit-able and the company expected to wipe out all accumulated losses by the end of the next financial year. FY 2009–10 can be termed as the year that

Ujjivan came of age, turning in a net profit of Rs 9.6 crore and wiping out all accumulated losses. In keeping with this, it also set its eyes on a long-term return on equity of 15 per cent.

At the end of FY 2008, the Parinaam Foundation was set up by Elaine Marie Ghosh as a not-for-profit company under the then Section 25 of the Companies Act (read with Section 8 of Companies Act, 2013). It was at completely arm's length from Ujjivan with an autonomous governance structure. Mrs Ghosh worked pro bono as executive director. The decision grew out of the realization that poverty can be successfully attacked only as a holistic exercise and something was needed to address issues outside the scope of microfinance. Through the microfinance 'plus' programme, Parinaam Foundation addressed areas like healthcare, micro health insurance, education, vocational and entrepreneurship development, and community-strengthening initiatives. The Foundation also initiated a major new focus with the ultra-poor programme. The endeavour was to bring within the development fold families that did not meet the eligibility criteria for availing microfinance. The focus was to bring these families up to a level where they could qualify for microfinance assistance.

During the high-growth period Ujjivan also undertook the financial literacy programmes Sankalp and Diksha, which sought to educate customers and insulate them from the ravages of the Andhra type of crisis which could severely cripple microfinance. It focused on excessive borrowing (taking multiple loans) and sub-lending or ghost lending (allowing the use your identity for a loan that someone else uses). It explained the significance of the credit bureau and why it was important to maintain a clean record in order to be eligible to take loans in the future.

The year 2008 marked the completion of a one-year pilot for a new product—the individual business loan—with the guidance and support of Women's World Banking. It was first introduced in 10 branches in Karnataka. These loans, for Rs 10,000–50,000, were offered to families with running businesses to meet working capital or investment needs. The year also marked the national launch of the educational loan to enable borrowers to send their children to schools of their choice. It covered tuition fee, cost of textbooks, and uniforms. A third product—a housing loan—was also introduced. Plus, right from the beginning, all borrowers were given life insurance cover at considerable administrative cost to the organization.

To get a sense of the road covered during the period, it is useful to step back and take note of a few milestones. May 2007 was a landmark month—as Delhi and Kolkata disbursed their first loans. By June 2010, in eastern India, Ujjivan has 100 branches and 3 lakh customers. By October 2010, with 23 branches in Delhi/NCR, Ujjivan became the largest MFI there. In the west, the last region where Ujjivan went, by January 2009, it served over 1 lakh clients through 48 branches in Maharashtra and Gujarat. What is more, by August 2010, it became the largest microfinance organization in Mumbai, with 21 branches.

A CRISIS FOREWARNED

Chapter 8 describes how Ujjivan, even as it grew exponentially during 2007–11, faced its first crisis in early 2009. A payments crisis created by mass default gripped the microfinance industry in four urban centres in southern Karnataka—Kolar, Sidlaghatta, Ramanagara, and Mysuru. Ujjivan, which had a presence in the latter three, was also affected. But the crisis began to recede by the end of the financial year and Ujjivan emerged from it relatively unscathed. This was a vindication of its policy of not putting all its eggs in one basket, spreading out its operations across the country. The sum total of learnings from the crisis is startling and show the crisis to be a forerunner of the Andhra crisis.

In the four years before the Andhra crisis, Indian microfinance had three dress rehearsals, so to speak. These are known as the three Ks. They each provided an important lesson, all of which were ignored, resulting in the crisis in Andhra Pradesh. The first rehearsal happened in 2006 in the state's Krishna district. The proximate cause was the collector, the administrative head of the district, shutting down 50 offices of microfinance institutions like Spandana, Asmitha, and SHARE and instructing their borrowers not to repay their loans. Fortunately, the intervention and active support of the RBI prevented the offices from remaining closed for long.

The second dress rehearsal took place in Kanpur and some other cities in Uttar Pradesh in 2009. It was triggered by a local MFI, Nirman Bharti, defaulting on large loans from banks and other financial institutions to fund its small-loans portfolio, prompted by repayment problems. This, in turn, happened because it did not have proper systems and processes to exercise due diligence while granting loans and then supervising recovery.

The third K was Kolar or the southern Karnataka crisis, also in 2009. The crisis broke in the first half of 2009. The key local trigger was the 'irrational exuberance' of the industry leading to excessively rapid growth in lending. This was marked by MFIs going after the low-hanging fruit—populated areas in which residents were already familiar with microfinance because of the groundwork done by earlier MFI entrants. As a result, multiple lending took place without adequate screening. This led to borrowers with multiple loans sometimes spending as much as 1–2 hours a day attending mandatory meetings of borrower groups. The easy availability of loans led to some agents who were appointed to recruit customers becoming proxy borrowers—using real borrowers as fronts to aggregate easily available finance which could then be on-lent. To this was added the troubles of the silk-reeling industry after the global financial crisis broke in 2008, impacting economic activity and trade in some of the affected areas.

When repayment instalments began to fall due with inexorable regularity, tension grew among affected families and neighbourhoods. This tinderbox type of situation was further ignited by the spark of an attempted suicide in Kolar. This exacerbated the tension and led to the local Anjuman committee (the religious body of the community) banning interaction between Muslim women and MFI representatives through a religious edict. The Sidlaghatta Anjuman committee followed suit by stopping repayment of loans. In Ramanagara, silk-reeling factory owners, who faced labour shortage because MFI loans tended to make women 'independent', persuaded the local Anjuman committee to impose a Kolar-type ban. In Mysuru, an unrelated communal clash led to business losses, enabling a local political organization to pose as a saviour by raising the possibility of a loan waiver and urging MFI customers to stop repayment.

THE CRISIS ARRIVES IN ANDHRA

Chapter 9 begins with the crisis in microfinance in Andhra Pradesh that broke in late 2010, first with the issue of an ordinance and then the passing of a state law which affected all stakeholders. The case of Ujjivan is significant. It had avoided going into Andhra Pradesh, assessing the field and concluding that it was overcrowded. With hindsight, this greatly de-risked its business, just as it did in 2009, when the company was able to easily weather the crisis in southern Karnataka because it had branched out across the country so as not to be solely dependent on the presence in its home state.

However, though Ujjivan did not take a hit in Andhra Pradesh, it was not able to avoid the ripple effects that had spread across the country. Recovery problems emerged in Tamil Nadu and West Bengal as MFIs withdrew because they were overextended. Samit Ghosh, in his May 2011 letter from the managing director in the 2010–11 annual report, did not mince words when he said the organization had gone into 'crisis-management mode' since the previous October.

The immediate build-up to the crisis began early in 2010, when local TV channels in Andhra reported suicides among microfinance borrowers. Some women came forward to say they had been forced into prostitution as a result of pressure for repayment. Then in July came the SKS public issue. The MFI opponents in the state now felt they had cast-iron proof of how investors and managers made millions at the expense of poor borrowers who had no respite from repaying loans that carried very high interest rates. In August the state government set up a committee to draft an ordinance to address the distress caused by MFI operations. For a decade, NGOs and the state government had worked to implement the World Bank's Velugu programme that had resulted in the creation of a million SHGs. MFIs were supposedly poaching on SHGs assiduously built up through a decade of hard work and walking away with the profit. The Andhra Pradesh Microfinance ordinance was approved by a special cabinet meeting convened for this single agenda, and issued the next day, on 15 October 2010.

The crisis broke with the issue of the ordinance. Passed in response to distress among borrowers over repayment, which, according to the government's own count, had resulted in 54 suicides, it severely restricted the MFIs' operations. This was followed by a state law being passed within the year, which, among other things, made it obligatory for an MFI to obtain permission from the relevant district authorities before operating in the area. Plus, MFIs could not engage in door-to-door collection but only in designated public areas, and that too monthly and not weekly. This sent a signal to borrowers that MFI loans need not be repaid and collections fell precipitously.

The Andhra Pradesh legislation revealed the regulatory gap that existed in the field of microfinance and in late 2010, the RBI appointed a committee under H.Y. Malegam, one of its board members, to go into the issue. It submitted its report in December 2010. In May the next year, the RBI issued guidelines for the functioning of the industry for MFIs registered with it as NBFC–MFIs. The guidelines were largely welcomed by the sector and this remains the current rule book, because the law for the industry remains to be passed.

When the crisis broke in late 2010, Ujjivan saw several tasks ahead. One was managing liquidity with bank loans drying up and repayments slackening. Organizations like SIDBI, IDBI Bank, and the developed world markets came to the rescue and helped the organization tide over tightness. For its part, Ujjivan set its priorities in spending—meeting basic operating expenses, debt servicing, and standing by the needs of good customers. The second was to protect its portfolio from collateral damage in states like Tamil Nadu and West Bengal. The third was to keep lines of communication open with the staff which was confused by the tumultuous developments all around them. Special care was taken to ensure that salaries were paid on time and routine expenses like rent for hired premises met on schedule.

The RBI guidelines represented a new ball game that MFIs had to quickly learn. A massive effort had to be made to reduce costs, as the RBI stipulated that margins over cost of funds should not exceed 12 per cent, thus effectively putting a 25 per cent ceiling on lending rates. A similar effort was needed to reduce the proportion of dropouts (borrowers who did not return for another loan after closing one) as a high 20 per cent figure reflected on the nature of customer experience. Funding flow had to be rejuvenated.

Despite all these problems, there was no long-term existential threat for MFIs. By creating a separate category for NBFC–MFIs, RBI had formally designated a space for them.

BATTLING THE CRISIS

Chapter 10 looks at FY 2011–12, which in many ways was the most critical in Ujjivan's 10-year history. During the year Ujjivan validated the robustness of its model by passing a severe stress test. It tackled the fallout of a crisis afflicting the entire microfinance sector in the country, undertook several changes, and, most importantly, came out on top with its basic model intact and ready to get on to the growth path again.

In the face of the Andhra crisis which dried up the major source of finance for MFIs—loans from banks—Ujjivan took two steps. Stepping back from the path of rapid growth, it cut down its total number of branches (from 351 to 299), reduced staff strength by 14 per cent (compared to a 42 per cent growth in the previous year), severely curtailed new customer acquisition (the rate of growth fell from 60 per cent to 5 per cent), restricted fresh lending mostly to existing customers with a good record, and, in the process, saw a sharp reduction in the growth rate of disbursals (from 122 per cent to 52 per cent). The overall impact of all these moves was a reduction in costs. The operating-expense ratio (cost-to-average portfolio) fell from 17.6 per cent to 13.5 per cent. Even without a crisis, this was essential as the RBI had put a 12 per cent ceiling on the margin. What the crisis did was to facilitate the whole process by putting the organization in a crisis-fighting mode.

The cost reduction was achieved through a business-efficiency programme which was introduced in 2011. It focused on two things—business consolidation and technology infusion. Branches (52) and customer centres (with less than 25 customers) were merged keeping in mind geographical proximity, scope for productivity improvement, and growth prospects. As a result, borrowers per staff went up by 24 per cent, outstanding loans per field staff rose by 52 per cent, and per branch by 41 per cent. The core banking solution was extended to most of the branches, allowing for instant uploading of repayment data, enabling better cash management and lower cash-handling costs. On operating procedures, a key decision was taken to extend the monthly repayment window for borrowers from one week to three weeks. This gave greater flexibility to borrowers and more scope to field staff, allowing them more time for centre meetings, thereby getting to know customers better. The business consolidation led to a lower deployment of field staff. The extending of core banking allowed for a smaller staff at the back end to take care of accounting functions. All this enabled more staff to be deployed in audit, vigilance, and credit, thus allowing better management of critical business needs.

A major challenge during the year was managing liquidity, as bank loans dried up following the Andhra crisis. The suspension of bank credit in the first half of the financial year created a gap between planned and actual disbursement, leading to a slowdown in business momentum and a decline in the loan book and profitability. Ujjivan managed to mitigate the adverse

funding situation partially by going in for issuing of non-convertible debentures and loan securitization. Additionally, it raised debt against equity
which was 'critical' for disbursement. In the entire financial year it raised
Rs 283 crore from banks and financial institutions to counter the winding
in of bank credit. But the crowning achievement was being able to raise
Rs 128 crore equity in a year of turmoil. Ujjivan was the first microfinance
firm to be able to raise fresh capital after the Andhra crisis.

One positive fallout of the Andhra crisis was the industry, under the
leadership of its association MFIN, taking positive steps to set up a credit
bureau, a good intention that had been discussed but stalled since 2008.
Ujjivan signed up with three credit bureaus—Highmark, CIBIL, and
Equifax. The main improvement was in asset quality, as references to the
credit bureau enabled Ujjivan to weed out applicants who did not fit the
bill. During the year, credit bureau checks resulted in the rejection of
2.6 per cent of applications.

The attempt to build a better work experience bore results. In 2011
Ujjivan was ranked the 'best company to work for in the microfinance
industry and 14th overall across industries' in a survey carried out by the
Great Place to Work (India) Institute in collaboration with the *Economic
Times*. This was the second time that it received this distinction.

A RETURN TO HIGH GROWTH

After weathering the Andhra storm, Ujjivan re-emerged on the high-
growth path by the end of 2011–12—the story tracked in Chapter 11.
In the four years up to 2015–16, there has been a phenomenal growth and
all-round improvement in the MFI's operating efficiencies. In the world of
microfinance, it is not just a formidable growth engine but an increasingly
efficient one too. A comparison between the figures by the end of financial
year 2012 with those of end 2016 shows a rise in its gross loan book to
Rs 5,389 crore, an increase by a compound annual growth rate (CAGR) of

66.4 per cent. The total number of customers went up from 1 million to 3.3 million, which is a CAGR of 34.7 per cent.

As impressive as growth and profitability have been, the improvement in operating efficiencies and cost control have been equally so. Cost-to-income ratio has gone down from 94.2 per cent (2011–12 was a crisis year in which the company barely broke even) to 51 per cent. This has enabled unit cost to support a much higher level of loans. Thus, the ratio of operating expenses to average loan book have gone down from 13.8 per cent to 7.5 per cent. It is therefore to be expected that the gross loan book per branch has gone up from Rs 2 crore to Rs 11 crore and gross loan book per employee up from Rs 20 lakh to Rs 60 lakh. This improvement has been made possible by the total number of employees and branches going up at a much slower pace than total loans. Employee head count over the same period has gone up by a CAGR of 23.6 per cent and the total number of branches has gone up by 56 per cent (that is not even doubled).

As a well-run microfinance company, Ujjivan's gross NPAs are a negligible 0.15 per cent. When customers repay loans with such alacrity, it is to be expected that Ujjivan's retention is one of the highest in the industry at 86 per cent. The MFI also has a high staff-retention ratio of 82 per cent. It is also therefore not surprising that Ujjivan ranked in the top 25 best places to work (across all industries) list for five consecutive years and last year was listed as one of the top three companies to work for, with the other two being multinationals.

Ujjivan has also been great for investors. Foreign investors who have exited over the last two years have been able to secure an annualized return of over 20 per cent. The few angel investors who invested in Ujjivan for 10 years have seen the value of their investments grow by 30 times based on the post 2016 IPO price. The IPO, preparatory to becoming an SFB, made shareholding in Ujjivan broad-based, with 41,000 individual shareholders and institutional shareholders equally distributed between domestic and foreign sectors.

The rapid growth and emerging sophistication of products point to the growing importance of individual lending whose dynamic is very different from the group lending that has dominated microfinance across players in the sector's initial years. Such is the importance and potential of individual lending that an individual lending organization is emerging within Ujjivan. This has had significant human resource ramifications. An entirely new team has been brought in for individual lending, as it requires distinct skills. To this have been added members of the existing staff with special training.

PROCESSES AND INFORMATION TECHNOLOGY

Ujjivan has been able to move forward on the path of high growth with stability because of several enablers. We look at three of them: improving processes and using more information technology; addressing the human resources need; and managing risk. Chapter 12 examines how Ujjivan has been able to continuously change and improve its processes, aided by more and more use of IT.

When Martin Pampilly joined in early 2009 as regional operations manager for the south and took a hard look at both the front and the back ends, he was in for a shock: work was completely paper based and computerization was minimal; yearly and half-yearly closings of accounts were a nightmare. He captures the change that has taken place in over seven years in a then-and-now comparison. Then, 250 people processed 60,000–65,000 loan applications in a month; in mid-2016, 165 people processed 300,000 loans per month. Output per head went up over seven times.

Deepak Ayare, chief information officer, joined just a few months before Pampilly, in late 2008. (Ayare left Ujjivan on 30 November 2016.) Then, there were 85 branches, 850 employees, and 1.5 lakh borrowers. By end 2015–16, eight years later, there were about three million borrowers but only 469 branches. While customer growth has more or less kept pace with earlier projections, far fewer branches are managing this enhanced workload. A part of the growth in productivity is captured in these numbers.

Pampilly considers the decision taken in 2012 to switch to monthly from weekly repayment as a watershed. This meant customer groups meeting monthly instead of weekly and a three-fourth reduction of the meeting-supervision load on the customer relations staff. It gave three additional weeks, so to speak, to the staff every month, raising their productivity. This, plus customers (for repayment) being distributed over the entire month, was like 'switching from a gas stove with one burner to four burners. The number of vouchers a cashier had to handle was reduced to a third. Each CRS could now handle 700 customers in a month, compared to 450 earlier,' says Pampilly.

Describing the IT scenario, Ayare said when he joined, they were using client-server technology restricted by LAN—not web-based technology—with different servers based in Delhi, Kolkata, and Bengaluru. There was no centralized system. The IT team had to sit up the whole night—every night—to synchronize the data. At that time connectivity was neither steady nor at high speeds. When a connection broke, the whole work had to be repeated. They used to face different challenges at the month-end and year-end. Then in 2010, the core banking vendor, Craft Silicon, came up with a web-based solution, BR.Net, which can be accessed from anywhere and was still in use in 2016. Then Ujjivan's data centre was outsourced to IBM, Mumbai, so that it was properly managed in a secure environment.

When Pampilly became head of operations in 2011, the first step he took was to outsource the production of customer ID cards, which had become a bottleneck. Those earlier engaged in producing the ID cards were transferred to data entry. This made them feel valuable as computer operators. The next step was to end working in shifts that were difficult to supervise. For this, work volume had to go down. This was done again by outsourcing the creation of digital profiles to

Vindhya, a BPO firm. The staff members thus freed up were moved to different functions. This was also done keeping staff convenience in mind. As employees were needed for new branches, some were moved to branches near their homes.

Before the core banking system linked up branches, customer-relationship staff collected repayments at centre meetings and brought the cash to the branches. Vouchers would then be prepared at the branches, but were posted initially at the head office and then the regional offices. Once core banking reached branches, the day's vouchers were posted there that very day. From April 2012, Ujjivan started closing monthly accounts the same day the month ended. Earlier there was a six-day cash float in the system. Cash was received but the overall cash position could not be immediately ascertained. Now treasury can know the fund position every day as the books are reconciled daily.

The year 2012–13 was, in some ways, a watershed. It brought about a revolution with the introduction of a document management system and scanners at branches from where couriering documents to regional offices would take more than two days. Now, scanned documents get tagged on to the workflow and customer data is entered by vendors. There are as many as seven of them. With the scanned documents in the workflow, regional offices go ahead with the loan processing. The customer-relationship staff is able to check the status of processing by referring to the workflow. Computerizing the workflow and dematerializing the documents has led to reducing the time it takes to process a loan application (receipt to disbursal) from 25–26 days to 6–9 days.

THE HUMAN FACTOR

Ujjivan has believed that a sustainable business is one in which workers get a chance to improve their skills, see prospects for career progression, and find some meaning in what they are doing from the social point of view, other than personal financial gain. In Chapter 13, we see how a conscious pursuit of such a policy has brought Ujjivan recognition almost year after year for being a leader as an employer and a preferred place to work.

High growth over the last four years has opened up opportunities for career progression. As new branches are opened, performers in existing operations are given the opportunity to move to the next level through the process of 'internal job promotions'. The scope for moving up is always high in a growing organization. But to this has been added the wholly new dimension of Ujjivan turning into an SFB, that is, a bank proper. This will overnight convert the entire workforce from being microfinance employees into bank employees, who figure higher in the pecking order of industries to work for. Being a young business which must remain organizationally flexible, Ujjivan encourages a certain amount of role change so that career progressions are not rigidly linear. High performers identified for development programmes are sometimes allowed to take on the roles of their superiors when the latter have to be away. This enables them to prove their abilities at the next level.

Training and the training department play a key role in the management structure of Ujjivan, with guidance being imparted at all levels. An induction programme with basic-level training in two parts, with a three-month gap in between is in place for new recruits. There is a customer relationship managers' training for supervisors, including branch managers, whose job is to generate revenue and engage with customers.

Then there is a management development programme which includes both an induction and a field component for those recruited from campuses. The training landscape evolves along with growth in new lines of business. A training programme has been devised for individual lending which is the new growth area and has been designed to skill employees handling personal and housing loans.

As the organization has grown and become more complex, a leadership development programme has been put in place which has involved selected managers spending short stints in leading institutions like IIM Ahmedabad and Harvard Business School, and attending conferences and seminars. For close to a decade now Ujjivan has been hiring management trainees from business schools.

One of the things that makes Ujjivan a great place to work is its pioneering role in introducing employee stock options plan (ESOP) as early as 2006, when the company was still in its swaddling clothes. The sixth ESOP was launched in 2015 and altogether 54 per cent of all employees at the end of FY 2015–16 were recipients of ESOP, which have been issued to employees across segments almost since Ujjivan's inception.

RISK MANAGEMENT

Samit Ghosh's remarkable story about the impact of Ujjivan's risk-management process is told in Chapter 14. While preparing to become an SFB, it got in touch with Bajaj Finance to understand how it appraised customer requests for loans to acquire consumer durables and how long it took to process each loan. This would help Ujjivan devise its own process for giving loans. During the discussion the idea of measuring risk naturally came up as well as the areas where the quality of Bajaj Finance's portfolio was poor. There was mutual surprise when it was realized that these were all areas which Ujjivan had avoided owing to their poor risk profile. On realizing this, the Bajaj Finance people said that they should have had this conversation with Ujjivan earlier! 'Before we enter a state or a city we do a survey to assess the risk. We are also not there in areas found by MFIN to be troubled. Our risk-management process is outstanding,' Ghosh observes.

After building an elaborate and systematic risk-management structure and process, how is Ujjivan preparing for the significant change in the risk scenario on becoming an SFB? The risk-management parameters cover credit, market, and operations risk. It has developed a unique process to evaluate and monitor risk at its branches. This includes management of internal and external factors like portfolio quality, branch supervision, staff attrition, and external events. Field risk staff help corporate and regional offices calculate risk scores for branches. Based on these, branches which are considered to be high risk are monitored and controlled more rigorously and audited more frequently. This has helped Ujjivan steer clear of major crises afflicting the industry. It also has a comprehensive risk-control and self-assessment mechanism conducted by all departments from 2013–14 once every six months. From this it has built a risk register for all its departments, IT systems, and applications. Each department has high-risk indicators for key risks and when it is breached, corrective action plans are formulated.

'Over time Ujjivan has prided itself on an independent credit department which has been there for the last eight years,' says Arunava Banerjee, chief risk officer. He further adds, 'We were the trendsetters in realizing the need for this because there are other external factors that play a role. We were also one of the first to have a credit-risk function and this has evolved over time. Recently, we started an independent credit-risk management department and building up the operations risk management framework. This is the risk we are vulnerable to from people, processes, and systems, so how do you set up a framework whereby you actually measure and monitor these risks?'

To counter the risk emanating from choosing the wrong kind of people to handle too much cash, Ujjivan evolved an elaborate system of recruitment based on pre-verification. This was backed by a robust customer-selection process. Thereafter came an equally elaborate process to select the location of a new branch. And data and analytics are being increasingly used to anticipate where risk can emerge and try to nip adverse developments in the bud before things precipitate.

People Fraud

A key area of learning in the past decade concerns people who work for Ujjivan and in this it has learnt things the hard way. Perhaps the biggest challenge that the microfinance organization has faced in its 10 years of existence is fraud relating to cash involving its own staff. Says Ghosh, 'As bankers we did not know how to handle cash and the risks associated with transacting purely in cash.' Microfinance is a cash-intensive operation in which poor people have traditionally taken their loan in cash and made repayments in cash. Loans are disbursed from Ujjivan branches where cash has to be maintained. Repayments are made at centre meetings from where the cash has to be brought to the branch. Cash travels to and fro between the Ujjivan branch and the bank branch.

As a result of handling a lot of cash at centre meetings and at its own branches, and with linkages with bank branches evolving very slowly, 'we were subject to a lot of frauds, thefts, and all kinds of stuff which came with handling cash. So we had to develop all kinds of mechanisms to prevent such things, including recruitment of staff—background verification. In terms of process we were very loose,' reminisces Ghosh.

Customer Selection

Assessing the credit worthiness of prospective microfinance customers without much or no documentation was a major challenge. 'The key processes that evolved over time was almost a replica of the Grameen model, which was introduced way back and was very successful,' recalls Sneh Thakur, head of credit. At the core of this model was selecting the women by getting them to form groups with their neighbours and friends whom they knew and trusted to get a loan and then stand guarantee against each other's repayment in times of financial difficulties. Once a group was formed, a loan officer would conduct a compulsory group training to help them understand how this whole process worked: the products offered, the interest rates, and the EMIs they would have to pay. Then came a group-recognition test.

A branch manager (customer relationship manager) would independently interact with the customers and take a look at their existing documents. The only document that they had, and this is true even now, is a know your customer (KYC) document. There would be a discussion on how they wanted to utilize the money, what kind of occupation or business they wanted to engage in so as to improve their lives. The discussion was also meant to verify that group members knew each other and the group was cohesive. The compulsory group training is given by the loan officer and the branch head does the group recognition. Thereafter he or she visited the houses of the prospective borrowers to get a sense of their lifestyle, the number of dependents and earners, and to check that the family members were aware that their wife, daughter, or daughter-in-law was taking a loan. The last was to ensure that repayment did not create any hassles. Also, they were shown a video on financial literacy which discussed the ill-effects of over borrowing, multiple borrowing, and ghost lending. Then the branch manager decided whether to take the applications forward.

This is the core process, but over time, there have been changes. There are norms on group size: initially, it was minimum of five, but group sizes now range from two to ten. Attendance rules for centre meetings have been relaxed over time in response to customer feedback. Another big change was reducing the frequency of group meetings from weekly to monthly. New processes have also been introduced. One of the biggest changes was the introduction of a branch credit policy which defined credit ceilings across society for every occupation Ujjivan wanted to lend to.

Selecting a Branch Location

Ujjivan has managed to keep away from troublesome places that may pose a risk to the portfolio by doing rigorous research before deciding to open a branch. The company follows a two-pronged approach to assess the risk in an area before setting up a branch: one entity puts the study together, another checks it. First there is an area survey report by the business vertical. It identifies the city or location where the new branch is proposed and does an initial survey report. Then there is a cross-check report by the controls function, which is the vigilance department, in conjunction with the audit department.

In the area survey a detailed study is done by experienced business staff, like a programme manager or area manager, to assess the area of operation, political situation, socio-economic condition, working environment, number of potential customers, their major occupations, and the prevailing source of income of a majority of the population. The population density data is taken from the block development officer or public sources. The area survey report also includes the experience of any existing MFI operating in that area by interacting with them. It gives details of the negative areas through communication with the local police station and also includes elements of external risk associated in that area. A risk-rating score (high/medium/low/safe) is recorded in the area survey report based on the crime assessment of that area.

Preparing for SFB

In order to become an SFB, Ujjivan has to become compliant with the risk-management framework laid down by the Basel committee for banks across the world. 'What will be new for Ujjivan,' says Arunava Banerjee, 'is the market risk factor, separate from the external or environment risks. It will have to rely on the market for both short-term and long-term funding. So we will be exposed to market risks like interest rate fluctuation and its impact.' Ujjivan is also preparing for contingencies. Hence some kind of contingency funding plan will also have to be put in place.

Coming to branches, Ujjivan, at the time of writing this book, is trying to do an assessment of the external risk faced even by branches doing well, so it is repeating annually what was done at the time of branch opening. This will be captured in the risk scorecard. But it will undergo a change as the focus will be partly on the micro, small, and medium enterprises (MSMEs) and secured lending verticals that already exist, and liabilities (deposits). Liability will become a part once branches start getting depositors on a regular basis. The market risk factor will kick in and monitoring and factoring it will have to be done on a regular basis. Samit Ghosh told a staff gathering, 'As a bank, risk management and compliance will be critical. As an MFI, if we lost any money it was the investors' money. But as a bank if we lose any money it will be the depositors.' We have a fiduciary responsibility towards this entrusted money. The colour of money changes the quality of the risk.'

MFI TO SFB, VIA IPO

Wednesday, 16 September 2015, was a red-letter day in the life of 10-year old Ujjivan. That was the day that RBI announced the names of 10 institutions (eight of them MFIs) which had been granted 'in principle' approval to become SFBs; Ujjivan was one of them. Chapter 15 looks at this development. One provision among the requirements that the selected companies needed to fulfil in 18 months was keeping their foreign shareholding to 49 per cent. For Ujjivan it was as high as 91 per cent. This created the most important landmark for Ujjivan in 2016, which was both a challenge and an achievement—seeing through an IPO of their shares to resident Indians which would make it a publicly listed company.

To prepare for the role of an SFB, a transition team was set up with Ittira Davis as the head. A key decision was to take on Ernst & Young as transition adviser. Then an important transition had to be made, both in mind and substance. You could not look after business as usual and simultaneously plan for the new avatar of the organization, a full-time job. So all departmental heads who had a role in transition joined that team and their deputies took up their bosses' existing work.

The biggest change that would have to be planned for and achieved would be to create an entirely new business vertical that would, over time, be bigger than almost the entire existing business. Now Ujjivan had to acquire the liabilities side of the business, depositors, and in a fundamental sense, be able to take care of people's savings. Davis, who spearheaded the entire transition process, looked into the future and visualized, 'Over five years we want to fund at least 60 per cent of our advances from our own deposits, as opposed to funding now being secured from multiple sources.' To be able to attract deposits, Ujjivan, as an SFB, would have to take banking to the doorsteps of the truly ordinary folks living in the remotest corners of the country.

An SFB would not just garner deposits, it would offer several new kinds of products. The first would be a transformed version of the key existing MFI product—small loans. While these would remain the bread-and-butter business, Ujjivan would also try to create a space for itself by entering a mass market a couple of steps above MFIs in terms of loans. This is a market in which the distinction between 'me and my company' (for micro- and small-enterprise owners) remains obscure. The owners run their own business, which is often not separately incorporated. As the space for micro-enterprise grows, such small business owners would need hand-holding so that they can sell their products through large online retail platforms. Ujjivan would tie up with other industries—like Uber tying up car finance for their drivers to own their own vehicles—and have a role with anyone supporting small enterprises.

The transition would take place with the building of new channels for service delivery to customers and developing a new relationship with them. The aim was to give SFB customers the same kind of experience that the middle class has come to expect—closer to mainstream banking than traditional microfinance. These channels would be—other than the branch itself—ATMs, hand-held devices, mobile phones, and the internet. On phones, keeping in mind the nature of customers, it may be decided to have an interactive voice response (IVR) system 'to primarily tell us in which language the customer wants to speak and then get someone to speak to her in that language. We need to create solutions for customers one level higher than current Ujjivan borrowers but not necessarily on day one,' said Jolly Zachariah, who supervised the rolling out of channels. 'The aim was to keep it simple for our customers, create simple products beyond loans. We wanted to change the nature of engagement with the customer and build a relationship that goes beyond hygiene.' A key new way of enlarging the engagement would be to focus on customers' life events—marriage, the birth of a child, the death of spouse—'develop sensitivity towards them', and be more than a transaction-oriented bank, says Zachariah.

While planning for life as an SFB, the most important enabler that was achieved even before that life had begun was to successfully deliver a back-to-back duo—a pre-IPO private placement and then the IPO itself. So Ujjivan roped in the services of a galaxy of leading investment banks—Kotak Mahindra Capital, Axis Capital, ICICI Securities, and IIFL Holdings—to lead, manage, and help build the book for the issue. When the structure of the issue was finalized by the end of the year, it was made up of three parts—a pre-IPO private placement which would validate Ujjivan as an attractive investment proposition and also discover the range around which the IPO could be priced, an IPO made up of existing shareholders giving up a part of their holding to enable an offer for sale, along with the issue of fresh equity.

Ujjivan began the IPO process in October 2015 by initiating work on the draft red-herring prospectus and talking to investors. It began in January 2016 by filing the draft prospectus with the Securities and Exchange Board of India (SEBI) in record time, less than three months from kick-off, compared to many others who took five to six months. 'No one has done this in the last few years,' said Hiren Shah, head, investor relations. The first milestone crossed was closing the pre-IPO placement with Indian institutional investors by February 2016, a month after the filing of the draft prospectus. This raised Rs 292 crore at an issue price of Rs 205, which became the benchmark price and established Ujjivan's credibility in the domestic market.

It was seen as a considerable success for three reasons. One, it represented winning over Indian institutional investors who had earlier mostly stayed away from the microfinance sector. Two, the placement took place when bank shares were being severely undermined in the market because of soaring NPAs of public sector banks. The day it received Rs 292 crore from pre-IPO placement, the Sensex crashed by 800 points, led mostly by bank shares. Three, the pre-IPO managed to rope in a mutual fund, Sundaram Mutual Fund, when such funds typically stay away from private placements which come in with a lock-in period that they do not like. By agreeing to invest, Sundaram Mutual Fund had to initially take a haircut of around 50 per cent as unlisted shares are valued, as per regulation, at the lower of two—issue prices and book value.

When the road show for the book-building process for the IPO began, Ujjivan and investment bankers had to grapple with several challenges. The issue was restricted to domestic investors, usually rather conservative about valuation and pricing. It was the only IPO in several years not open to foreign investors (who usually are the most aggressive and give their valuation), on the basis of which an issue can be launched. Along with this, there were two or three challenges which investors posed to the management, according to V. Jaya Sankar, senior executive director, Kotak Investment Banking. One, the MFIs had the ability to build on the asset side, but needed to show their ability to build on the liability side—that is, create a deposit base. It would take three to four years to complete the entire transition. The second concern was around the asset portfolio. The bulk of their lending was in the MFI category. They had not got into too much of assets in sectors like housing, auto finance, and SMEs.

The investors, felt Jaya Sankar, expected that Ujjivan would probably go through a two-to-three-year learning curve and in the process, probably make a few mistakes, which would take time to rectify. There was the need to factor this in. Nipun Goel, president, head, investment banking, IIFL Investment Banking, also felt that in the initial term the financial matrix—the ROE and ROA—'could potentially dip'. A bank is bound from day one by all those appropriations, reserve requirements like CRR and SLR. But if the management were to get it right, then in the longer term, in a four-to-five-year perspective, the growth prospects are phenomenal.

But as the road show progressed, the lead managers found that, by and large, investors were convinced that the company had the necessary requirements to become a successful SFB. 'There were three or four things that we really liked,' said Jaya Sankar. It was a play on financial inclusion and investors knew that public sector banks had only so much ability to penetrate the unbanked or underbanked villages. If you, as an MFI, are already serving there then you are far better positioned to take on that market. Besides, as an SFB, Ujjivan would be able to begin with an already prepared customer base of about three million of its own MFI clients. Investors also liked the fact that the successful microfinance companies were operating at pretty high return on equity (ROE), which in the case of Ujjivan was in the high teens. Typically, no equity investor expects upwards of 12–13 per cent. This, combined with very low NPA levels, created the confidence that NBFCs like Ujjivan would become successful SFBs. It became clear through the IPO process, recalled Goel, that 'they [were] extremely committed to the cause of building a very successful institution. They don't take risks which they do not understand and therefore they [were] building an institution which will be here for the long term.'

What impressed institutional investors about Ujjivan was that it was different form a normal Indian company, says S. Subramanian, managing director, institutional equities, Axis Capital. Samit Ghosh personally had a very small percentage of holding. It was a professionally run company with strong backing from a set of very decent private equity investors who had great hopes on both the leadership and its commitment to corporate governance. Every round of investment for Ujjivan (there were six) happened at a higher price. Ujjivan also had the most diversified customer base. 'Ghosh has an ability to choose what he will and what he will not do. His background as a commercial and consumer banker has helped him understand the market. To run a business without securities and have less than 1 per cent NPAs is truly commendable. His understanding of consumers and ability to deliver to them have been phenomenal,' says the MD of Axis Capital.

A lot of investor confidence was centred on Ghosh himself, said Goel. He led an 'incredible management team across levels which resonated extremely well with the investment community'. Throughout the book-building process, Ghosh had been very clear that he did not want the top valuation but the right valuation. As he puts it, 'During the IPO we told investors we are building a bank. It is not an overnight thing.' A microfinance organization, built to offer financial services to the poor, was now converting to a bank. He said, 'During the first two years our return on assets, return on equity, will dip.' A bank can never provide the kind of returns a very successful finance company can. But the risk element for both these is also different. A finance company has a higher risk and if it is well-run, it provides a higher return. 'We have dinned this into our investors again and again. So hopefully that will help us and we don't have to be bound by the quarterly thing.'

But Ghosh also wanted investors to make money. Jaya Sankar felt investors got comfort from the fact that Ujjivan 'had a statesman-like person in Ghosh to provide the leadership and he also had a strong wide-ranged team empowered on business, strategy, risk management, and technology. Among the various MFIs this is the one strong differentiator for Ujjivan because it is not too dependent on one personality.' In particular, Ghosh had been very pragmatic throughout the life of Ujjivan, careful and focused about getting the right investors who were aligned with him from a medium- to long-term perspective. It had a very well-thought-out strategy towards developing into an SFB, understanding what the challenges were, what it took to get to that.

'For these reasons,' explained Jaya Sankar, 'Ujjivan became a very compelling investment proposition for institutional investors. That is the reason why you saw such subscription levels.' The anchor group of 17 which subscribed Rs 265 crore had names like ICICI Prudential Mutual Fund,

Birla Sun Life Mutual Fund, UTI Mutual Fund, Tata Mutual Fund, Birla Sun Life Insurance, and Sundaram Mutual Fund which 'would probably be the who's who of institutional investors,' Goel added. 'The demand was mind-boggling and most of the large investors who matter from a domestic standpoint participated in the IPO.'

The result of all this was that the IPO of Rs 882 crore, which was priced at Rs 210 and closed on 2 May, sailed through, attracting 0.67 million domestic investors, being subscribed 41 times! Ujjivan Financial Services got listed on 10 May, opening at Rs 227, rising to a high of Rs 244 and closing at Rs 232. It reached a peak of Rs 547 in July before settling down at a bit over Rs 400—around twice the issue price. On that occasion, Hiren Shah remarked, 'The listing of shares has started a new era for Ujjivan and all its stakeholders.'

BEYOND MICROFINANCE

Even though the country has a successful microfinance programme meant to address poverty, large sections of the population remain poor. Mindful of this, former banker Elaine Marie Ghosh created the Parinaam Foundation in 2008, a not-for-profit organization under Section 25 of the Companies Act, 1956 (read with Section 8 of the Companies Act, 2013) to deliver, in partnership with Ujjivan, the micro credit 'plus' programme to its customers. Chapter 16 looks at this foundation. Led by Mrs Ghosh, who as executive director worked pro bono, the foundation set out to offer healthcare, education, vocational training, and sustainable livelihood development support for the urban poor and community services to both Ujjivan's customers and below poverty line (BPL) families who were outside the scope of traditional microfinance. Till 2015–16, over half a million people have benefited from the Ujjivan–Parinaam partnership.

The first initiatives were in the areas of eye, ENT, and dental care, and vocational training. Parinaam has been running health camps since

2006—even before it was formally constituted—first in Karnataka and Tamil Nadu and thereafter in Kolkata and Pune. Those needing further care have been provided access to partner hospitals and have been provided financial help when they were unable to meet the costs. It also initiated its own service-provider network in partnership with pharmacies, laboratories, and hospitals. In 2010, vocational training was started with special emphasis on engendering self-confidence among the poor, particularly the youth, and its livelihood development programme was supported by leading retail chains and garment factories to provide jobs to those trained.

A key effort of Parinaam Foundation is its financial literacy programme Diksha, launched in 2012, which has been widely appreciated, including by the RBI. Diksha seeks to teach the poor how to plan expenditure, work out budgets, appreciate the importance of savings, and, very importantly, the difference between good and bad borrowing. Nearly 400,000 women were trained by 2015–16, with 80 per cent of these certified under the programme. Diksha has helped nearly 100,000 customers open bank accounts. In 2015 it started a savings programme for children. The aim is to catch them young and make them aware of the importance of saving, teach them how to handle money, and get them to start saving a little, even if by setting aside a few coins whenever possible. The programme has two segments. One is a 90-minute module delivered in five parts under which children are taught the basics through role play, assignment, and discussion. The second is helping children open bank accounts. The trainer prepares a list of children who do not have bank accounts and then works with a bank branch to open accounts for those who want to. In 2015–16, 30,000 children participated in the programme; 8,500 of them opened accounts in 294 branches across 18 states, becoming, both materially and metaphorically, richer.

While Diksha has tied up with the government's Jan Dhan Yojana programme, a pilot toilet and sanitation programme has been launched in line with the Swachh Bharat Abhiyan. It is aimed at providing toilets to families that do not have any. Another pilot was initiated to help Ujjivan customers buy affordable solar lamps. Working in tandem with Ujjivan, Parinaam chipped in to make the microfinance organization's low-interest education loans free. A scholarship fund was initiated to support those who could pursue higher education.

Perhaps the most ambitious task that Parinaam has undertaken is the Urban Ultra Poor Program to tackle the issue of poverty, launched as a pilot in a Bengaluru slum in late 2009 to cover 1,200 people in 240 families. It targets those earning less than Rs 1,000 a month, with irregular or no work and no access to any developmental credit. These people live in slums, have access to few amenities, suffer from food insecurity, and are heavily in debt. The aim was to stand by them so that they became 'bankable', that is, be able to fruitfully utilize the assistance offered by microfinance organizations. The strategy, aimed at attacking generational and family poverty by helping an entire family and not just one woman, addresses several areas: livelihood support, healthcare, childcare and education, financial literacy, and social support. This is a 12-month programme, with another 12 months of support on a needs basis. After this the women are expected to 'graduate' into microfinance customers.

Until 2014–15, altogether 14 communities have been assisted under the programme with a total membership of 5,000. The programme has had an attrition rate (dropouts) of 27 per cent but among those who have continued, 76 per cent are employed. And half of them have come under the ambit of microfinance. In all, 423 have 'graduated', and pulled themselves up from being ultra poor. More than the numbers, what is important is a model has been developed and tested to lift people out of absolute poverty.

Another social initiative of Ujjivan which goes beyond microfinance is its community development programme (CDP). After Ujjivan turned profitable in 2009–10, it decided to allocate a part of its annual profit to its community development fund under its corporate social responsibility (CSR) initiative. To make it effective, the CDP works bottom up. A branch forms a committee with members from staffers and customers who together decide which programmes to support.

For Ujjivan, this is not entirely altruistic. The idea is to bond with the community so that they can help one another in times of need. If there is a fire or a flood then the branch staff help out, and when Ujjivan faces a hurdle the community stands by it. A piece of corporate memory is the experience in southern Karnataka in 2009 when religious community leaders stopped repayments and the women who benefited from the loans were unable to stand by their MFIs. If they had built up a space in the consciousness of the community, then the story would have probably been different. Ujjivan has been building bridges with the communities within which it works by undertaking social development programmes through its branches, bringing together customer, staff, and community.

Finally, Ghosh addresses a core question running through this book: How far can microfinance go in removing poverty? 'I believe, as did my wife, that financial services are only one element and you need multiple interventions, whether through healthcare, children's education, provide occupation and skills, or address addictions. [The less privileged] are exposed to all kinds of emergencies, natural and man-made. And you have to protect them against all of these. We cannot provide everything. We are only providing what we can.'

We began this chapter by noting that microfinance can only go so far and looked at the rationale behind the creation of Parinaam. To get back to Parinaam, when Ujjivan received the 'Microfinance Organisation of the Year 2011' award, the education loan interest-refund programme (thereby making the loan totally free) and the financial literacy programme run along with Parinaam received special mention. Parinaam's Urban Ultra Poor Program received international recognition in late 2013 when it was declared as the Asia-Pacific winner of the 2013 Financial Times and Citi Ingenuity Awards: Urban Ideas in Action programme, for being the most innovative urban programme in the region. Elaine Ghosh passed away shortly before the award was received. On her contribution to the Ujjivan family, Samit Ghosh says, 'A lot of the values of Ujjivan originate from her.'

THE DEMONETIZATION TSUNAMI

At a time when Ujjivan was buoyed by having secured the licence to become an SFB, it was hit with the tsunami of demonetization. This period, when the entire microfinance sector was severely affected, is discussed in Chapter 17. Its customers, poor working women who dealt mostly in cash, were adversely affected twice over—first by the shortage of cash and second by loss of income as the businesses they worked for, also working mostly in cash, were severely disrupted. This led to loss of income, in addition to the inconvenience of being paid in demonetized notes that had to be exchanged for usable currency at a discount. Then as the plight of borrowers became clear, local political leaders with an eye on securing tickets for forthcoming elections started a campaign by telling borrowers not to repay; they claimed, the government would waive microfinance loans. All this led to borrowers being unable or unwilling to make their scheduled repayments, putting MFIs under severe financial strain.

For Ujjivan, repayment problems started in western Uttar Pradesh, home to innumerable micro and small units, and then spread to the entire state. Quick to follow were parts of Maharashtra, where the textile industry was present in a big way. Repayment problems also surfaced in drought-affected Karnataka, and especially in Bengaluru, with its concentration of garments factories. To combat this, Ujjivan focused on communicating with its staff and borrowers. Staff were advised not to put pressure on borrower, already harassed, to repay immediately as per schedule but repay as and when they could in order to protect their own credit history and scope for future borrowing.

Other than sending the right message to the field staff so that they could reassure borrowers, Ujjivan relaxed its own conservative provisioning norms in order to recognize the unusual conditions and aimed at providing enough to take care of any eventual default. As the financial year ended, Ujjivan saw a fall in the rate of growth of business, rise in NPAs, and an impact on the bottomline. The overall picture was that the targets set for the year when it began would not be met but results would be higher than what was achieved in the previous year. The long-term cost to the business seemed being set back by two to three quarters.

Ujjivan learnt several critical lessons from the experience of demonetization. One was a vindication of its policy of carefully choosing its geographical areas of operation. This enabled it to avoid the severe stress that some other MFIs faced in the worst affected areas. Ujjivan also realized the critical need to remain in touch with customers and understand their hardships. This would enable it to be flexible in rescheduling repayments and thus avoid mass default. Perhaps the most fundamental lesson learnt was that to best serve its objective of helping remove poverty, MFIs needed to lend not just short-term funds but also long-term debt. This would truly help the micro businesses as during times of stress there would be less pressure to repay because customers could skip dividend.

LIGHT AT TUNNEL'S END

Chapter 18 describes how, despite the damage that demonetization did, Ujjivan stuck to its own timeline and launched as an SFB on 6 February 2017. It was a transformative new beginning. The event, held in Bengaluru, unfolded in the presence of Muhammad Yunus, the father of modern-day microfinance. A group of industry leaders chose the occasion to chalk out a path for the future. What they agreed on was the need to change—on the part of both the regulator and the industry—in order to keep growing healthily and sustainably.

2

Situating Microfinance

It is ironic that the poor in India should still be severely deprived of credit when the country has a long history of government loans being given to the poor. Muhammad bin Tughluq, the sultan of Delhi in the early 14th century, was the first Indian ruler in recorded history to advance 'taccavi' loans to villagers to rehabilitate them after a disastrous famine. The British kept the tradition going through legislation in 1883–84, which played an important role during flood, drought, and famine. These were both short- and long-term, and even meant for things like land improvement as well as buying seeds. The Government of India formed a committee on taccavi loans and cooperative credit in 1962, and the practice of granting such loans continued into the 21st century.

Before we go any further, let us note the global and historical contexts in which India transited from taccavi loans to modern-day microfinance. Post World War II till the 1970s, donors and governments offered financial services through subsidized credit programmes for the rural poor. But these were not successful in that they often resulted in high defaults and losses and were unable to reach those who mattered—poor rural households.

The modern global pioneer in microcredit can be said to be ACCION International, which was founded in 1961 by a law student, Joseph Blatchford, who gathered USD 90,000 from private companies to start building schools and water systems in the shantytowns of Caracas, Venezuela. It turned to microcredit in 1973 and is today a premier microfinance organization with lending partners across Latin America, the United States, and Africa.

The terms 'microcredit' and 'microfinance' first began to be widely used in the 1970s—and it is largely Bangladesh-based Muhammad Yunus and the organization he founded, the Grameen Bank, that have made 'microfinance' both a household term and a part of a widely accepted development strategy to address poverty. In 1976, Yunus, who was with the University of Chicago, returned to a newly liberated Bangladesh still in the grip of famine-like conditions to design a credit-delivery system for the poor.

He found the poor were trapped in poverty for, among other reasons, lack of affordable finance. He began in Jibra village near Chittagong by lending the equivalent of USD 27 to 42 women to weave bamboo baskets. Its success caused the programme to be extended to several districts across the country. The historic moment came in 1983, with the Bangladesh government issuing an ordinance to create Grameen Bank. It innovated the group-lending joint liability programme under which a group of women borrowers took the responsibility for each other's loans and ensured very high recovery rates.

In 2006 Yunus and Grameen Bank were awarded the Nobel Peace Prize for their work in fighting poverty. Grameen Bank (its enabling ordinance was made into an act in 2013) is today owned 90 per cent by its borrowers and 10 per cent by the Bangladesh government. Its success has inspired over 40 similar projects around the world. In 2013 it had 6.7 million active borrowers, USD 2.3 billion in assets, 3.6 per cent portfolio at risk (PAR; percentage of lending on which repayment is overdue), and gave a return on equity of 13.7 per cent.

The 1980s also saw the emergence of another global microfinance flagship, BRI, which is described as the largest MFI in the developing world. The Indonesian government converted a state-owned agricultural bank into a system of autonomously managed village banking units. The system serves a massive 22 million savers.

In the 1980s, the Grameen Bank and BRI helped shape a critical conceptual and institutional breakthrough. They showed that you could serve small people not just on a large scale but profitably too. They were commercially funded and did not need regular subsidies and hence were sustainable businesses which could keep expanding. The 1990s were marked by both the number and size of microcredit organizations increasing. Microfinance began to be considered as an industry and the decade came to be known as the 'decade of microfinance'. The Microfinance Summit was launched in 1997; in 2005, it resolved to reach by 2015 women from 175 million of the world's poorest families and offer them credit for self-employment and other financial and business services. Microfinance received global recognition, so to speak, when the UN declared 2005 as the International Year of Microcredit.

Though microcredit and microfinance have been used interchangeably, there is a difference between the terms, and spelling that out partly reveals how the idea of empowering the poor, as opposed to giving them charity (which addresses specific needs at a given time) emerged. Microcredit came first, in the form of official small loans to those in distress. After World War II, when the Marshall Plan for the reconstruction of Europe was launched, as were multilateral financial institutions such as the World Bank Group, development came into its own as the first UN Development Decade was launched in 1961. Over time it became clear that there was more to banishing poverty than offering small loans (or microcredit). The poor, in order to permanently rise out of poverty, also needed to save, be able to access insurance, and plan for pensions. Hence the term 'microfinance', which embraced offering all the basic financial services, began to be used more often.

How has the Microfinance Summit goal of reaching women from 175 million of the world's poorest families by 2015 fared? According to

'Mapping Pathways Out of Poverty: The State of the Microfinance Summit Campaign Report 2015', global microfinance had 211 million clients in 2013, of which 112 million lived in extreme poverty, that is below USD 1.9 per day. (To put this in perspective, according to the World Bank, in 2012, 869 million people across the globe lived in extreme poverty.) So microfinance has more than met its goal, but to overcome poverty, you need more. We will address that in a later chapter.

To get back to India, rural poverty and indebtedness have been a concern of economists right from the pre-Independence days, when they sought to understand the cause of poverty under colonial rule and tried to make an economic case for independence. Unsurprisingly, the RBI undertook the first of its decennial All-India Rural Credit Survey when the independent nation was barely four years old, in 1951. These surveys, conducted till 1991, indicate some progress. Number-crunching in a 2007 Planning Commission paper made a few revelations: Over a 40-year period, the share of the non-institutional sector (made up of moneylenders and the like) in rural credit fell by precisely half, from 90 per cent in 1951 to 45 in 1991. Simultaneously, the share of the institutional sector went up six-fold, from 9 per cent to 53 per cent over the same period. Within this overall picture, the data for credit cooperatives and nationalized banks underline the realities surrounding them. Credit cooperatives were established to deliver the goods, and they did, up to a point, until their troubles caught up with them. From accounting for 4.6 per cent of rural credit in 1951, their share went up to 29 per cent in 1981, to fall back to 19 per cent 1991. It is a similar story with commercial banks, which were a great source of hope on state takeover, or nationalization, but after a good start, failed to maintain momentum. From accounting for 1.1 per cent of rural credit in 1951, their share went up to 25 per cent in 1981, but remained at the same level in 1991.

The remarkable rise in the share of institutional credit to the rural sector should have been a game changer in fighting rural poverty. But a 2003 World Bank–NCAER (National Council of Applied Economic

Research) survey conducted in Uttar Pradesh and Andhra Pradesh indicates that around 87 per cent of marginal farmers and landless labourers did not have access to formal bank credit. The share of the non-institutional sector in microcredit or microfinance remained at the same level as it was in 1951. The rapid expansion of the banking sector post nationalization had touched mostly large farmers. Around 66 per cent of them had bank accounts and 44 per cent had access to bank credit. Thus when microfinance made a beginning in a significant way in the 1990s, it had a huge task laid out in front of it—reaching out to the rural poor.

Microfinance through the bank–SHG programme took off in the 1990s and thereafter MFIs proper, constituted as societies, trusts, or non-banking financial intermediaries came into the picture and since the early 2000s, have taken the lead in providing credit to the poor. But long before microfinance took off in a big way, there were a few pioneers. The origin of microfinance in India can be traced first to the establishment of the Self Employed Women's Association (SEWA) in 1972, and then to the SEWA Cooperative Bank in 1974 to provide banking services to the poor women employed in the unorganized sector in Ahmedabad, Gujarat.

The message by Ela R. Bhatt, founder of the SEWA movement and the bank, encapsulates the essence of the microfinance ethos as it stands even today. She said poor women were economically active and hence were bankable. But, since they were busy and hesitant to go to the bank, it was up to the bank to approach them and not the other way around. The bank had to be run by 'barefoot bankers' committed to the cause, and not 'suited-booted' executives with a bureaucratic attitude. As poor women are most concerned about the running of their households, they made the most eligible borrowers. Trust, not paperwork and collaterals, are the cornerstones of lending to them. Mutual guarantee, by fellow women borrowers, was the best kind. As women's needs were diverse, they had to be given small loans for various purposes with recoveries made through small instalments. This would lead to 98 per cent recovery. Microcredit, micro-deposit and micro-insurance would pave the way to security for the poor women who made up the SEWA movement and the bank.

Another early player is MYRADA, or Mysore Rehabilitation and Development Agency, an NGO started by Aloysius P. Fernandez in 1968, which was initially dedicated entirely to the resettlement of Tibetan refugees. As MYRADA raised resources for the Tibetans and worked with them, the villagers around the settlements asked MYRADA, 'Why can't you work with us also?' The government soon stipulated that 10 per cent of all funds raised by MYRADA be used for Indian communities.

When rehabilitation of Tibetan refugees ended by 1978, MYRADA decided not to wind up but to use its skills in other similar projects for which the government also sought its help. Since 1979, MYRADA has been involved in setting up rural SHGs by building upon rural chit funds and informal lending networks to evolve a model of a credit management group.

In the early 1990s, NABARD took a crucial step and launched the bank–SHG linkage, where SHGs took loans from banks to lend to their members and ensured recovery and repayment. In this, MYRADA, under the leadership of Fernandez, played a path-breaking role. The development critically left the banks out of the individual micro-loan recovery exercise and the bank–SHG model achieved very high repayment rates. In 1996 RBI included loans to SHGs under priority sector lending, giving a major boost to the delivery of rural credit under the bank–SHG linkage. This can be said to be the first large-scale microfinance programme to take off in India.

MYRADA emphasizes that it does not work with microfinance, which is accessed by, among others, social units like SHGs or self-help affinity groups; rather, it helps organize these groups so that they can access bank finance. Fernandez also heads Sanghamithra Rural Financial Services, which took shape in the 1990s and is a proper MFI. MYRADA further also involved itself in various aspects of social development and currently works with a million families in 18 districts of Karnataka, what was undivided Andhra Pradesh, and Tamil Nadu, forming and strengthening community-based organizations.

Another pioneering institution working for the rural poor is PRADAN or Professional Assistance for Development Action. Founded in 1983, it works to empower the poor with a range of skills so that they can earn a livelihood and change their lives. Around 350 young professionals are working with nearly 400,000 families (mostly belonging to the scheduled castes and tribes [SCs and STs]) in nearly 6,000 villages in the seven poorest states of the country. They work with poor women so that they can form SHGs which can access institutional finance for their livelihood. PRADAN volunteers also work with donors, governments, banks, and institutions to garner resources so as to create livelihood assets and local infrastructure for the poor. Significantly, PRADAN, like MYRADA, does not directly offer microfinance but helps build and empower SHGs to access finance from banks.

In the late 1990s, the Small Industries Development Bank of India (SIDBI) launched a term-loan programme to create a national network of large and viable MFIs from the formal and informal sectors. Among those that grew up to size were SHARE, Spandana, and SKS Microfinance Limited. Historically, perhaps the most successful initiative to come out of this programme is the Rs 25 lakh that was given as loan and grant to Bandhan Microfinance in 2002 which got it going, setting it on a journey that would enable it to become the first MFI to get a universal banking licence.

After a promising start in the 1990s, microfinance experienced a tremendous period of growth in the new millennium. The total number of microfinance borrowers grew from a mere 300,000 in 2001 to 40 million in 2016 (Bharat Microfinance Report 2016, prepared by Sa-Dhan, the industry association that recognizes all types of microfinance organizations). The main driver of growth was the category of MFI-NBFCs—microfinance institutions registered with the RBI as NBFCs—which accounted for 85 per cent of the borrowers. The same proportion, 85 per cent, were served by large MFIs (those with over Rs 500 crore of outstanding).

Along with this emergence of NBFC–MFIs as the main engine of growth, the new millennium marked another significant change. At the root of this change was Ujjivan, focusing from day one, not on the rural poor—the traditional area of interest of MFIs—but the urban poor. Initially rural borrowers far outnumbered urban ones. But a big change happened during the three-year period from 2013 to 2015—urban borrowers overtook rural borrowers in numbers. From accounting for 67 per cent of all borrowers in 2013, the share of rural borrowers fell to 33 per cent in 2015, while in a complete reversal, the share of urban borrowers rose from 33 per cent in 2013 to 67 per cent in 2015. A correction of sorts took place in 2016 with the urban–rural ratio getting a bit less skewed at 62:38. But the broad trend remained unchanged, tying up with the rapid urbanization that India has seen after the launch of economic reforms in 1991. As more and more people migrated to urban centres seeking a better life, the number of poor in urban areas rose rapidly, thus creating a space for microfinance in urban India.

The second decade of the millennium saw both continuity and change. During 2011–16, women continued to make up the vast majority of borrowers, going up from 94 per cent to 97 per cent. The share of SC/ST borrowers also rose, from 20 per cent in 2012 to 30 per cent in 2016. The share of borrowers from the minorities, however, went through a trough before recovering. It came down from 23 per cent in 2012 to 14 per cent in 2014, but then improved sharply to 27 per cent in 2016.

Just as the number of borrowers has multiplied, the gross loan portfolio (GLP) of MFIs has gone up too. From Rs 24,332 crore in 2011, it has gone up by around two-and-a-half times to Rs 63,853 crore in 2016, recording a compound annual growth rate (CAGR) of 21.3 per cent. Here too, the large NBFC–MFIs account for the lion's share of the business.

While the overall growth rate has been phenomenal, there have been ups and downs, coinciding with the crises experienced by the industry, notably the developments in Andhra Pradesh around 2010. Thus, the GLP remained virtually static (zero growth) during 2011–13, and recorded an increase only in 2014, when it rose over the previous year by 30 per cent. The total number of borrowers also fell after 2011, and growth resumed only in 2014, by 20 per cent over the previous year. This growth momentum has remained robust till 2016. To take a longer perspective, the growth rate in both total borrowers and outstanding loans peaked in 2009, went into negative territory in 2012, and resumed in right earnest in 2014.

Rapid growth is the hallmark of the industry but how sustainable is such growth? The industry measures the health of its portfolio, first and foremost, through the ratio of portfolio at risk. For this, the primary benchmark is PAR at 30 days, which is essentially aggregating those accounts where repayment has fallen behind by over 30 days. The portfolio at risk came down from 1 per cent in 2012 to 0.02 per cent in 2014, indicating a return to health after the Andhra crisis. But it went up again to 0.13 per cent in 2015 and rose further to 0.29 per cent in 2016. While this is still low and healthy, the issue is—are we seeing stress on assets re-emerging in the wake of the rapid growth achieved in the post Andhra crisis years, just as rapid growth preceded the Andhra crisis?

Low PAR is made possible by controlling costs. For the industry as a whole, the operating expenses ratio (administrative plus staff costs)—as a share of the total portfolio—stood at 10.2 per cent. In this, as in a lot else, it is the NBFC–MFIs and large MFIs that have a low operating expense ratio. For NBFC–MFIs, it is 8.5 per cent and for large MFIs (those with a loan portfolio of over Rs 500 crore), it is as low as 7.5 per cent.

Profitability is also determined by financial costs, which is high for MFIs depending mostly on bank borrowings. For NBFC–MFIs, it is the second highest at 13.5 per cent, while for large MFIs it is only a little lower at 12.4 per cent. It is the MFIs constituted as cooperatives that have the lowest financial costs at 9.5 per cent. In terms of trends, the operating expenses ratio has gone down in the last two years (2015 and 2016), indicating that MFIs are able to cut costs as they grow bigger. But in the last three years (2014–16) their financial costs ratio (borrowing costs), which is not in their hands, has gone up.

Overall profitability is indicated by the yield on portfolio. Post the Andhra crisis this ratio has gone up from 17 per cent in 2012 to 24 per cent in 2014, and remained at that level in 2015, a year of very high growth. Thereafter, significantly, the yield fell in 2016 to 21 per cent. This ties up with the trend we have seen in the health of portfolios indicated by PAR. As growth has picked up significantly, PAR has risen and yield has begun to fall. Yield is low for NBFC–MFIs at 21 per cent, lower for large MFIs at 19 per cent, and the highest for small MFIs (with less than Rs 1 crore portfolio) at 26 per cent. This underlines the reality that small MFIs have high costs and thus have to go for a higher yield in order to be able to have the resources to build capacity and grow.

Yield ties up with costs and margins. As regulator, the RBI has laid down the rule that MFI margins should not exceed 10–12 per cent (this is in response to the perception that they should not make money at the cost of their poor borrowers). In 2016, legal MFIs have complied with this, their margins falling in the 9–10 per cent range. NBFC–MFIs have recorded a median margin of 10.07 per cent.

In keeping with the general health of the industry, in 2016, the operating self-sufficiency (OSS)—how much of the operating, financial, and provisioning expenses are covered by operating and investment income—for all MFIs stood at 113 per cent, at 119 per cent for NBFC–MFIs, and at 127 per cent for large MFIs. A significant takeaway is that MFIs make very little money on very small loans; OSS is 106 per cent for loans below Rs 5,000. But things get better as loan sizes increase, with OSS reaching 119 per cent (the NBFC–MFI figure) once loan size goes above Rs 15,000.

Return on assets and equity, the final measure of profitability, is the best for NBFC–MFIs and also the highest for large MFIs. Return on assets for the industry as a whole is 2.21 per cent, 2.58 per cent for NBFC–MFIs, and 2.9 per cent for large MFIs. It is the same with return on equity. For all MFIs in 2016, it is 11.57 per cent, for NBFC–MFIs, it is 12.51 per cent, and for large MFIs, it jumps to 19.3 per cent. Overall, if we look at the industry in terms of size, MFIs are able to lower their operating costs as they grow, but their financial costs, dependent on what banks charge, goes up. At the end of the day, they are able to earn a higher surplus, which gets reflected in higher return on assets and equity. Thus, the lesson here is—big remains beautiful, even while serving the small (poor).

SELF-HELP GROUPS

Microfinance in India has run on two parallel tracks—through MFIs and bank-linked SHGs. The latter, as mentioned earlier, began in the 1990s and by 2016, 7.9 million SHGs were linked with banks and they accounted for total outstanding of Rs 57,119 crore. This compares with a total outstanding of Rs 63,853 for MFIs which have 40 million borrowers. If we assume each SHG has around six members, then the total number of borrowers served was around 48 million. What is specific to the bank-linked SHGs is that their members save with banks even as they get finance from them. In 2016, total savings stood at Rs 13,691 crore, around a fifth of total outstanding loans. Thus, SHGs have a good bit of their own funds with banks from whom they borrow.

Both the streams were affected by the Andhra crisis. The total number of SHGs linked to banks during a year peaked to 1.6 million in 2009 and fell to 1.2 million in 2012, to go up again to 1.6 million in 2016, thus things returned to where they were in 2009. Total disbursement was flat in only one year, 2011, and then grew rapidly till 2016. In comparison, the growth rate in microfinance borrowers, as also the total portfolio, was negative only in one year, 2013, and has thereafter resumed till 2016. Thus the medium-term impact of the Andhra crisis was much more on the SHGs (in terms of new group linkages) than it was on acquisition of MFI borrowers. During the three-year period (2013–16) both MFIs and SHGs returned to growth in disbursals and acquisition of customers.

But the biggest difference between the two groups is the level of NPAs among loans taken by SHGs. These stood at 6.5 per cent in 2016, compared 4.7 per cent in 2011. MFIs, on the other hand, ended 2016 with a PAR of 0.29 per cent. This would indicate that the NBFC–MFIs, till now, represent the most successful and self-sustaining model for lending to the poor in India. The underlying quest in the chapters that will follow will be to glean why this is so from the example of one successful NBFC–MFI—Ujjivan.

3

Experts Remember

In the previous chapter we have given a somewhat dry and fact-laden account of how the practice of giving small loan to large numbers of poor women without securities began and evolved into India's robust and rapidly growing microfinance sector. Here is the same story retold in greater detail by the actual players—people with emotion and compassion who remember a south Asian drama as it played out, seeking to redeem lives condemned to poverty, and look into the future to get a sense of what it holds.

Poverty at the grassroots has endured in India but not for lack of official attention. The RBI is the only central bank in the world where in the act itself, first passed in 1934, there is mention of agricultural credit, as Vijay Mahajan, one of the pioneers of Indian microcredit or microfinance, ruefully notes. That is because the British colonial regime was always very concerned about peasant rebellion. So it tried all kinds of medicines to cure the malady—whether with taccavi loans, or subsequently with cooperative credit. When the country became independent, the government tried a lot to ensure that the rural credit system worked. But to very limited purpose. As he explains: 'Despite bank nationalization and branch expansion, availability of credit to the rural poor remained a huge issue all through.'

NGOs that concern themselves with the poor found that wherever they went, people were crying out for credit to enable them to make a living.

Hence the need to organize credit for the poor was high on their agenda. When their attempt to move the nearest bank manager proved futile, many of them 'actually tried to dabble with providing credit themselves,' says Mahajan. That is how NGOs came into the picture, by trying to fill a bit of the credit gap.

This is what happened in a highly amplified way in Bangladesh. After East Pakistan was dismantled, the government and administration in the country went to pieces. Whatever development activity was taking place was being delivered by aid agencies and NGOs. It is in this context that Muhammad Yunus set to work in 1976, barely five years after Bangladesh was born, to set up the Grameen Bank. Fascinatingly, things were then happening in India too. In 1973 Ela Bhatt started the SEWA Bank. The difference between these first two examples of microcredit delivery on the subcontinent is that while Grameen Bank grew in leaps and bounds, SEWA, by choice, remained relatively local. That apart, the two established something critical—proof of concept. In Mahajan's words, 'it was possible to serve the poor with a reasonably sustainable institution', and not by distributing private charity or government dole, which had ebbs and flows and occasionally dried out, depending on the state of public and private solvency.

In the 1990s, when economic liberalization policies came to India, the second Narasimham Committee effectively told banks that the era of social banking was over and their first concern was their profitability and NPAs. 'The banks took that as a mandate to turn their backs on the poor. So whatever little credit was coming to the poor till 1989–90, just vanished,' says Mahajan. These constituted the direct and indirect impact of liberalization on the banking system.

SELF-HELP GROUPS

Nature abhors a vacuum and the result of the banks winding down their concern for the poor created a ferment in the NGO-dominated microcredit space. The first stirrings had begun earlier when Aloysius

Fernandez, through MYRADA, started working among the rural poor in Karnataka from 1982. The poor, who found primary agricultural credit societies and their low-cost loans being cornered by powerful families, broke away and formed groups of their own from 1985 onwards. Critically, notes Fernandez, 'the members selected themselves on the basis of affinity. MYRADA called them credit management groups [CMGs]', whose focus was on savings management and later, credit from those savings. These later came to be called SHGs. (It is all too clear that Fernandez wishes that his nomenclature had stuck.)

In the early 1990s, three policy decisions were taken by the RBI and NABARD:

1. Let banks extend bulk loans to self-help affinity groups (SAGs), and allow them to decide on which group member to lend to.
2. Allow banks to lend to unregistered SAGs so long as they maintained proper books of accounts and records of meetings.
3. And critically, lend without physical collaterals.

The idea was to create an alternative channel to banks' rule-and-procedure-bound systems of lending. With this system, the banks had to merely satisfy themselves about the genuineness of the SAG. This was the basis of the SHG–bank linkage programme launched by NABARD in 1992 in which MYRADA, under the leadership of Fernandez, played a path-breaking role. Fernandez feels that it was all going well while NABARD remained in charge. Over time the government adopted the programme, and official targets were set and chased, but the critical task of enabling capacity building by groups of poor lost priority.

The work of MYRADA began to be emulated and there was a period of ferment in the first half of the 1990s. Some NGOs like PRADAN—Mahajan worked with them till 1991—started self-help work in the footsteps of MYRADA. Fernandez wore two hats, CEO of MYRADA and chairman of PRADAN. This was followed by M. Udaia Kumar establishing SHARE Microfin Limited in Hyderabad. Several NGOs also came up with the explicit agenda of providing credit. 'Those were the early beginnings,' says Mahajan.

SIDBI'S ROLE

Fortunately for India, while there were these stirrings of voluntary action at the ground level, things began to happen at the official institutional level too. SIDBI, which was founded in 1990, realized while working with the poor that nobody was giving them small loans. Recalls Brij Mohan, who went on to become executive director of SIDBI, that this realization prompted them to run a pilot during 1994–98—lending to NGOs to give small loans to the poor. 'Then, microfinance had not arrived in India, though it was very much there in Bangladesh.' After the pilot, SIDBI asked the National Institute for Rural Development (NIRD) to carry out an evaluation 'and it gave a very positive report. NGOs were getting their money back and clients were benefiting. The SIDBI management asked if this business will be big and we [those involved in the exercise] said yes.'

This represented a conceptual breakthrough. Till then most NGOs working with the poor had been on a 'largesse' mode. But if they got into microfinance they could be on a 'continuous mode'—keep borrowing and lending. 'So we decided to go ahead (put them in a continuous mode),' explains Brij Mohan, 'and create a separate setup called SIDBI Foundation for Micro Credit [SFMC] in 1999' and immediately faced two issues. SIDBI was lending to NGOs at 9 per cent and had asked them not to charge more than 18 per cent. But NGO costs were more and their other operations were subsidizing microfinance. The second issue was putting the financial relationship between SIDBI and SFMC on a stable footing. Thus, two decisions were taken. SFMC would borrow from SIDBI at 10 per cent and on-lend to NGOs at 11 per cent, who would then have freedom on pricing. The challenge was to have 100 large, formal, strong, and profitable financial corporates giving small loans to the poor. For this to happen,

NGOs aspiring to the new role had to overcome their intrinsic habit of thinking small. They also had to acquire capabilities in good governance, infrastructure, and technology. The UK's Department for International Development (DFID) and the UN's International Fund for Agricultural Development (IFAD) became partners offering capacity-building grants and low-cost funds, respectively.

Another institution that played a pioneering role was Friends of Women's World Banking (FWWB), the Indian affiliate of the global Women's World Banking. They had a tradition of lending small amounts to start-ups which would lend tiny amounts to the poor. FWWB were often the first to lend money for capacity building, before SIDBI lent money. While SIDBI had to abide by some norms like the NGOs it lent to had at least 3,000 clients and a few balance sheets, FWWB had no such conditions to abide by. The first microfinance loans to several NGOs came from three development institutions—Rashtriya Mahila Kosh set up by the government of India, FWWB set up by SEWA under the leadership of Ela Bhat, and Rashtriya Gram Vikas Nidhi promoted by development institutions and operating in the Northeast.

During 2000–07 SIDBI ran the National Microfinance Support Project. This was the beginning of the so-called microfinance movement. 'We started with some small institutions in Andhra. Those that grew included SHARE, Spandana, SKS, and much later, Bandhan in West Bengal,' Brij Mohan says, and is extremely modest when told that all these names that became big later on owed their origins to hand holding by SIDBI.

INTEREST RATE DEBATE

Before the SIDBI initiative, few private interests looked at the microfinance market, says Professor M.S. Sriram, long-term academic tracker of microfinance, because there was an unwritten taboo about high interest rates. The rhetoric was the exploitative moneylender charging usurious interest rates. The Prahlad type 'bottom of the pyramid' thought did not percolate into financial services because when you are selling a shampoo, the mark-up is not known, only the MRP is evident, but for financial services it is depicted by the interest rate. As Sriram notes, 'Because of the taboo on high interest rates, the private sector did not come in and the market remained as it was. All [financial assistance] was government-driven, subsidy-driven.'

The first private phase, according to Sriram, started with the bank-linked SHGs—savings-based inter-lending. A similar model was being pursued by the cooperatives but it never took off. For a long time, SHGs remained outside the purview of the state because they dealt with women—a new market—and they were notionally based on saving. Therefore, one did not need too many outside resources to set up an SHG, except the intervening NGO, which was inter-lending and subsequently mainstreaming over three to six months. MYRADA and PRADAN were the two big SHG-centred organizations. SEWA belonged to a separate category because over time it deepened its engagement with its members in Ahmedabad, did not spread geographically, and was initially savings heavy—hence, a safe place for women to keep their savings.

In their wisdom, continues Sriram, those who promoted SHGs advised them to charge interest rates closer to those charged by moneylenders and not banks, thus encouraging them to charge upwards of 24 per cent. The logic was simple: prevent arbitrage between the outside market rates and SHG rates so these women would not turn into mini moneylenders; SHGs took care of the internal default of the group without defaulting to the bank as they had a buffer; even if an SHG made tremendous profits, it remained within the group, so it was not seen as exploitative at all. So for the first time, the debate over interest rates occurred in a very constructive manner. It legitimized high interest rates and 24–26–28 per cent rates were seen as cost and taken as acceptable.

MFIs—NOT-FOR-PROFIT AND FOR PROFIT

When the NGO MFIs came—SHARE, SKS, Spandana—they rode on the legitimacy of SHGs but added that the groups took too long to grow, and required a lot of hand-holding (the famous cycle of forming, storming, norming, performing). On the other hand, the MFIs were an impatient lot, who wanted to grow much faster, and followed the Grameen model. There were three organizations which nurtured them. 'One which prevented stillborn babies and infant mortality—Friends of Women's World Banking, led by Vijayalakshmi Das—would have bailed out many organizations which are big now with a two-lakh or a five-lakh loan. The other two were SIDBI and ICICI Bank which actually did not nurture but recklessly helped them grow.'

The MFIs which rode on SHGs could charge the same rate of interest as they said they were not-for-profit. So the 24–26–28 per cent rate went out of the debate for a temporary period. The debate was more about how to provide access and scale rather than at what cost. Ujjivan, Janalakshmi, and Equitas represent the third wave of microfinance organizations— these started as NBFCs, were for profit, and focused on performance and scale. (The first wave was SHGs and the second wave was early non-profit MFIs like SHARE, Spandana, and SKS following the Grameen Bank model of group lending.)

The third wave MFIs did not come with huge developmental finance baggage but were all led by ex-bankers who saw there was a market potential that could be exploited with professionalism and a certain amount of empathy for the poor. They were all able to raise capital without resorting to grants, like the second-wave organizations which were all grant based and later converted to commercial entities. The suppression of the interest-rate debate allowed the for-profit private sector to come in with the help of freely available risk capital and grow phenomenally, until the 2010 Andhra crisis.

BASIX, A PIONEER

To go back a little bit in time and see the historical process through the eyes of one of the microfinance pioneers, Vijay Mahajan, it is necessary to narrate the story of Basix. When he started Basix in 1996, Mahajan had studied not just the Indian developments but also spent two years looking at various models around the world. He came to the conclusion that given the size of the country, you couldn't rely on an NGO or a grant-based model because it would be too constrained by resources. It would have to be something which could raise money from the capital market and debt from the banking system over the long term.

Mahajan's intention was to start a bank but he was unable to get a banking licence because of little experience and equity, so he started off as an NBFC. Basix, in that sense, was the first attempt at delivering commercial microfinance in India. The intent was as developmental as anybody else's but the principle of sustainability was equally important. Everybody else—SHARE, Spandana, SKS—remained NGOs until 2005. Even Bandhan began as an NGO. 'Most of them acquired their first half a million to one million customers as NGOs, then set up an NBFC, transferred the portfolios to it, and left behind the costs and bad debts in the NGO. When the NBFCs were born in 2005–06, they were like new babies dressed in princely clothes paid for by the NGO donors. People talk of NGO transformation but are unaware of the financial implication. If you start as an NBFC, all your start-up costs remain on your balance sheet. Ujjivan started as an NBFC. Samit Ghosh, being a banker, came to Basix before he launched Ujjivan and immediately picked up the point,' says Mahajan.

Among the early challenges that the microfinance sector faced was one of mindset. In the previous 30–40 years, because of increasing pressure from the government to the banks to lend—first it was directed credit, then tied to government schemes like Integrated Rural Development Programme (IRDP)—repayment rates were extremely poor. In IRDP, for example, the repayment rate was 18 per cent. Most regional rural banks, in their non-IRDP credit, were getting recoveries of 30–40 per cent in the eastern region, and about 60 per cent in the south. Commercial banks in the south were getting 70–80 per cent and 50 per cent in the eastern region. So for the banking sector, microfinance meant you give the loan and pray. Hence post-liberalization when banks had to make provisions for bad loans, this couldn't be a working model as then the government had to recapitalize the banks.

So it was that in 1996, nobody believed in Mahajan's ideas. He recalls, 'People said, "You are crazy. You are going to borrow from banks in your own name and the name of your company and lend to poor people. They will not repay you or even if they repay 20 per cent, where will you get the remaining 80 per cent from?"' But his own experience was different. He had worked in PRADAN with poor people and seen the work in SEWA in great detail, been to Grameen Bank and Bangladesh Rural Advancement Committee (BRAC) in Bangladesh, Bank of Agriculture and Agricultural Cooperatives (BAAC) in Thailand, Business Innovation Centre (BIC) in Indonesia and ShoreBank in USA—institutions across cultures, ownerships, and regimes. 'I was convinced that if you treat the poor as customers with dignity, don't play games with them, and don't trouble them while they are getting a loan, most of them will try their best to maintain their credit with you,' says Mahajan.

Not only was he convinced that lending money to the poor was a viable business proposition, if you had to make an impact in rural India, then you had to provide comprehensive credit, not just for agricultural and livestock, but also to encourage diversification from farm to non-farm. In the long run, that is where the hope is. He adds, 'We designed products which, even today, can challenge any MFI in India. Their product range will not match what ours was in 1996; forget about later, when we added many products like sanitation, energy, vocational training. Our microfinance business suffered a lot after 2010 but we are still around, even if in a small way.'

In the early 1990s when there was a quest for what was the right way to lend to the poor who needed credit, some NGOs went in for the self-help model like MYRADA and PRADAN, and some NGOs like SHARE went in for the MFI model of Grameen Bank. Mahajan adds, 'Ideally, in a large country like this, pluralism should flourish but the self-help model became the darling of the government and the public-sector banking system. This is because they could make it appear that they were lending at only 12 per cent [the rate applicable to the SHG] and hide the fact that the women were getting the loan at 24 per cent from the group.'

When NGOs entered this sector they were very small. They realized that if they had to break even or keep their head above water, even 24 per cent would not work. So some of them started charging unacceptably high rates of 30 to 36 per cent. 'They were basically moneylending NGOs.' So they eventually ended up doing their first Rs 100–200 crore at such rates and built an enormous surplus. 'To confirm this, all you have to do is look at where the founding equity of some of these six or seven transformed NGOs came from. And wherever it has come from a trust or society with an NGO-sounding name, that is the surplus which has been left behind due to the high interest rates charged; that was what was converted into the equity of the NGOs.'

GENESIS OF THE ANDHRA CRISIS

Mahajan was engaged with the issue of credit to the poor generically, and was not a votary of any specific model—MFI or SHG; he was working on both. In 1995, when the RBI appointed a working group—of which he was a member—on what was the best way to lend to the poor, it recommended the SHG model. C. Rangarajan, RBI governor ('a former professor of mine'), took good note of it and issued a guideline allowing banks to open accounts for unregistered SHGs. The lead agency appointed to take this model all over the country was NABARD, which went about the business of promotional activities, training bank managers, and so on. It did not meet with great success except in two or three southern states where the chief ministers—like the late J. Jayalalithaa in Tamil Nadu and Chandrababu Naidu in Andhra Pradesh—took to this model and supported NABARD in a big way, which led to both the states having lakhs of SHGs by the late 1990s.

That is where the trouble began, recalls Mahajan, because Andhra was also where four or five MFIs had come up, including Basix, but most importantly SHARE, Spandana, and SKS, which were working only with women. These same women were becoming members of SHGs and the groups made by these MFIs. ('In the case of Basix we used to give crop loans to men—farmers. Almost 50 per cent of our borrowers in the early years were men. We also lent for non-farm activities.') States like Andhra set up a whole machinery funded by the World Bank to nurture SHGs. That bureaucracy initially had a missionary motive, which subsequently turned into a vested interest. 'Even today, senior IAS officers utter sentences like, "How can MFIs work with my women", meaning those who had joined SHGs. There was the sense that MFIs were stealing their women. The fact was that loans from SHGs were fairly small and never met the full credit requirement of a household. Which is why households had to go to sometimes one or two MFIs.'

There is a global pattern to the way a microfinance crisis builds up. The generic process is as follows. Initially, there is a starvation of credit and people are borrowing only from moneylenders, loan sharks. Then some MFIs are set up. 'Then people start liking the fact that MFI interest rates are much lower. They are friendly, the whole process is much more dignified, so it becomes a "success". Then a second MFI comes, then a third. At that stage, particularly if there is no credit bureau, there is a danger that MFI2 starts lending to some of the existing borrowers of MFI1 and MFI3 starts lending to existing borrowers of MFI1 and MFI2. Why would the borrower do that? She has not seen such money in her life. While getting a loan, everybody is happy. The problem begins when you have to repay.'

Then adds Mahajan tellingly, 'it is possible for a country's microfinance sector within a year, or a short period, to go from being a good thing to a bad thing.'

An MFI going from good to bad can be prevented in two ways—one, through the strict use of credit bureaus, so that one can at least know whether there are formal or MFI loans. Moneylenders' loans cannot be checked. The second is by imposing a code of conduct. The credit bureau will only tell you if the borrower has previous loans or not. The code of conduct has to say that you cannot give a third loan and the RBI has to back it up.

SELF-REGULATION

Before we look into the future of microfinance, there is a need to digress into a brief discussion about self-regulation, which is as vital as preventive healthcare. Crises would rarely happen if an industry had good self-regulation. Microfinance in India did not have self-regulation and hence Andhra happened. Sa-Dhan, the first association of microfinance organizations, was set up in 1998, when there were only two organizations which could be so called, SEWA and Basix. Adds Mahajan, 'Ela Bhat and I set up Sa-Dhan and asked anybody who had anything to do with microfinance—NGOs, banks—to please come and join. It was really a promotional federation. The idea was to get the government and the banking system to accept the organization. Hence, Sa-Dhan never thought that there could be malpractice. We came from a world where we thought there would always be a shortage of credit. It was only when the Krishna crisis happened in 2006—and as co-chairman of Sa-Dhan, I went to Vijayawada and Elluru and met the authorities and managed to diffuse the crisis—that for the first time we declared a code of conduct.'

But Sa-Dhan had no enforcement mechanism and RBI was not involved, as MFIs at the time were all NGOs. They—the RBI—said,

'We don't regulate you, and except Basix, which we regulate as an NBFC, and SEWA Bank, which we regulate as a cooperative bank, we don't even know who the others are.' Later on, when the NGOs began to transform into NBFCs in 2006, and when there were early signs of overlending in 2009, in Kolar and Kanpur, Mahajan got a film-maker to make a 20-minute documentary on what happened; 'he did a great job'. Through authentic borrower interviews he showed what was going on—it started with MFI1, followed by MFI2, and then MFI3. That became a kind of a warning bell. This was shown at the Sa-Dhan AGM (annual general meeting), 'but most people said, "this is not us but them"'.

So, Mahajan realized there was this gap between the mainstream MFI and NGO MFI. What was needed was a specialized body only of the NBFC–MFIs, which could have hopes of becoming a self-regulatory organization (SRO), since RBI was also thinking along those lines. That's how he got the NBFC–MFIs together and the MFIN was set up in late 2009. 'We hired Alok Prasad as CEO just two–three months before the Andhra crisis broke!'

PRIVATE EQUITY

Till 2005, MFIs (with the exception of Basix) were all NGOs. But a stage came when the balance sheets of NGO MFIs became so big that their lenders started getting nervous, as there was no equity in the system and they were not properly regulated. So they were urged and supported by institutions like SIDBI to transform themselves into profit-making NBFCs. However, capital for these institutions could only be raised from national and international development financial institutions and some international private equity players. But change was on the way. Recalls Ujjivan's Ghosh, 'The microfinance industry was seen to be a close parallel to the mobile telecom industry which was riding high in the equity markets. Microfinance too caught on as the flavour of the month for international private equity without a clear understanding of the risks associated with the business serving the most vulnerable sections of society. In order to achieve high valuations, MFIs—especially those that started out as NGOs—were encouraged to ensure very high growth and profitability. This aggressive growth in business with massive customer acquisition was done blindly without adequate credit information on customers, their debt levels, and their ability to service debt. This started a mad scramble among the MFIs in Andhra Pradesh to lend imprudently. Unfortunately, this was happening in [the same] geography which also had the highest density of SHGs. The largest SHG programme was promoted by the government and financed by the World Bank. When repayment time came these women became very distraught trying to decide who to repay from their limited resources. There was pressure for repayment at weekly meetings and they took their problem to their SHG, which took it to the government employee who amplified their complaints and took it to his bosses. This brought the government department running the programme in direct conflict with the MFIs.'

The first to become an NBFC (other than Basix) and take in private equity was SHARE Microfin Limited, headed by Udaia Kumar, securing equity from Legatum in 2006. Then Spandana secured equity from JM Financial. SKS secured a first round from Kismat Capital and the Ravi and Pratibha Reddy Foundation, and a second round from Sequoia. Between 2007 and 2009, private equity came in, as did specialized funds such as Globe Capital and Aavishkaar Goodwell. By 2010, banks were lending happily as MFIs were able to raise capital to maintain capital adequacy. In the quest for growth people start doing reckless lending. ICICI Bank, for example, was lending heavily to Spandana. 'In front of my eyes it went from a Rs 4 crore institution in year one to a Rs 100 crore institution in year three. Lenders were very happy,' Mahajan recalls.

It was only a matter of time before private equity players started urging MFIs to go in for IPOs so that they could exit. To do so profitably MFIs would have to ensure high growth and high profitability. The quick way to do this would be to lend more and more to the same borrowers. So SKS incentivized the staff to lend more. 'A borrower was getting Rs 5,000 one day and in six months' time she was getting Rs 25,000.' Echoing Ghosh, Mahajan adds that unfortunately, this was happening in the same geography—Andhra Pradesh. Thus, there was pressure for repayment at weekly meetings, and the borrowers took their problem to their SHG, which eventually reached senior government officials.

Early attempts by MFIN to curb this were met with complete non-response, recalls Mahajan, because MFIs like SKS were in a big rush to make a success of their IPO. SHARE and Spandana were watching over SKS's shoulders thinking, 'If their IPO is a success we will do ours within two or three months.' These three were competing with each other to build their portfolios in the same geography where the government was pumping in money through SHGs. So the crash had to happen. Then, when the SKS IPO in August 2010 was a grand success—13 times oversubscribed—suddenly political leaders realized that they were being left out: '*Ye log to* "poor, poor" *bolte hain*, but they have got thousands of crores; *lekin hamko to kuch nahi diya*, so let's teach these guys a lesson.'

The MFI founders also got a bad name because they were seen to have enriched themselves during the process of converting from non-profits to for-profits. There were 'extraordinary financial gains for the promoters and managements' of MFIs, says Ghosh in an article in the book, *Client Centricity*, edited by Jan Hagen and Ulrich Schurenkramer (Murmann 2011). After studying data on four MFIs—SHARE, Asmitha, Spandana, and SKS—Sriram wrote in a June 2010 article in *Economic & Political Weekly* that 'the promoters came in with a development objective—wanting to promote institutions that helped the community. Each tried to have a community share holding and give some part of the profit back … They moved to the mainstream due to the requirements of capital and the pace of growth … However, in the process of getting the mainstream players into the poverty market, there was a drift. Whether they were pushed into a corner because of pressure from new investors, or they thought their job was done, is not known. However the incidents in the history of these organizations do not make very good reading, particularly with organizations that started out with resources from the society. The founders never invested risk capital ... In the case of MFIs it is possible to trace the profits to the poor. The contrast between the client who is supposed to benefit and the promoter who is actually benefited is stark.' Advocating moderation, he warned, 'the backlash in case of undue enrichment from the poor is going to be much larger and harsher.'

THE ANDHRA CRISIS

The fallout is best captured at some length in Mahajan's own words. After the SKS IPO, 'politicians turned against MFIs, with the bureaucrats already put off because of the SHG members' complaints. The worst was that in some cases, borrowers felt so harassed that they committed suicide. That completely turned public sentiment against MFIs and the media started painting MFIs as moneylenders and sharks. *India Today* ran my photo in their Telugu edition [with the headline] "Microfinance Mafia of Andhra Pradesh". For 15 years while one was quietly doing some work, nobody came. Then suddenly within two months of the SKS IPO, all of us became villains. The deification [lionizing the microfinance sector for bringing in all the world's money] was not correct and neither was the demonization.'

The crisis broke in October 2010 when the state government of Andhra Pradesh issued an ordinance severely restricting the operations of MFIs. The ordinance was followed by a state law being passed within the year, which, among other things, made it obligatory for an MFI to obtain permission from the relevant district authorities before operating in the area. Plus, MFIs could not engage in door-to-door collection but only in designated public areas, and that too monthly, not weekly. This sent a signal to borrowers that MFI loans need not be repaid and collections fell precipitously.

The Andhra Pradesh legislation revealed the regulatory gap that existed in the field of microfinance and in late 2010 the RBI appointed a committee under H.Y. Malegam to look into the issue. Dr D. Subbarao was the RBI governor when the Andhra crisis happened and he and his wife were both from the state's IAS cadre. 'He knew exactly what was going on and when the Andhra crisis occurred, he decided to let it take its course. My assessment is that he thought: "These guys have misbehaved, so let them suffer". Eventually, the system had to do something about it because it was a loss of over Rs 7,000 crore of banking business,' says Mahajan.

MFIs had their reservations over the Malegam Committee. With the exception of Sashi Rajgopalan, who was basically from the cooperative credit sector, there was nobody on it who had any familiarity with lending to the poor. Members like industrialist Kumaramangalam Birla or Indian Space Research Organization (ISRO) scientist U.R. Rao were very learned gentlemen but did not really know this field very well. Says Mahajan, 'When they came to talk to MFIs—I remember having more than one dialogue with them as MFIN president—they would discount whatever we were saying as self-serving.'

Sriram recalls appearing before the Malegam Committee, where they asked him to comment on usurious interest rates, multiple lending, and coercive recovery: 'I said as RBI you should not be asking me these questions. Have you been monitoring the inflow of FDI into the microfinance sector and valuations, particularly given that the clients are vulnerable? If the valuations are doubling every six months, you need to be aware that these valuations will put some pressure on the profitability and growth of the organizations. The reason for growth and this peril [2010 crisis] was the huge pressure that came as a result of high valuations and the amount of investment flowing in.'

Mahajan reflects the sentiment of the MFI sector when he says, 'The initial Malegam Committee report was not very fair to MFIs. It exaggerated the wrongdoings—I am not saying there weren't any—and understated the good work, particular in light of the failure of the banking sector to serve the poor in the previous decades. Malegam's reputation in Bombay was of a very learned and objective man. So I went to see him after the report came out, asking him to hear me out. I was told, whatever you do, go equipped with data. Samit [Ghosh of Ujjivan] and Vasu [P.N. Vasudevan of Equitas] were with me. He listened to us and took extensive notes. Basically, in that one-and-a-half hour meeting, he revised some of the perceptions—he realized we were not a bunch of unprofessional moneylenders who were out to make money off the poor and that there were some genuine operating issues.'

Fortunately for the sector, the eventual RBI circular which was based on MFIN's code of conduct incorporated many changes from the Malegam Committee recommendations. On the other hand, the circular initiated a regime of intensive regulation. Mahajan's final take: 'One can say we brought this upon ourselves because of our misbehaviour. Over time, RBI has eased up on many of the regulations but even today NBFC–MFIs are among the most regulated of NBFCs. In all this, we lost about two to three years due to the Andhra crisis. By 2013 the sector recovered and the last two or three years have seen very robust growth.'

Sounding like an elder statesman, Brij Mohan says, 'The crisis did a lot of good to the sector. To borrow from genetics, it resulted in mutation which was needed for the development of a new gene from the early inbreeding. We felt bad at the time—the sector fell into disrepute. But it emerged stronger, more responsible, more regulated, more formal. To be fair, whatever we demanded, RBI acceded to over a period of time.'

DISSENTING VOICES

In the general optimism over microfinance, there are some voices of concern and scepticism. Sriram acknowledges what microfinance has been able to achieve. It opened up a new market—women—and so its advent did not affect the existing market. The customers of microfinance and SHGs had not borrowed from anybody before. The men had been borrowing for agriculture. The portfolios of microfinance organizations consist largely of loans for livestock, petty shops, vegetable vending, and tea shops. These loans helped to make best use of the spare time and capacity that existed and developed enterprises and cash flows which were regular. These were not very profitable but reduced the vulnerability of borrowing families, as cash started to flow in regularly.

But the problem, as Sriram sees it, 'is that in this business model you can service a loan at 24 per cent provided you do not grow. A vegetable vendor cannot handle two carts at the same time. What happened in Andhra and what is happening now [2016] is giving a Rs 50,000 loan at 24 per cent to a person who can at best service a Rs 10,000 loan. This is because the model is bereft of credit appraisal and relies on recovery. If you were to theorize this model, you would say the credit appraisal is the self-appraisal done by the borrower. If she does not do this she is in for trouble some time or the other. If a little bit of disequilibrium happens then the default starts and then there is the domino effect.'

There is angst written into this. In the book edited by Yunus, *Jorimon and Others: Faces of Poverty*, each episode begins with a query: 'Will I be able to repay?' 'That angst,' notes Sriram, 'is a subtext which we need to look at, as to what it does to a borrower when she is not sure of being able to repay. So this coercion of group lending and the 1 per cent NPA is a big thing. As long as you are spreading it across and not deepening the engagement, not as a single organization but as a sector, then it is okay. But the moment you deepen and borrowers get more and more indebted at these rates, then interest rates become important. Paying 2 per cent to fill up gas is okay but you will never use a credit card to buy an apartment.'

The Andhra crisis, which exposed the cyclicality of the industry, followed a period of very rapid growth. What is the nature of this cyclicality of the industry today? Can the current rapid growth [2013–16] be followed by another crisis? The cyclicality is driven by supply, not demand side dynamic, says Sriram. There is not much of cyclicality at the client level; the poor borrowers are not so related to the cyclicality of the mainstream economy. At the client level, it is manageable so long as you do the appraisal and do not deepen the engagement. If you do, then interest rates and repayment schedules should be nuanced. But it becomes very expensive and time-consuming for a mainstream agency to have a nuanced multilevel engagement with clients. The industry follows the trend of the investment pattern and valuation. 'Why are we saying we are sitting on a volcano even though we are unable to say where it is going to erupt?' Sriram asks. Credit bureau data did not capture the multiple lending last time because people were trading identities: 'One person is still gathering a set of Aadhaar cards, taking loans for multiple people but actually using it himself. This is proxy borrowing. We do not know when or where but it is going to blow up at some point. There is some concern that microfinance portfolios are growing disproportionately to the growth of offices and clients. If some organization grows at scale at 100 per cent, red flags should go up all over.'

Anal Jain, former corporate leader and now with a decade of involvement with MFIs, has a slightly different take. While acknowledging that there are concerns that the industry is getting overheated and worries about getting into another Andhra-type situation, he sees credit bureaus as a bulwark against the wrong kind of lending. These were key to bringing in some discipline in the sector after 2010. Prior to that, credit bureau functioning was at a rudimentary level and there were precious little checks on multiple lending. With this check exercised now through information available from credit bureaus, the industry is healthier. But there is still some gaming of the credit bureau check by some clients who give one ID (a voter's ID) to one MFI and another (Aadhaar) to another MFI and thus secure multiple loans from multiple types of sources. From 2017 this will get a bit more difficult. The RBI has ordered all loans, including those by SHGs, to be reported to credit bureaus. As he says, 'One sign that credit bureau checks are working is that the percentage of rejections because of multiple borrowing is going up. Besides, MFIs have also diversified geographically. A lot of consolidation and weeding out has taken place and the industry is today definitely much more professional.'

Despite the way a large swathe of the microfinance sector, including Basix, was bruised by the Andhra crisis, Mahajan has faith in its long-term strengths. 'Everybody who came to this sector, including Vikram Akula of SKS who is demonized unnecessarily, did so to serve the poor, though that was not the only motivation.' Ghosh, who has had a main-stream career—Wharton, Citibank, Bank Muscat—came three times to Basix for quarterly reviews and joined the field because his heart was in this. It is the same with Ramesh Ramanathan of Janalakshmi, who was with Citibank; Vasudevan of Equitas who was with Cholamandalam and then with DCB; and Govind Singh of Utkarsh who was with ICICI. 'The stock of people who have promoted these institutions is broadly good, professional, and have what I call hybrid motivation. They want to do some good, but in a scalable manner and make a decent living for them-selves. I think that is a fair enough motivation to permit or encourage. I am totally against putting these people on a pedestal, including myself. The fact is, this is a new profession where you are helping at least a subset of the poor who have enough entrepreneurial ability to make good use of it,' he says.

For Mahajan, SFBs are the new future, which is distinctly bright. By dint of having an all-India licence and larger starting capital, they have a much better chance to thrive than local area banks which were their predecessors. And the fact that 10 of them have been licenced shows that RBI is serious about giving them a chance; this was the next logical step for MFIs. The big problem with NBFCs was that they were impaired on the liabilities side—they could not take deposits. They were wholly dependent on banks and as the Andhra crisis showed, if the banks turned off the tap then even the good MFIs could not do anything. Small-finance banks, by being able to take deposits, will be able to improve their balance-sheet flexibility.

Though this sort of current growth is risky, the difference between now and 2010, according to Mohan, is that there are counter bodies like SROs which are trying to bring moderation. There is some effort to ensure that 2010 is not repeated. But given the growth, you can't really tell. With SFBs coming in and taking over a large part of the sector, there will be very close supervision by RBI which will address these concerns. But a repeat of the crisis cannot be ruled out. There is a risk in small banks lending to enterprises as they have no experience in that. So they will concentrate on their existing clients and gradually move up in terms of loan sizes.

Anal Jain agrees that with the MSME segment coming in the industry is changing and SFBs will change the size of loans and the nature of clients. The focus will also change with the need to chase deposits, as Bandhan is doing. SFBs will give less attention to the bottom of the pyramid, and thus the acquisition of new customers from there. But other MFIs will grow by stepping in, as exclusion is still high in states like Maharashtra, Madhya Pradesh, Bihar, Jharkhand, and Chhattisgarh. Today, a majority of applicants there have no loans from MFIs. In a way, therefore, the players will change and it is good that there is greater scope for growth of mid-sized MFIs as SFBs move out.

FUTURE OF POVERTY

We end by going back to the fundamental issue of whether microfinance can end poverty. Fernandez recalls that when NBFC–MFIs were set up, development programmes already existed; the NBFC–MFIs brought in the money. With this there was a shift from targeting poverty to promoting financial inclusion. 'Now,' he says, 'MFIs are not helping income generation but consumption. Asset creation is difficult given the small size of loans.' You cannot buy a cow for Rs 20,000. Asset creation is helped, on the other hand, by the way MYRADA, for instance, works with the Karnataka Milk Federation (Nandini). Banks give relatively larger loans for acquiring cattle. Their money is safe as it is routed through the federation which acquires the milk and pays for it. A part of this payment goes to liquidating the bank loan. However, MFI loans do help. They go to buy fodder for the cattle. MFIs are responding to aspirational needs that are genuine. Fernandez's final analysis: 'MFIs are dumping loans on people as banks in the west at one time dumped credit cards on people. If Marx was here he would have said, "Consumption is the opiate of the masses".'

Brij Mohan indirectly agrees that microfinance is not really doing what it claims to. Repayment of small enterprise loans does not come from current income. 'Money goes into the family, it is invested, some part of it is consumed, and it is returned monthly or fortnightly. In a way, it is a loan to the family and repaid by the family from its own resources and not out of the income from the assets built with the microfinance loan.'

Mahajan offers a larger critique of microfinance. In itself, it is insufficient in enabling the poor to make a living. They need many other things—access to information, market linkages, skills training. 'To give a loan and call for instalment repayment in a week is a half-baked solution. To offer an integrated solution, you need a hybrid model where an NGO does something along with an MFI. Ujjivan does that and Basix has been doing that from the beginning.'

4

An Idea Is Born

Samit Ghosh, an MBA from Wharton, spent 30 years in the Middle East and India with international banks like Citibank, Arab Bank, Standard Chartered Bank, Bank Muscat, and new-generation Indian start-up, HDFC Bank. Not long after the economic reforms came to India in 1991, he was back in the country, setting up a world-class retail-banking operation for HDFC. In 1998 he joined Bank Muscat as their CEO in India, setting up its operations in the country and making it viable. His base was then Bengaluru, where he and his wife also got busy building a home for themselves. But in 2004, at the height of his banking career, Ghosh decided to quit and set out on his own—start a bank for the poor. What made him do this?

Around the time that he joined Bank Muscat, when India's economic reforms had more or less set in, he saw how the full range of financial services became available to the Indian middle class. But the emerging middle class was quite small. He recalls how it struck him that 'in our country such a huge number of people are financially excluded and we are not able to provide them with basic financial services which they require. I felt that as I had worked in virtually every area of banking, this was a challenge I should take up.' Why not make available a full range of financial services to India's 600 million working poor too, a section that had remained outside the pale of organized financial services despite the large-scale nationalization of banks in India more than two decades ago. This had the potential to transform their lives and create a mass market for financial services which the nationalized banks were unable to provide because of their own constraints.

This was the insight he gained from his working life, but there was something more he acquired from his family background and early life. He recalls, 'Our parents' generation was the one that went through the Indian independence movement and the first decades of independent India. They inculcated in us a sort of social objective that we became independent not only to remove the British but also to eliminate poverty.' His parents imbued in him 'from early childhood a sort of social purpose which should be there in life'. His father was a doctor who 'never practised medicine to make money. For him it was more important to practise where he was needed the most.' He came from Hazaribag, now in Jharkhand, a town in the Chhotanagpur area, where there was extensive coal and mica mining. These miners were very poor and did not have access to any medical services. So in the early 1950s, the Government of India decided to build a lot of hospitals for them. 'My father joined the Indian Medical Service and set up many of these hospitals. So my early childhood has been in all these places like Jharia, Katrasgarh, Tisra, Tilaiah—very obscure poor places where no medical services were then available. To him setting up these hospitals was more important than making money.' Similarly, his mother was a teacher and with 'education being so important a part of the development process, she devoted her entire life to it, first as a school teacher and then teaching in college.'

Ghosh's father died when he was just 10 years old and 'since he was in government service, it did not leave us with anything. So we had to rebuild our lives from scratch.' Having lived through the tumultuous 1960s and 1970s of revolutionary Calcutta, his objective in life became 'very materialistic. I wanted to finish college, university and make a good living so that my children didn't have to go through the kind of insecurity which my family had gone through.'

With that goal he went through 30 years of banking, and realized he had achieved success 'both professionally as a banker and materially whatever I needed for my family. Then I had a moment of epiphany. I had a discussion in my mind with my father—who was long since dead—asking him, "Are you proud of me, of what I have achieved?" Materially, I had achieved everything. As a banker I had achieved a lot and was well regarded both internationally and in India. The answer I got was, "So what?" What had I achieved? What am I leaving behind? It was then that I started thinking of utilizing my education and experience in the financial sector to make a real societal impact.'

That is how the idea of Ujjivan was born and as Ghosh makes this clear: 'Ujjivan was set up for a specific purpose—to provide financial services to the various segments of our society who are either excluded or underserved by the organized financial services.' He did not let anything get in the way of serving that purpose. That is why 'earlier, when we had the opportunity for applying for a full commercial banking licence, we did not do so.' The objective was not to use the microfinance route 'to get a commercial bank licence'. There was the apprehension that by becoming a commercial bank the pressure to move away from the original objective [of serving the unserved and underserved] would be lost. 'I felt if we had taken that route there would be a dilution of our original objective. If you go under the quarterly [results] kind of regime and forget the long-term purpose, you definitely risk losing the objective, the purpose, for which the organization was set up.'

Ghosh had two assets and a personal philosophy when he set out on this journey. The assets were a retail and a technology vision. The retail vision came from his experience in Citibank and from the couple of years spent in setting up HDFC's retail banking structure in India. This involved developing a strategic plan based on extensive market research, getting together teams, reorganizing branches, introducing new technology, and reframing operating processes. The technology vision was reinforced by being in Bengaluru, India's technology capital, which made him realize how technology could extend the boundaries of what could be achieved with a given level of resources.

The philosophy is captured in Ghosh's embrace of 'conscious capitalism', enunciated by, among others, John Mackey and Raj Sisodia in their 2013 book of the same name. Conscious capitalism is purpose-driven and socially desirable. Conceptually, it stands on two legs. The first is that a business must take care of all stakeholders, not just the shareholder. This includes employees and customers and lays great store by employee job satisfaction (and not just an attractive compensation package) and customer satisfaction. The focus was, Ghosh says, 'Do the job at hand well while taking care of all stakeholders. The idea is to have respect for the customer, to grow with the customer.' The second pillar is a long-term approach—'no short-term focus on return for the shareholder, no role for the Wall Street-type of greed, which is sickening and has brought about the downfall of capitalism.' In adopting a long-term approach, conscious capitalism also focuses on sustainable development. A business has to be mindful of the long-term needs of a society, not excessively exploit the earth's finite stock of natural resources, and create pollution in the process, which imposes its own costs on society.

To give shape to the idea of taking financial services to the poor, Ghosh, in a way, went back to school. First, he did some reading, looking up books like Yunus's *Banker to the Poor* and Marguerite Robinson's *Microfinance Revolution*. He also wanted to see how microfinance worked on the ground. The first person he got in touch with was Basix's Vijay Mahajan early in 2004, who invited Ghosh over to visit him at his head office in Hyderabad. 'We toured the operations of the Krishna Bhima Samruddhi [KBS], a local area bank of the Basix group in Mahbubnagar in Andhra Pradesh,' he recalls. He attended a customer meet which he also addressed. Finally, he spent a few days in Raichur to see the branch operations of Basix's NBFC and interacted with cotton seed farmers to try and understand how a village 'mandi' worked.

As part of the learning process, Ghosh went on a sort of a pilgrimage. 'Later that year I signed up for the Grameen Commonwealth Poverty

Dialogue Programme for a 10-day exposure to the "Vatican" of microfinance—Grameen Bank in Bangladesh.' After a few days at the head office in Dhaka, where he got a macro view of microfinance and lessons on how to set up an MFI, he travelled northwest, to Rangpur. There he spent a few days seeing how the branch operated, attended centre meetings, and interacted with customers. On returning to Dhaka, the group attending the programme met Professor Yunus, whose advice was, 'Go do it'.

The last leg of his learning journey brought him back to Bengaluru, where he met Aloysius Fernendez, another pioneer of microfinance in India who started the SHG revolution. He was the head of MYRADA and also chairman of Sanghamithra, an MFI working with both the urban and rural poor. Thereafter he spent a month observing and learning from Cecil Lazarus, the operations manager of Sanghamithra. In those days, they were largely involved in financing the setting up of SHGs under the supervision of NGOs. Ghosh also looked at the workings of BSS Microfinance and Grameen Koota, both of which followed the Grameen model. Ghosh recalls, 'my education was largely free and I was over-whelmed by the goodwill and warmth showered on me by these pioneers of microfinance.'

What emerged from this learning process was that microfinance, as it was practised then, was made up of two parts. The front end of it—how they acquire customers, service them, collect repayments, maintain relationships—was very unique. But the back end—in terms of things like processes, risk management, service quality, and technology—was very archaic. 'So we built a model where we kept the front end of microfinance intact but brought in technology, the discipline of centralized operations and efficiency, the risk-management process of banks, service quality to retain our customers, and training and married all of them together.' Because this was such a distinctive model, the sense that emerged was that Ujjivan would be set up as an independent entity, not in partnership with banks, as the latter supported SHGs which were also in the business of microfinance, lending small amounts to the poor.

K.R. Ramamoorthy, chairman of Ujjivan since its inception and also former head of the public sector Corporation Bank and private sector ING Vysya Bank, recalls how Ghosh, on returning from Bangladesh, said, 'The amount of work they have done is to be seen to be believed.' Ramamoorthy though, puts it a bit dramatically, saying Ghosh was 'brainwashed' by them.

If the Grameen Bank model offered the proof of concept for bringing financial services to the poor through a viable business, then there is one area in which Ghosh was a sort of pioneer in India. He applied the Grameen model not to India's rural poor (which several microfinance organizations were already doing), but the urban poor. This completely ran against conventional wisdom and was not considered right, as there were perceived differences between the rural and urban poor. It was believed at the time that the urban poor were not as socially cohesive as their rural counterparts. The credit and repayment culture was strong in rural areas as a bank default was a reputational slur. But there was no such culture in urban areas. Besides, metros in particular had a floating population. Recovery rates among banks in urban/metro areas (for micro loans) were at that time as low as 30–35 per cent, recalls Ramamoorthy. He had, in his Corporation Bank days, promoted some SHGs with NABARD and could understand group lending, but not in urban areas. However, Ghosh felt this was not a major issue. 'He said,' reminisces Ramamoorthy, '"There is an untapped potential. The space is wide open." Then a professional study backed his idea and I was won over.'

Sunil Patel, a board member of Ujjivan and its original finance mentor who played a key role in giving it shape as it set out on its journey, has a personal note to add on how it all happened. 'In a way, Ujjivan was born on the many types of food and coffee that was consumed when the idea was thrashed out during meetings at various coffee shops.'

5

A Firm Is Born

Ujjivan started functioning from Monday, 2 August 2004. In a communication entitled 'Update 1', to the team dated 22 August, Ghosh said, 'It's
been twenty days since we started on the road to establish this microfinance
institution ...' and promised a monthly update. The update announced that
the registrar of companies had approved the name of the firm and went
on to outline the essential character of the company: 'The company will
be branded Ujjivan. We wanted to select a name which reflects the aspirations of our customers and would be understood nationally. "Ujjivan"
in Sanskrit means better (or progress) in life.' Ujjivan Financial Services
Private Limited was incorporated on 28 December 2004 and the first board
meeting was held in the new year, on 25 January 2005.

The immediate task was to put together a business plan that would be
necessary to secure equity investment. Also high on priority was to have
an impressive enough board of directors. All these were needed to get RBI
approval to set up an NBFC. Recalls Ghosh, 'As far as the board is concerned, I think, two people were very supportive right from the beginning.
One was Sunil Patel, who was my college mate from Wharton. He helped
me build the first investor proposals and business plan which helped me
raise the initial capital. The other was Mr [K.R.] Ramamoorthy, with his
experience as a banker in Corporation Bank and then ING Vysya Bank,

whom also I had known from before. These two actually formed the core of my support from the board. Subsequently, of course, the investors came in and helped the board.'

Ghosh reveals that 'actually the most difficult time I faced in the entire existence of Ujjivan was raising the first Rs 2.7 crore of capital. I had some savings which I had put in. The balance had to come in from friends and colleagues, because otherwise nobody knew me or would trust me with money. Very frankly, most of those who put in the money thought this was some kind of a charitable act on their behalf. I was trying to do something good and they had enough faith in me professionally and also trust in me personally that I would not run away with their money. And so they said, "Instead of donating [it] to a temple, let's give him some money". It took me almost a year to reach that Rs 2.7 crore.'

The ball was set rolling by Ghosh and Ramamoorthy putting in Rs 1.1 lakh in January 2005. 'Many of my friends and colleagues, especially from my Citibank days and alumni from Wharton, chipped in. Friends who were already successful entrepreneurs, like Jerry [Rao], went through their Rolodex to get in more investors. But we were still substantially short. Providentially, S. Viswanatha Prasad was in the process of setting up Bellwether Microfinance Fund, a domestic equity fund, to invest primarily in start-up microfinance companies. After our initial discussion in Bangalore, Ajit Grewal, an old colleague from Citibank, and I took an overnight bus to Hyderabad in August 2005 to sign up our first institutional investor.' In August, a critical Rs 2.4 crore came in from Bellwether Microfinance Trust through Caspian Advisers, Nucleus Software Exports, Jaithirth [Jerry] Rao, Jayamani Ramachander, Nalini Sood, Dipika Sood, and several others. 'With that we were able to raise that initial capital of Rs 2.8 crore, which enabled us to apply for the NBFC licence from RBI.'

Here is how the mood changed in internal communication as the battle to raise the initial capital progressed. While the first response in August 2004 from individual domestic investors who made commitments of

Rs 1.05 crore was 'overwhelming', by March 2005, Ghosh saw the progress as 'slow and steady'. By then, just Rs 50 lakh had come in along with commitments of Rs 1.3 crore. The change of sentiment was even more apparent in July, when Ghosh spoke of a 'long march', but added that the 'light at the end of the tunnel is visible'. By then, Rs 1.6 crore had come in. By August, capital paid in had crept up to Rs 1.7 crore. Deliverance came, so to speak, in late August when the shareholders' agreement was signed with Bellwether, taking paid-up capital to Rs 2.4 crore and Ujjivan applied to RBI on 8 September, 13 months after the firm started, for the licence to operate. There was a bonanza of sorts when in October, Rs 32 lakh more of domestic capital came in, as also the first bit of foreign equity, of Rs 31 lakh.

Since investment by Bellwether at an early stage played a key role in getting Ujjivan going and attracting international investment in subsequent rounds of equity raising, it is useful to trace how the paths of the two companies crossed. Prasad, the managing director of Caspian Impact Investment which is aligned with Bellwether, recalls that by around 2004, the percentage of urban poor in India exceeded the rural level. But the entire political system had been thinking of financial inclusion purely from a rural perspective even as urban poverty was getting starker. 'So we said we would invest in entities and business models bringing capability to cater to urban needs. Plus, we said we would back entrepreneurs who would build this on a national scale, that is, scale their business. Lastly, we wanted to encourage mainstream bankers and entrepreneurs to enter the industry. By that time there were many successful NGOs like PRADAN, Asmitha, Gramin Vikas, and Cashpor who were running good-quality operations but came from the—I don't mean it in a derogatory way—NGO mindset.' They were struggling with issues like coping with regulation, raising capital, and ensuring high standards of governance.

If mainstream people and companies are to venture into this sector, they have to be convinced that this was a viable business model. 'That's when we met Samit Ghosh,' explains Prasad. Like anybody who wants to set up something in the inclusion space, Basix was the first stop to understand what was happening and Ghosh had been there. 'Everything I said, he wanted to do. He wanted to put the customer first, like any consumer bank, seeking to understand the product he or she wanted,' continues Prasad, adding, 'Ujjivan was the first MFI in those days to be set up like a bank.' This meant that credit was separate from sales, risk was separate from credit and sales, and a top-notch board was recruited. The institutional genetic code was built well. A blue-chip financial institution had put the excluded customer at the centre of the business. 'Ghosh was also very clear that you can't scale the business without top-class technology. So he never hesitated in investing in technology or people.'

Caspian–Bellwether came in first and was part of the exercise, along with the Ujjivan board, to secure the NBFC licence. Prasad adds that they 'had to be careful about getting the right type of new investors for growing the business. We wanted to do a lot of things at scale, very differently, invest significantly in people and technology. So you need a board and investors who would support it.'

When it was decided to set up Ujjivan as an NBFC, several issues came to the fore. A public profile was needed to get investment and well-qualified people. The profile that Ujjivan aspired to from day one was to be a social business venture which was nevertheless professional in every way. The social business part came from lending to the poor and following the path of conscious capitalism while the professional part came from Ghosh's years spent with various international banks. The combination of these led to the first business plan being formulated. Ghosh recalls, 'We adopted the Citibank process but not their culture of competition. We laid great store by employee job satisfaction and customer satisfaction. The idea was to have respect for the customer and grow with the customer. The HR philosophy was to create job satisfaction, not use the driving force of materialism. We created a lot of internal equity in an open environment, like having the same formula for all for increments. Hence, we have repeatedly won the best employer rating [from Great Place to Work].'

The other early challenge, after incorporation, was to build a team—from the core outwards. 'For the management team I initially started looking at my ex-colleagues in banks', Ghosh explains. 'Then, because none of us had any experience in microfinance, we hired some people from SHARE who virtually inducted us into the process of microfinance. And since we were a partner of Grameen Bank, they sent us an expert. So with all that help we started building a microfinance team.' The process of building a core team was set rolling by a few top-level people joining. In the initial core team, there was Ajit Grewal (an old colleague from Citibank), Carol Furtado, and Srikrishna, Ramamoorthy's son, who has now moved on to Unitus.

Once the nucleus was in place, a policy had to be articulated to build the rest of the team. As an MFI, while Ujjivan was unable to offer alluring salaries, what it could do was outline a vision and create the feeling that it was doing something of value for customers, build a culture around that idea, and then use it to attract people. Prospective recruits were told that they needed to remain committed to the sector. There was a lot of emphasis on training. The field staff went through a month of training before getting down to work.

The DNA of Ujjivan was evident in the way it went about its work in the year leading up to obtaining the RBI licence. It initiated its practice of undertaking research before doing anything by engaging Delphi Research Services in early 2005 to understand its target customers—the poor women in Bengaluru and its suburbs—which was akin to the 'usage and attitude' studies done by banks. In a few months the market research was expanded to include garment workers. The initial findings were fascinating, clearly indicating that no study like this had been done in the country earlier. As the study (Ujjivan later published the full report) contributed importantly to identifying who the MFI wished to worked for, it is worth outlining its salient features. The study looked at economically active women in the monthly household income bracket of Rs 3,000–7,000, and included housemaids, roadside vendors, agarbatti rollers, workers in garments factories, and helpers in shops, schools, and hospitals. Mostly married and living in semi-pucca dwellings, these individuals took up work when the financial burden of the household fell largely upon them and they found they could make a significant contribution by working. They lived a hand-to-mouth existence, were often the sole earners of the family, and needed to borrow even for basic needs like food, healthcare, and education. With hardly any education or tangible securities, they had to rely mostly on the unorganized financial sector.

Moneylenders charged 2–10 per cent interest a month. Most women were usually servicing at least one loan at any given time. Loan sizes were in the Rs 500–5,000 range, with business loans tending to be smaller than personal loans. Self-employed women found their return from their business enough to pay the high interest rates. Correspondingly, the salaried found it difficult to repay loans and also found them harder to come by. The most popular business loans were for 100 days, the interest was held back on disbursal, and repayment was daily. Personal loans were usually larger, taken by salaried women, repaid over longer periods, and attracted higher rates of interest. Most women liked to save a little for a rainy day but found it hard to come by savings schemes. They did save regularly in some areas where the pygmy deposit scheme and LIC agents were active. Investment in chit funds was risky but widespread. 'Item chits'—requiring smaller payments—for things like steel utensils, saris, and Diwali crackers were particularly popular. The gap waiting to be filled by microfinance was for bigger loans of longer tenure and at lower interest rates.

A lot of early work went into explaining to RBI what Ujjivan wanted to do. Eventually, it secured RBI approval to become an NBFC in record time as it was well structured from day one, with a wired legal framework. In fact, it helped chart the way for regulation of MFIs constituted as NBFCs. Says Partha Mandal, senior partner of Universal Legal, who has been associated with Ujjivan from its early days, 'Not only was it compliant with the regulations of the day, even corporate compliances not needed for microfinance institutions under Indian regulation were nevertheless adhered to, as foreign investors needed it for *their* compliance.' For example, Ujjivan complied with CSR-disclosure norms and the requirement of a CSR policy before these were made mandatory in India.

During the initial weeks, Ujjivan'a office was a guest house in Bengaluru's Whitefield area, where lived three of the 'Magnificent Seven', as Ghosh describes the first team that set off Ujjivan on its journey. The dining table was the common workstation, with Ghosh's old PC the sole common infrastructure. Expectedly, the dining table was not big enough to accommodate even that small a team, and a new office had to be found. Thanks to Rao, who was still very much the founder and CEO of MphasiS, as also friend and early investor in Ujjivan, the team moved to the firm's Bannerghatta office in April 2005. There the team rattled around in a huge furnished office trying to write various manuals, discuss plans, and do market research. 'The only thing I remember,' says Ghosh of this period, 'is how the whole Ujjivan team used to walk down to the Udupi joint next to the flyover for lunch.' That would be difficult to do 10 years down the line, as Ujjivan ended FY 2016–17 with a staff strength of 8,049 spread over 469 branches in 24 states!

Furtado, now head of human resources and service quality, the only one apart from Ghosh left of the Magnificent Seven, has fond memories of the office at MphasiS. 'The ground floor was given to us. It was a very nice office with wide open spaces, and just around seven of us. But we were hardly there, as we used to go out to the field, [Bangalore] markets like KR Market and HAL Market, and meet potential customers. We would ask them what their needs were, and then try and bring all our thoughts together around a table. Then we would use that to draw up our policies and put a framework around it.' But the space was not meant to last: the team found that the MphasiS office was a designated software technology park, so only software businesses could have offices there. So in a few months they had to move to a flat in Indiranagar kindly vacated by friends.

There is palpable excitement in the bland print of Ghosh's November 2005 update. The first borrowers' group had been formed, the first group-recognition test had been done, the first centre meeting had been held, and most importantly, the first batch of officers had been trained. Ujjivan secured the certificate to run as an NBFC on 31 October 2005, 'in a record time of 49 days'. The die was cast and the ball started rolling on a 10-year journey which was, in its own way, historic.

6

A Pilot Gets Going

Ujjivan started out on its journey by opening its first branch on 8 November 2005 in the Koramangala area of Bengaluru. Significantly, it called this phase of its operations a 'pilot', indicating that it was part of a learning process which would be used to gain insights and validate every aspect of its operations. This was in keeping with its culture of going about its work methodically—study, learn, absorb, and then go forward. As noted earlier, one of the first things Ujjivan did on opening for business was to commission a market research project to find out all about its target customers. The first 100 Ujjivan customers, who would save for a three-month period before getting a loan, had already been inducted, and the first loans were disbursed to Ramakka and Lily on 17 January 2006 at a small function held in a corporation school in Rajendranagar. This made Ujjivan the first micro-finance organization in India to lend without any grant or donation. Then survey work to determine the location of the second branch was started.

When the first branch opened and the pilot period started, it was a test of a unique hybrid model consisting of the front-end processes of Grameen Bank of Bangladesh and the back-end technology of modern banking which Ghosh had himself ushered in. While the smooth operations and the rapid growth during the pilot period validated the basic Ujjivan model, several key learnings also emerged. One was the imperative of being able to retain staff in a vibrant job market like Bengaluru, where IT firms were head-hunting day in and day out. Second was the need to control quality in operations (selection of borrowers, processing of loans, disbursal, and follow-up), which held the key to survival. Hence a process of an ongoing audit of field operations was instituted. Third was the need to go beyond the income-generation single-product model of Grameen Bank and become a multi-product operation which gave education, festival, and housing loans to low-income women. Additionally, to devise a holistic approach to fighting poverty, Ujjivan also offered life insurance cover through LIC. Fourth was the need to acquire the ability to handle cash, in which the early team—which came from a banking background—had no experience. Hence, systems had to be put in place to handle cash and guard against cash-related fraud.

There were other learnings too, which led to changes in the operating model. Smaller centres were developed as there was no space in the slums where the urban poor lived and among whom Ujjivan worked. Centre meetings were held monthly instead of weekly, as customers had less time. Importantly, as the urban poor had a smaller circle of friends, Ujjivan moved away from the system of holding the entire centre liable, to dividing the centre into groups of five instead, and holding these five members accountable for one another. Ujjivan's offering multiple products instead of the sole Grameen-type income-generating one also grew out of the learning that urban slum-dwellers had critical needs in education and home improvement. There was also the learning on dealing with people who engaged in diverse occupations, many quite non-conventional, and came from different ethnic backgrounds. Eventually, Ujjivan learned how to cater to the diversity residing in India's urban slums, the complex economic machine that it was, and how to help the slum-dweller improve her lot in that milieu.

At the end of the 18-month pilot period in April 2007, Ujjivan had 17 branches in three cities—Bengaluru, Kolkata, and Delhi—and a staff strength of 285. It had also opened its first semi-urban branch in Ramanagara near Bengaluru. It served almost 24,000 customers who had been disbursed Rs 13.5 crore in loans. While this was great progress,

Ujjivan's goals were also aggressively ambitious. It sought to break even in three years, have 600,000 customers in six years of operations, and offer a long-term return on equity of 15 per cent. It sought to offer its employees a professionally and financially rewarding career and, perhaps most ambitiously, aimed to take its customers out of poverty in five years. We will have occasion to get back to these goals later on in the book to assess how well Ujjivan has fared in terms of its own goals.

Towards the end of the pilot, Ujjivan became the first MFI in India to grant stock options to its employees, with sign-on stock options granted to the 22 employees who had started with the organization. This was part of the stock-options programme in which all employees were eligible to participate. Performance stock options were to be granted annually.

The experience during the pilot gave clarity to Ujjivan about who its customer was—the poor working woman—and what went into making an eligible customer. The household to which the customer belonged typically earned Rs 4,000–6,000 a month and the household's per capita income was less than Rs 1,000. Most of it was taken away by expenses in the range of Rs 2,000–4,000 a month on things like food, housing, medical expenses, repayment of debt, and social and religious festivals. Nearly half of these were salaried—working as housemaids, sweepers, or teachers—and paid once a month. Nearly 40 per cent were self-employed, selling fruits and vegetables, worked as tailors, ran petty shops, or engaged in handiwork. Around 10 per cent worked as beedi or agarbatti rollers or peeled garlic, and earned on a daily or a weekly basis. The typical borrower was an economically active woman between 18 and 55 years of age, who was married or single (widow or separated) and had lived in the same area for five years. To get a loan, a woman had to join a group of five and take joint responsibility for the group members' loans, go through a customer group-training programme and pass a group-recognition test.

In moving away from a single-product to a multi-product offering, Ujjivan crossed a conceptual hurdle by offering loans for both income generation and consumption. A borrower could take a business loan (to fund the business), or a family loan to meet virtually any kind of family expenditure like education or medical needs, to repay a costly previous loan, or even for a loan which was a combination of the two (business and family). If a borrower had a good track record for six months she could also get an emergency loan, a festival loan, or a top-up loan, which added 10–20 per cent to an existing loan. She could even take a housing loan to pay for rent deposit, leasing charge, or home improvement.

The family, business and combo loans were in the Rs 6,000–12,000 range with a repayment tenure of 12–24 months and attracted an interest rate of 24–26.9 per cent (declining balance). The emergency and festival loans, for Rs 1,500, were repayable in six months, with interest for festival loans at the higher end of 26.9 per cent (declining balance). The housing loan could be for Rs 10,000–30,000, for a longer period of 36 months and attracted a lower interest rate of 21.5–24 per cent (declining balance). These details indicate that Ujjivan's lending terms were similar to those of other well-run microfinance organizations and were at the lower end of the range. The rates will, later on in the book, be compared to the guidelines issued by RBI after the Andhra crisis.

There were also customer fee and security deposits, levied typically by the industry, which added to borrowing costs and appeared hidden. These were: a one-time training fee of Rs 50; one-time documentation, passbook, and customer ID card fee of Rs 60; annual meeting fees—Rs 70 for business, combo and housing loans, Rs 50 for family loans; replacement of lost loan/ID cards, Rs 50; security and additional security deposits—10 per cent of all loans except housing loans, which attracted 5 per cent with a minimum deposit of Rs 1,000. Additional security deposit of Rs 20 per week was levied to aid timely repayment and contribute towards initial deposits. These charges have attracted criticism on the grounds that they are routine expenses and should be subsumed in the interest rate charged. If this is done it will add to transparency. Over time the industry has brought down these charges.

All Ujjivan borrowers had to take out a life insurance (this secured the loan in case of demise) by paying a modest premium. What went beyond the scope of microfinance was the option offered for health coverage. For a modest premium, borrowers and their families were offered primary, secondary, and tertiary care, free outpatient service at Ujjivan's network hospitals and Arogya Raksha Yojana Trust clinics, diagnostic tests at discounted rates, a range of surgical procedures and hospitalization for three days in a year per family member. Under its Microfinance Plus services, Ujjivan offered health care, vocational and skills training, and educational assistance. This was done by tying up with partners like Biocon Foundation, Vittala International Ophthalmology Hospital, Parikrama, and Arogya Raksha Yojana. This set out Ujjivan's understanding of the reality that while a microfinance organization is primarily geared to the task of offering small loans without security to enable the working poor to earn more and rise out of poverty, fighting poverty is a multidimensional task. For the poor, the need is to be educated and skilled and not allow health emergencies to drag a person back into the clutches of impoverishment.

While the concept has endured, Ujjivan has stopped offering health insurance. Instead, the task of offering help on healthcare and health emergencies has been shifted to Parinaam Foundation, which has a healthcare agenda. Its work will be covered in detail in a subsequent chapter.

The importance of life cover for all borrowers was highlighted when, in September 2006, Taj, a 32-year old beedi roller, wife of an auto rickshaw driver and mother of three, died while delivering her fourth child owing to the debilitating impact of extreme anaemia. Her loan was, of course, automatically paid off, but more importantly, the microfinance-plus dimension of Ujjivan's work promised proper education for her children at the Parikrama, School. The internal newsletter of the company also sought sponsors to support the children.

As the pilot headed for its close, Ujjivan updated and finalized its field operations and process manual, a sort of bible that remained the bulwark of its strategy to operate successfully. It also marked the completion of the renovation of its first proper head office in Koramangala. After moving like a nomad from a guest house to a software firm's office to an apartment which was vacated by friends, the company had zeroed in on a garments factory that had been elegantly redesigned and renovated.

The pilot period came to an end with two significant FDIs, by Unitus and the Michael and Susan Dell Foundation (MSDF). Together, they invested Rs 3 crore in equity, taking Ujjivan's equity capital to Rs 5.5 crore. This didn't happen without a hiccup, though. On learning that MSDF was interested in Indian microfinance, Ghosh went up to Austin, Texas, only to find that they were more interested in recruiting him to run a foundation of theirs which would invest in microfinance around the world. But Ghosh managed to convince them to invest in Ujjivan, their first investment in the sector. Over the years, MSDF invested twice more in further rounds of equity funding. When it eventually existed in 2012, the investment had secured an internal rate of return of 20 times (in rupee terms) in six years! Taking into account the three rounds of investment made at different price points, MSDF secured a return of 2.2 times. The pilot had yielded a model that has worked successfully.

7

On a High Growth Path

After the pilot ended in April 2007, Ujjivan embarked on a rapid growth path over the next four years. Then, in late 2010 the storm that broke over Andhra Pradesh posed an existential threat to the microfinance industry in India. Fortunately for Ujjivan, it had no presence in the state and its growth continued through 2010–11. It would suffer collateral damages but those would be visited upon it in the next year. So during 2007–11, Ujjivan's growth was unimpeded.

The dimensions of the four-year growth phase (2007–11) can be captured by comparing the figures at the beginning and end of the period. From 19 branches by mid-2007, Ujjivan had 351 branches by the end of FY 2010–11. The customer base had grown over 30 times to over 992,000, and total disbursements had gone up by over a hundred times to Rs 2,073 crore. Similarly, staff strength had gone up by over 14 times to just over 4,000. Perhaps, most critically, Ujjivan had established a track record of over 98 per cent repayment.

At the start of the period, Ujjivan looked forward to wiping out all accumulated losses in under three years. In keeping with this, it broke even from January 2009 and in the last quarter of the 2008–09 financial year, earned a net profit after tax of Rs 1.7 crore. By the end of the first quarter of the next financial year, two major regions—south and east—turned profitable and the company maintained its target of wiping out all accumulated losses. Financial year 2009–10 can be termed as the year of coming of age for Ujjivan when it turned in a net profit of Rs 9.6 crore and wiped out all accumulated losses. In keeping with this, it also set its eyes on a long-term return on equity of 15 per cent.

Eyes set on becoming a pan-Indian organization and not be satisfied with being present only in the south and east, Ujjivan ventured out early in the period to establish a presence in the west and north as well. By the end of FY 2009, its footprints covered the entire country with the opening of a regional office for western India in Pune and establishing a presence in 13 states. South and east naturally predominated with 61 and 51 branches respectively, but the north had established a presence with 28 branches and the west had opened its account with five.

With growth rose the need to reorganize the administrative structure. This was done by the end of FY 2008 with the help of Cocoon Consulting. Under a new matrix organizational structure, regional offices were sent up in Kolkata and Delhi under regional operating officers so as to strengthen decentralized operations, while overall management came from a central leadership team for every operation. The first management development programme was initiated with 30 recruits from leading academic institutions.

At the end of FY 2008 Elaine Marie Ghosh took a key step to create Parinaam Foundation as a not-for-profit company under the then-existing Section 25 of the Companies Act of 1956 (read with Section 8 of the Companies Act of 2013). It maintains an arm's length relationship with Ujjivan and has an independent governance structure. Mrs Ghosh worked pro bono as executive director. The decision grew out of the realization that poverty can be successfully attacked only as a holistic exercise and something was needed to address issues outside the scope of microfinance. Through the microfinance-plus programme, Parinaam Foundation addressed areas like healthcare, micro-health insurance, education, vocational and entrepreneurship development, and community-strengthening initiatives.

Parinaam Foundation also initiated a major new focus, the ultra-poor programme, to bring within the development fold families that did not meet the eligibility criteria for availing microfinance. The aim was to offer families help in acquiring skills for earning a livelihood, taking care of their own and their children's health, gaining financial literacy, and, in the process, promoting social development. The focus was to bring these families up to a level where they could qualify for microfinance assistance.

During the high growth period, between 2007 and 2011, Ujjivan also undertook a two-part financial literacy programme on debt management, Sankalp and Diksha, which sought to educate customers and insulate them from the ravages of an Andhra-type crisis that could severely cripple microfinance. It focused on excessive borrowing (taking multiple loans) and sub- or ghost lending (allowing someone to use your identity to take a loan which they use). Importantly, it explained the significance of the credit bureau and why it was vital to maintain a clean record with the bureau so as to be able to take loans in the future. The programme is delivered in two stages. Stage one or Sankalp creates awareness. For this a 30-minute programme dramatizes the fate of two borrowers who fall into the debt trap. Diksha consists of five training modules, which focus on managing a family's cash flow, imparting numerical skills, learning how to make budgets, understanding the importance of savings (how to save and where to save), pros and cons of different types of loans, dangers of ghost lending, and getting to know the credit bureau. The film is freely available and the training modules come with a training kit.

The year 2008 marked the completion of a one-year pilot for a new product—the individual business loan—with the guidance and support of Women's World Banking. The product was first introduced in 10 branches in Karnataka. These loans, which ranged from Rs 10,000 to Rs 50,000, were offered to families with running businesses so that they could meet working-capital or investment needs. The year also marked the national launch of the educational loan to enable borrowers to send their children to schools of their choice and covered tuition fees and the cost of textbooks and uniforms. A third product—the housing loan—was introduced. Right from the beginning, all borrowers were given life insurance cover at considerable administrative cost to the organization. This later prompted a switching of partners, from LIC to ICICI Lombard, to bring down costs.

Rapid growth also needed funding, and Ujjivan went in for its third round of investment in 2007, largely from existing investors, taking its share capital to Rs 12.3 crore from Rs 5.5 crore, with domestic holding at 51 per cent. In 2008, Ujjivan went in for its fourth round of funding. The target of raising Rs 75 crore was exceeded and ultimately Rs 87.8 crore was raised. Four new investors came in—Sequoia Capital, Lok Capital, Elevar Unitus, and Indian Financial Inclusion Fund. This reflected a policy of securing a mix of social- and market-driven investors. A unique feature was Bellwether Microfinance Fund and UEF offering to buy out any investor, thus creating a market mechanism for anyone seeking to exit. This would have the effect of developing a secondary market for shares of microfinance companies which were unlisted. With this round of funding, the holding of foreign investors rose to almost 75 per cent.

During 2008, Ujjivan took some distinctive steps in the field of human resource development which resulted from its effort to tailor existing templates to specific needs. The field-study component of its management development programmes was given greater weightage under the rubric, 'believing by seeing and doing'. The distribution supervisory team was put at the head of the 'train the trainer' programme which was very critical to the organization as it had a large field staff who would not always know of changes in trajectory and the standards that the organization had to live up to in the public eye.

One reason why microfinance organizations have done far better than nationalized banks in serving the financially excluded is that many of their employees come from the same socio-economic stock as customers and are therefore able to communicate effectively with them. This, plus the ability to grow professionally through the various training programmes, have taken them to levels which they could have never foreseen when they had started working. A case in point is Veerapatheeran M., popularly known as Veera, who joined Ujjivan in November 2005 even before the first loan was sanctioned. He was the first from his village in rural Tamil Nadu to join a college and get a degree. He first worked with an NGO engaged in livelihood development for the poor and then got attached to a rehabilitation project for the urban poor in Bengaluru. On joining Ujjivan as its 25th employee, he became one of its first branch managers. He was soon promoted and transferred to the cash department of the head office, a sensitive area in a microfinance organization which has to handle a lot of cash. He was next given the task, as programme manager, of launching Ujjivan's operations in Tamil Nadu and then as distribution manager overseeing all Tamil Nadu branches. A village boy who made it good, Veera is clear that he has been able to rise so fast in Ujjivan because it helps develop skills and then recognizes them in a transparent manner. He has since moved on but his career in Ujjivan is an example of how a microfinance organization with the right DNA helps its customers and staff to grow and keep growing.

Ujjivan has been technology-driven from day one with the primary focus on enabling the field staff to serve the customer better. During 2008 an ERP (enterprise resource planning) and core-banking solution, based on open-source Linux software and customized to meet Ujjivan's needs, were implemented across the firm's network. It began working towards a paperless document management system using scanning and digital imaging to reduce document turnaround time. Work was also on to incorporate the use of mobile/wireless technology and also GPS (global positioning system) to track field movements.

But halfway through the growth period, during 2009, clouds began to gather on the horizon in the form of a crisis in southern Karnataka. It proved to be a harbinger of the wider crisis in the microfinance industry that hit Andhra Pradesh—where microfinance had grown the most—the next year. In the next chapter we will take a look at what happened in southern Karnataka to understand the root of the Andhra crisis. But in this chapter there is still a lot more of the growth story to pursue.

During 2009–10, Ujjivan saw phenomenal growth with its customer base growing by 110 per cent, that is, it more than doubled. In the following year, on the high base, it again grew its customers by 60 per cent. Ujjivan now had close to a million customers at the end of its four-year growth phase. If customer acquisition was dramatic, disbursements grew exponentially, by 198 per cent in 2009–10 and on top of that, by 122 per cent in 2010–11. To service the new business, the number of employees grew by 67 per cent in 2009–10 and 42 per cent in the following year, while the number of branches increased by 81 per cent and 53 per cent respectively.

Portfolio at risk (PAR30), which refers to loans outstanding by over 30 days, and is the prime indictor of asset quality, showed an interesting pattern. For 2009–10, it recorded 0.48 per cent. For 2010–11, ended with 1.03 per cent. Clearly, storm clouds were gathering. The region-wise share of the loan portfolio also made a statement. The share of the south remained static at around 40 per cent (Ujjivan had no exposure in Andhra, which was the trouble spot). The north and west, both of which had a lot of catching up to do, grew their combined share by around 10 per cent. Significantly, the share of the east went down by around 10 per cent, perhaps indicative of the fact that stress in asset quality was mounting and hence the system was drawing in the slack.

Statistics tell the story up to a point but the human stories behind them say much more. Among all the regions, Ujjivan reached the west last. And within that region Mumbai was approached with much circumspection. India's premier and richest city, it nevertheless has over half its population living in slums. Mumbai's working poor are highly sophisticated and their needs complex. Impacting them in a positive way is challenging. The pace of work picked up after a slow start, and by the end of FY 2011, Mumbai's 22 branches were serving 50,000 borrowers. Still, the sense among those running the operations was that it was a job half done. Sharda Gade, who used to sell a few packets of chocolates and snacks out of a small room in the suburb of Mankhurd, had never been able to make ends meet. But after taking a loan from Ujjivan, she was able to stock her petty shop better and greatly improve her sales. Within a year of the loan, her family budget was balancing. Gulnaj Sheikh from the Golibar area worked in a garments factory and sold handcrafted handkerchiefs to earn a bit extra. But that was not enough. Then with a loan from Ujjivan she went into the business full-time and thereafter earned enough to make ends meet.

At the other end of the country are Assam and Meghalaya, as landlocked as coastal Mumbai is engaged with the rest of the world. Ujjivan started operations in the two states in 2010 and served 15,000 customers by the end of FY 2011 through 10 branches. Manju Kalita offered private tuition, supplementing what her husband earned from selling fast-food from a cart. Then with a loan of Rs 10,000 from Ujjivan, Manju's husband was able to rent a place and meet the working-capital needs of a much-grown business, which, of course, enhanced the family income. To Abdul Kalam Azad, 27, customer relationship manager of the Kalapahar branch, working with Ujjivan was a little more than just a job. Having been very poor himself as a child, he was able to keenly feel the impact that Ujjivan was making through its operations. He felt the organization had been able to do this in less than a year because of the professionalism of its staff and the way they dealt with customers.

To get a sense of the road covered during the period, it is useful to step back and take note of a few milestones. May 2007 became a landmark as Delhi and Kolkata disbursed their first loans. By June 2010, in eastern India, Ujjivan had 100 branches and 0.3 million customers. By October 2010, with 23 branches in Delhi/NCR, Ujjivan became the largest MFI in that region. In the west, the last region where Ujjivan went in, by January 2009, it served over 0.1 million clients through 48 branches in Maharashtra and Gujarat. What's more, by August 2010, it became the largest microfinance organization in Mumbai, with 21 branches.

8

A Crisis Forewarned

Even as Ujjivan grew exponentially during the years 2007–11, towards the middle of the period—in early 2009—it faced its first hurdle. A payments crisis created by mass default gripped the microfinance industry in four urban centres in southern Karnataka—Kolar, Sidlaghatta, Ramanagara, and Mysuru. Ujjivan, with a presence in the latter three, was also affected. But the crisis began to recede by the end of the financial year and Ujjivan put it behind itself without feeing any serious strain. This was because of its policy of not putting too many eggs in one basket and spreading out its operations across the country. Hence the impact of a default in a particular area on overall performance was negligible. Its total portfolio was only marginally affected and its investors did not bat an eyelid.

Despite this, it is useful to look in some detail into not just this crisis but two others that preceded it. The learning from them is startling and show them to be forerunners of the Andhra crisis which affected not just the microfinance industry in the state, but others as well.

In the four years before the 2010 Andhra crisis, Indian microfinance had three dress rehearsals, so to speak. These are known as the 'three Ks'. Each provided an important lesson, each of which was ignored. This eventually, and inevitably, led to the final full-scale production—the Andhra crisis. The first rehearsal happened in the Krishna district of Andhra Pradesh in 2006. The proximate cause was the collector, the administrative head of the district, shutting down 50 offices of MFIs like Spandana, Asmitha, and SHARE and instructing their borrowers not to repay their loans. The contention was that MFIs were charging usurious interest rates at the expense of poor borrowers, making super profits and using strong-arm tactics to ensure recovery. In the process, the recovery of bank-linked SHGs, which had lent to the same borrowers and were backed by the state government, suffered. This is a precise summary of the issues which led up to the crisis in Andhra Pradesh in 2010. The intervention and active support of the RBI prevented MFIs from remaining closed for long. The MFIs promised to lower interest rates and introduced a code of conduct which they implemented as well, but soon, interest rates began to creep up and the code of conduct became a dead letter.

What is unique to the Krishna district crisis is the revolutionary role (in the financial sphere) that ICICI Bank played through its partnership model with MFIs. Under this the MFIs acted as the agents of the bank in mobilizing borrowers and handling the disbursal of loans while the loans themselves remained on the books of the bank. This ensured an income for the MFIs (agency fees) while enabling the bank to meet its priority-sector lending obligations. As the MFIs were not operating with their own funds and did not take any financial risk, there was little need for them to collect sufficient risk capital or equity to provide for bad loans. At its peak before the crisis, the bank had a 100 such partnerships with MFIs and had on its books 1.2 million borrowers. It had plans to more than double the number of MFI partners.

When RBI stopped this practice, it did so on the grounds that the bank had not been able to fulfil the mandatory Know Your Customer (KYC) responsibility. A bank was duty-bound to satisfy itself on this legal requirement, and the borrower information on the books of MFIs was second-hand and not acceptable. The end of this practice made MFIs look for equity partners and their transformation into for-profit NBFCs with proper balance sheets from around that time paved the way for FDI in the form of private equity to come in.

The second dress rehearsal took place in Kanpur and other cities in Uttar Pradesh (UP) in 2009. It was triggered when Nirman Bharti, a local MFI in UP, defaulted on large loans it had taken from banks and other financial institutions to finance its small-loans portfolio. This was prompted by repayment problems over its loan portfolio. That, in turn, happened because it did not have proper systems and processes to exercise due diligence while granting loans and then supervising recovery over time. Rapid portfolio growth, which led to induction of inadequately trained staff, aggravated the malfunctioning and contributed to defaults. In the absence of proper information systems being in place, there was no sanctity in the low PAR or NPAs that were claimed. It could not be determined how much of the repayment was due to rollover (granting of a fresh loan to repay the existing one), a process that cannot go on indefinitely.

The third K was Kolar or the southern Karnataka crisis in 2009. In this case the lessons are particularly useful as they flow out of a rigorous independent study which the Association of Karnataka Microfinance Institutions (AKMI) requested EDA Rural Systems Pvt Ltd—the rural finance and investment learning centre—and Consultative Group to Assist the Poor (CGAP) to carry out on the suggestion of RBI.

The crisis broke in the first half of 2009 and reflected the pattern noticed in MFIs across the globe, of high growth followed by a crisis. The key local trigger in India was the irrational exuberance of the industry leading to excessively rapid growth in lending. In 2008–9, as many as 27 MFIs operating in Karnataka grew their customer base by 64 per cent to reach 3.2 million borrowers, against a national growth rate of 42 per cent. This was on top of the three million customers that bank-linked SHGs had in the state.

The lending was marked by MFIs going after low-hanging fruit—populated areas in which residents were already familiar with microfinance because of the ground work done by MFIs which had come in earlier. As a result, multiple lending took place without adequate screening. This led to borrowers with multiple loans sometimes spending as much as one-to-two hours a day attending mandatory meetings of borrower groups. The easy availability of loans led to some agents appointed to recruit customers becoming proxy borrowers—using real borrowers as fronts to aggregate easily available finance which could then be on-lent. To this was added the troubles the silk-reeling industry ran into after the global financial crisis broke in 2008, impacting economic activity and trade in some of the affected areas.

When repayment instalments began to fall due with inexorable monthly regularity, tension grew among affected families and neighbourhoods. Thus was a tinder-box type of situation created, to which was added the spark of an attempted suicide in Kolar (Ujjivan did not have a presence there). This exacerbated the already existing tension and led to the local Anjuman committee banning interaction between Muslim women and MFI representatives through a religious edict. The Sidlaghatta Anjuman committee followed suit by stopping repayment of loans. In Ramanagara, silk-reeling factory owners who were faced with labour shortage (as MFI loans tended to make women independent) persuaded the local Anjuman committee to impose a Kolar-type ban. In Mysuru, an unrelated communal clash led to business losses, enabling a local political organization to pose as a saviour by raising the possibility of a loan waiver and urging MFI customers to stop repayment.

The religious or communal angle needs to be understood. Kolar's essentially conservative society resented Muslim women borrowers attending long meetings addressed by male MFI employees; photos of women without burkas being taken; the prayers and pledges that were part of the process and had religious overtones. The Anjuman committee members found it easy to address these issues by issuing bans and bringing credit to themselves. In Ramanagara, a false news report alleging suicide was attributed by the MFI staff to a nexus between local clerics and silk factory owners. It is axiomatic that successful income-generating microfinance can ultimately lead to social changes beneficial to women and help rectify gender bias. This will not come easy. Reaction and retrograde action will be inevitable. MFIs have to be aware of this and have to be, if nothing else, philosophical when it happens.

Two aspects prevented and delayed a return to normal life. One was the zero-delinquency mandate to MFI staff, leading to inflexibility in allowing rescheduling of loans. The second was group liability—a borrowers' group standing guarantee for repayment by all members. The burden of bearing the default of one or two members of a group by the rest of the group members was possible, but not more. And once an entire group was declared a defaulter, even those members who could repay stopped doing so as they were part of the collective default. A contributory factor was the adamant attitude of the Anjuman committee leaders who, having taken a tough stand, stuck to it as a matter of ego.

As a result of all this, Muslim women borrowers were caught in a cleft stick—between adamant community leaders and inflexible MFIs—although they all found MFI loans very useful and were willing to abide by repayment discipline. The bottom line was that religion provided neither the trigger (it was actually the attempted suicide) nor aggravated (inflexibilities were responsible for this) the crisis. Normalcy returned with MFIs giving up the attempt to get the government to intervene in their favour and instead cultivating deeper relationships with community leaders.

A key finding of the EDA Rural and CGAP study was that multiple lending, if not serious indebtedness, played a major role in the mass delinquency that occurred in southern Karnataka. The MFIs operating in the district, particularly their field-level staff, had no experience in handling a complex crisis like this and so were slow to react, thus losing the opportunity to take quick action as had been possible in the case of the first crisis in the Krishna district under the leadership of RBI. The first lesson to be learnt is that MFIs should be able to share information so as to avoid multiple lending. This has become possible with the development and growing effectiveness of the credit bureaus which are in place now.

The second learning is that in giving small loans to the economically active poor, one size will not fit all. The genuine need of someone who wishes to grow her small business should not force her to take several small loans from as many MFIs. Again, getting around this (securing a loan that matches somewhat higher needs) has now become possible with the introduction of individual loans whose ticket size is much larger and whose numbers are growing rapidly. Thus, over time they have come to constitute a still small but significant part of MFIs' portfolios. It follows from this that the larger loans require proper appraisal, as is the case with small loans given by commercial banks. Such appraisal will ensure that only those who can generate the necessary cash flows for repayment will be eligible for getting the larger loans, which are linked to the business, and not just to give some cash flow flexibility to a family.

A lot of the problem was caused by MFIs' zero-tolerance-for-delinquency policy. In case of genuine stress and distress, loan repayments need to be rescheduled. In order to distinguish between the genuinely troubled borrower and the artful dodger, it is imperative for the MFI to have in place proper systems of follow-up and supervision. If, for example, a local industry is in trouble because of adverse market conditions—as was the case with the Karnataka silk reelers—borrowers affected by it will need hand-holding by way of at least rescheduling of instalments. The same holds for a health emergency which can throw the entire small business of a borrower, whose business and family finances are intensively intertwined, out of gear. A borrower in such a situation will not just need rescheduling, but also maybe a medical loan.

Lastly, an MFI must dig deep roots and bond with the community it serves. This will provide the foundation for the support that it may need at a time of difficulty. Ujjivan, through its social responsibility agenda, has cultivated precisely this kind of community bonding in subsequent years. If MFIs in southern Karnataka had taken pains to do this in their earlier days, then they perhaps would not have been left to the mercy of self-serving community or local religious leaders without their borrowers coming out in large numbers to support them. The goodwill did exist, but it was not mobilized.

Signing of the agreement between Ujjivan and Unitus, one of Ujjivan's very first investors.

At the end of Ujjivan's 18-month pilot period in April 2007, Unitus and the Michael and Susan Dell Foundation together invested Rs 3 crore in equity. The foreign direct investment took Ujjivan's equity capital to Rs 5.5 crore.

One of the many first agreements to build better lives.

The first centre leaders' meeting held on 17 January 2006.

{ Microfinance is a cash-intensive operation: the loans are taken in cash and repayments are made in cash. Loans are disbursed from Ujjivan branches, where cash needs to be maintained. Repayments are made at centre meetings from where the cash has to be brought to the branch. }

Some happy faces from among the many men and women Ujjivan has helped lead economically independent lives.

Michael Dell of the Michael and Susan Dell Foundation visiting the customers at the Koramangala slum in Bengaluru.

H.R.H. Queen Beatrix of the Netherlands at the Ujjivan office at Jakkasandra, Karnataka, in 2008. She was accompanied by her son Prince Willem-Alexander and Princess Maxima.

Ever since it turned profitable in 2009–10, Ujjivan has been allocating a part of its annual profit to its community development fund. Ujjivan has a community development programme that works bottom-up. A branch forms a committee with members from staff and customers who decide which programmes to support.

A session of Diksha, launched in 2012, which seeks to teach the poor how to plan expenditure, work out budgets, appreciate the importance of savings, and, very importantly, the difference between good and bad borrowing.

Even though the country has a successful functioning microfinance programme which is meant to address poverty, large sections of the population remain poor. Mindful of this, Elaine Marie Ghosh, former banker, created the Parinaam Foundation as a not-for-profit organization in 2008 to deliver, in partnership with Ujjivan, the micro credit 'plus' programme to its customers.

The dawn of a new era:
submission of application
to the Reserve Bank of India
for small finance bank status,
1 February 2015.

Wednesday, 16 September 2015, was a day of irony for Ujjivan Financial Services.
It was a red letter day in the life of the nearly 10-year-old organization, yet it
also signalled the beginning of the end of the organization as it had been known
till then. On this day the RBI announced the names of 10 institutions (eight of
them MFIs) which had been granted 'in principle' approval to become small
finance banks and Ujjivan was one of them. Later, on 2 February 2017, the bank
commenced its operations with a gala launch in Bengaluru.

While planning for life as a small finance bank, the most important enabler that was achieved even before that life had begun was to successfully deliver a back-to-back duo – a pre-IPO (initial public offering) private placement and then the IPO itself.

Ujjivan received the 'Microfinance Institution of the Year' award in 2011. This award came during the crisis period.

For the last five years, Ujjivan has been ranked consistently among the top 25 companies to work for in India by the Great Place to Work Institute in collaboration with the Economic Times. It was ranked number one among the best companies to work for in the microfinance industry in 2015. In 2016, Ujjivan was ranked the third best place to work, taking all industries together. This made it the first Indian company as the first place had been taken by Google India and the second place by American Express India.

Ujjivan completes 10 years of operations. Seen here is a photograph from Dushotsav (lit. celebration of 10 years).

9

The Crisis Arrives in Andhra

The microfinance crisis in Andhra Pradesh broke out in late 2010, first with the issue of an ordinance and then the passing of a state law which affected all stakeholders. The case of Ujjivan is significant. It had avoided going into Andhra Pradesh, assessing the field there was overcrowded. In hindsight, this greatly de-risked its business, as had happened the previous year when it was able to easily weather the crisis in southern Karnataka because it had done the opposite—branched out across the country so as not to be solely dependent on business from its home state.

Even though Ujjivan did not take a hit in Andhra Pradesh, it was not able to avoid the ripple effects which had spread across the country. Recovery problems emerged in Tamil Nadu and West Bengal as MFIs withdrew because they were overextended. This put an end to the scope for multiple borrowing and exposed those who were engaged in it—as also those who were 'ghost' borrowers using others as fronts to garner cash—to the risk of default. Several leading microfinance organizations in Andhra Pradesh were put in a severe liquidity crunch as banks withdrew from lending to them after the crisis. Samit Ghosh, in his May 2011 'Letter from the Managing Director' in the 2010–11 annual report, did not mince words when he said the organization had gone into 'crisis management mode' since the previous October.

We will seek an understanding of the Andhra Pradesh crisis and its fall-out because it explains what was incorrect in the way MFIs operated, which led to the crisis in the first place. This gives an idea of the agenda for the change that was needed. Second, the regulatory responses that followed allowed the industry to determine what is good and what is bad regulation. Third, the regulatory regime that emerged post the Andhra Pradesh crisis is the world in which the microfinance industry has had to live. All this will give us a chance to examine how Ujjivan has been able to respond to challenge and change and also the space that will be available to it to grow and prosper as time goes on.

The immediate buildup to the crisis began early in 2010, when local TV channels in Andhra reported suicides among microfinance borrowers. Some women came forward to say they had been forced into prostitution as a result of repayment pressure. Then in July came the SKS public issue. Those in the state who were opposed to MFIs now felt they had cast-iron proof of how investors and managers made millions at the expense of poor borrowers who had no respite from repaying loans which carried very high interest rates. In August the state government set up a committee headed by the principal secretary of the state's rural development ministry to draft an ordinance to address the issue of distress caused by MFI operations. Helping the committee was the Society for the Eradication of Rural Poverty (SERP) which had, for a decade, worked hand in hand with the state government to implement the World Bank's Velugu programme that created a million SHGs. MFIs were poaching on SHGs assiduously built up through a decade of hard work and walking away with the profit. R. Rajsekhar, CEO of SERP, told David Roodman of Bengaluru-based online news media and publishing company, Microfinance Focus: 'It's like SERP have cooked the food; it's ready; MFIs can just come serve themselves and start earning.' The ordinance was approved in a one-hour special cabinet meeting with a single agenda and issued the next day, 15 October 2010.

The crisis broke with the issue of the ordinance which severely restricted MFIs' operations in response to distress among borrowers over repayment, which, according to the government's own count, had resulted in 54 suicides. The ordinance was followed by a state law being passed within the year, which, among other things, made it obligatory for an MFI to obtain permission from the relevant district authorities before operating in the area. Plus, MFIs could not engage in door-to-door collection but only in designated public areas, and that too on a monthly instead of a weekly basis. This sent a signal to borrowers that MFI loans need not be repaid and collections fell precipitously.

The Andhra Pradesh legislation revealed the regulatory gap in the field of microfinance and in late 2010, RBI appointed a committee under H.Y. Malegam, one of its board members, to go into the issue. It submitted its report in December 2010. The report first recommended that a separate category, NBFC–MFIs, should be created by RBI for supervision. It also defined the scope of NBFC–MFIs. They were to provide financial services predominantly to low-income borrowers through small loans for the short term on unsecured basis, mainly for income generation. They were to implement a repayment schedule which was more frequent than in the case of commercial banks. Interest rates were to be priced according to the size of MFIs. There was a margin cap of 10 per cent for MFIs with over a Rs-100-crore loan portfolio, 12 per cent for those with a less than Rs-100-crore portfolio, and a 24 per cent interest rate cap on individual loans. A key set of recommendations sought to ensure transparency in the rate of interest charged. There were to be three components to the pricing of loans: processing fee not exceeding 1 per cent of the loan; interest rate charged; insurance premium to recover actual cost of cover. Every MFI borrower would get a loan card showing the effective rate of interest and other conditions. No security deposit would be levied and there would be a standard loan agreement.

A borrower's annual household income could not exceed Rs 50,000. Loans would have a ceiling of Rs 25,000 with a similar total debt ceiling for the borrower. Loans up to Rs 15,000 would be repayable in 12 months and the rest, over 24 months on a weekly, fortnightly, or monthly basis as chosen by the borrower. There would be no penalty for prepayment and loans would be without collateral. Income-generation loans would not be less than 75 per cent of all loans given by MFIs, which would be allowed to lend to individuals who were members of joint liability groups and it was the responsibility of the MFIs to ensure that a borrower was not a member of another joint liability group. A borrower could not be a member of more than one SHG/joint liability group and not more than two MFIs could lend to the same borrower. All sanction and disbursal of loans would be done at a central location. Coercive recovery would attract severe penalties and MFIs would have a code of conduct for the recovery staff. Bank lending to SHGs and MFIs would be significantly increased.

In May the same year, the RBI issued its guidelines for the functioning of the microfinance industry registered with it as NBFC–MFIs. This remains the current rule book for most of the industry as the law for the industry still remains to be passed. The guidelines were largely welcomed by the sector for several reasons. One, there were at least some rules to go by, good or bad, given that one of the main problems earlier was the absence of such rules. Two, the sector found them to be a considerable improvement on what was originally proposed by the Malegam Committee. This indicated that the regulator was willing to listen to the practitioners, making the interactions that had taken place since the committee's report came out, meaningful. It also implied that issues on which the sector still had doubts were likely to be addressed and over time, most of them were. Plagued as the industry was with enormous uncertainty ever since it imploded in Andhra Pradesh, any kind of return to business as practicable, if not as was usual, gave cause for satisfaction.

The regulations sought to address several key concerns of the time: MFIs charge exorbitantly high rates of interest; the way they calculate it—and in combination with practices like taking security deposits—leads to charging a higher rate of interest than officially declared; multiple lending leads to diversion of funds from income generation to consumption, paving the way for greater future indebtedness. By fixing an effective interest rate ceiling of 26 per cent, defining how the interest is to be calculated, putting a ceiling of 12 per cent on margins, and abolishing the practice of taking security deposits, the regulations sought to address some of the concerns. While industry players did not have much to complain about regarding these aspects, they were negative about the RBI allowing a repayment period of two years. An individual MFI loan cycle did not exceed a year and giving a longer repayment period created the risk of what should have been repaid ending up in consumption. This is how the Andhra crisis identified a regulatory gap and how it was filled largely, though not entirely, to the satisfaction of the sector.

Now let us get back to Ujjivan. As the crisis broke in late 2010, Ujjivan saw several tasks ahead of it. One was managing liquidity with bank loans drying up and repayments slackening. Organizations like SIDBI and IDBI Bank and developed world markets came to the rescue and helped the organization tide over tightness. For its part, Ujjivan set its priorities in spending: first, meeting basic operating expenses, debt servicing, and standing by the needs of good customers; second, to protect its portfolio from collateral damage in states like Tamil Nadu and West Bengal, where it was operating when the crisis hit; third, to keep lines of communication open with the staff, who were confused by the tumultuous developments all around them. Special care was taken to ensure that salaries were paid on time and routine expenses like rent for hired premises met on schedule. The fourth was to engage in a continuous dialogue with the regulatory authorities, along with industry organizations like MFIN, Sa-Dhan, and AKMI. The fifth was to keep bonding with the community in which the organization operated, particularly through the work of Parinaam Foundation, so that an Andhra type situation did not develop in which an MFI was seen as merely another moneylender.

The RBI guidelines represented a new ball game that MFIs had to quickly learn. A massive effort had to be made to reduce costs as the RBI stipulated that margins over cost of funds should not exceed 12 per cent, thus effectively putting a ceiling on lending rates. A similar effort needed to be made to reduce the proportion of dropouts (borrowers who did not return for another loan after closing one) as a high 20 per cent figure reflected on the nature of customer experience. Funding flow had to be rejuvenated.

Another critical lesson learnt and which had to be slowly put in place was to phase out the practice of forming joint liability groups under which individual members of borrower groups were responsible for the repayment of other members. Tension on this account (from one member failing to meet her obligations) was an important reason for customer suicides in Andhra Pradesh. Bangladesh, which had pioneered microfinance on the subcontinent, had already dispensed with the practice. (Now, under joint liability, other group members' obligation to step in for a defaulting member extends only up to three instalments.) Plus, staff-incentive schemes had to be revised as over-the-top incentives led to excessive unsound lending. At the institutional level, it was necessary for the industry to ensure that credit information bureaus were created so that they could act as the main bulwark against multiple lending.

Despite all the problems around them, MFIs were reassured that there was no long-term existential threat to their future. By creating a separate category for NBFC–MFIs, RBI had formally designated a space for them. What was more, the government declared its intention to issue separate banking licences which would allow MFIs to accept deposits and thus not have to depend on relatively high-cost bank loans. Once such licences were issued, MFIs would take a long step towards securing a viable future. But again, that is getting too far ahead with the story.

10

Battling the Crisis

In many ways, FY 2011–12 can be described as the most critical in the 10-year history of Ujjivan. During this period, it validated the robustness of its model by passing a severe stress test. It tackled the fallout of a crisis afflicting the entire microfinance sector in the country, undertook several changes, and, what is most important, came out on top of the crisis with its basic model intact and ready to get onto the growth path again.

In the face of the fallout of the Andhra crisis, which dried up the major source of finance for MFIs—loans from banks—Ujjivan took two steps. Stepping back from the path of rapid growth, it cut down its total number of branches from 351 to 299; shed 14 per cent of its staff (which had seen a 42 per cent growth in the previous year); severely curtailed its acquisition of new customers, so that the rate of growth fell from 60 per cent to 5 per cent; mostly restricted fresh lending to existing customers with a good record; and, in the process, saw a sharp reduction in the growth rate of disbursals, from 122 per cent to 52 per cent. The overall impact of all these moves was a reduction in costs. The operating expenses ratio (cost to average portfolio) fell from 17.6 per cent to 13.5 per cent. Even without a crisis this was essential as RBI had put a 12 per cent ceiling on MFI margins. The crisis facilitated the whole process by putting the organization in fire-fighting mode.

The cost reduction was achieved through a business-efficiency pro-gramme which was introduced in 2011. It had a two-pronged focus—business consolidation and technology infusion. Fifty-two branches and customer centres that had a staff of less than 25 were merged keeping in mind geographical proximity, scope for productivity improvement, and growth prospects. As a result, borrowers per staff went up by 24 per cent, and outstanding loans per field staff rose by 52 per cent and per branch by 41 per cent. The core banking solution was extended to most of the branches, allowing for instant uploading of repayment data, enabling better cash management and lower cash-handling costs. On operating proce-dures, a key decision was taken to extend the monthly repayment window for borrowers from one week to three weeks. This gave greater flexibility to borrowers and more scope to field staff, allowing them more time for centre meetings, thereby getting to know customers better. The business consolidation led to a smaller field staff being deployed. Extending core banking allowed for fewer staff at the back end to take care of accounting functions. All this enabled more staff to be deployed in audit, vigilance, and credit, thus allowing better management of critical business needs.

The stress that was witnessed can be gauged from the fact that Ujjivan's PAR (stressed assets to total assets) went up rapidly in two months from 1.48 per cent in March 2011 to under 2.5 per cent in May. Thereafter, the level held steady for the next three months, right up to August, and then declined steadily for the rest of the financial year to reach 1.33 per cent by March 2012, actually ending the year better than it began. Credit performance worsened during the first quarter of the financial year but recovered thereafter. Pockets in Tamil Nadu, West Bengal, and Odisha—which initially saw a deterioration in portfolio quality because of exces-sive competition among MFIs—stabilized by the end of the year. When borrowers in some branches in Bihar and Tamil Nadu were affected by calamities like floods and a cyclone, they were nurtured (given food and repayment rescheduled) so that portfolio quality regained stability by the year end. As a result of all this, Ujjivan was able to clock a repayment rate of 98.2 per cent for the year, which was par for the course.

The ability to grapple with and get on top of adversity quickly was the result of policy decisions taken and action initiated on that basis. Risk-management committees were set up for crisis-hit branches and branch-wise action plans were worked out. Changes were made in the level of strategic supervisors of stressed branches and mentoring programmes were undertaken for their staff. Special collection teams were set up for them. These ensured that first-time overdue cases were not allowed to deteriorate into substandard assets and default cases were followed up on a daily basis. Loans of customers facing genuine problems were rescheduled and further credit was given to those considered to be essentially 'good' borrowers. Back-end teams kept track of all this. Thus, the entire operational set-up got into and worked in a crisis mode.

A major challenge during the year was managing liquidity as bank loans dried up following the Andhra crisis. The suspension of bank credit in the first half of the financial year created a gap between planned and actual disbursement, leading to a slowdown in business momentum, and a decline in the loan book and profitability. Ujjivan managed to mitigate the adverse funding situation partially by going in for issuing of non-convertible debentures and loan securitization, issuing paper backed by underlying loans which is subscribed to by banks. This has the result of banks being able to meet their priority sector lending targets. In May Ujjivan, through its maiden securitization programme, raised Rs 17.4 crore and then in September Rs 40 crore. Both the issues were structured by the Institute of Financial Management and Research (IFMR). Ujjivan also went in for issue of non-convertible debentures, for Rs 55 crore in June and July (about the toughest part of the financial year) and then again for Rs 29 crore in January 2012. Additionally, it raised Rs 50 crore of debt against equity which was critical for disbursement. In the entire financial year it raised Rs 283 crore from banks and financial institutions when, in the early part of the year, there was a strong impact of the winding in of bank credit resulting from the Andhra crisis towards the end of 2010.

But the crowning achievement was being able to raise equity in a year of turmoil. It was a rigorous process of due diligence and intensive interaction, leading to Rs 128 crore of fresh equity capital being raised from WCP Holdings, Nederlandse Financierings, Indian Financial Inclusion Fund, Elevar Equity, Sequoia India, Sarva Capital, Mauritius Unitus, and others. Investors conducted due diligence over several rounds. Ujjivan's double bottom-line approach and transparency contributed to new investors deciding to come in even during a period of adverse financial outlook for the industry. The emotional equity that Ujjivan had with its existing investors acted as a certificate which enabled it to attract new investors. The rigorous manner in which it ran its operations resulted in investors, both existing and new, reposing their faith in the company. Ujjivan was the first microfinance firm to be able to raise fresh capital after the Andhra crisis. This both renewed its faith in its mission and enabled it to hope that microfinance in India had turned the corner and could look forward to growing with comfortable leveraging.

One positive fallout of the Andhra crisis was the industry, under the leadership of its association MFIN, taking positive steps to set up a credit bureau, a good intention that had been discussed but hung fire since 2008. Ujjivan signed up with three credit bureaus—High Mark, TransUnion CIBIL Limited, and Equifax. By the end of the financial year, High Mark had a database of 43 million customers and 76 million accounts received from 77 MFIs. In order to make its data compatible with the format required by the credit bureau, Ujjivan modified its customer profile and loan applications as part of a strong internal process of data capturing, extraction, and sharing. This has led to an improvement of data quality, documentation, and understanding of customer behaviour. The main improvement was, of course, in asset quality as references to the credit bureau enabled Ujjivan to weed out applicants who did not fit the bill.

During the year, credit bureau checks resulted in the rejection of 2.6 per cent of applications. Other than improving the quality of borrowers, the advent of the credit bureau helped in two more ways. Customers became aware that it was in their own interest in maintaining a good profile with the credit bureau in order to get future loans. Hence, they became more proactive in sticking to the repayment schedule. Plus, credit bureau work helped in geographic mapping in two ways: MFIs could discover white spots—areas which were underserved by microfinance, and dark spots—areas with a high proportion of rejection as a result of references, indicating that all was not right with the region. As is to be expected, in the aftermath of the Andhra crisis, the south accounted for the highest percentage of rejections for Ujjivan.

In times of hardship and tension, it is vital for an organization to be able to communicate effectively, both with the outside world and internally. Earlier, Ujjivan did not have a well-worked-out, consistent approach to being able to tell the rest of the world about itself. So in 2011–12, it decided to go in for a formal corporate communications framework. This meant relaunching Brand Ujjivan by setting branding guidelines, streamlining logos, and standardizing communication templates. The visual aspect of communicating with the outside world was very important as many of Ujjivan's customers were barely literate, or not at all. It was critical to appear friendly to them, in particular, approachable—informal, flexible, and concerned about relationships beyond the financial aspect. As few of its customers would know English, the brand and the brand promise, 'Build a better life', were rendered in 10 Indian languages.

As outdoor signage is the first point of contact with the general public, an attempt was made to make it look bright, eye-catching, and relevant to the customer. Along with this, all communication materials like stationery and forms were standardized so that they appeared to be extensions of the brand. Some branches were designed as model branches so that the experience on entering them became an extension of the positive feeling that the outdoor communication created.

Ujjivan already had a carefully designed website which was regularly updated and used as a key source of precise communication of message and data. Its annual reports have far more than what is statutorily required. An attempt was made to use social media (Facebook and Twitter) as useful ways of keeping a finger on the pulse of the world around Ujjivan.

By being prompt and regular in reporting to the Microfinance Information Exchange (MIX), it has won four awards for its reporting. Internal communication, vital for building staff morale, was taken forward with the launch of the U. Connect, the company's intranet, and an employee blog and forum. All this was part of trying to better communicate all the effort that was being made to fight adversity and not just survive but get back to the path of high growth.

The attempt to build a better work experience bore results. In 2011 Ujjivan was ranked as the 'best company to work for in the microfinance industry and 14th overall across industries' in a survey carried out by the Great Place to Work (India) Institute in collaboration with *The Economic Times*. This is the second time that it received this distinction. The survey covered organizations of different size across industries and looked at issues like credibility of leadership, fairness and transparency in practices and processes, work–life balance, and camaraderie and a sense of belonging among employees.

What was the industry outlook at the end of a financial year in which the microfinance industry as a whole had been trying to pick up the pieces and Ujjivan had been successful in scripting a turnaround? Ghosh told a conclave on the industry, which had several other industry leaders on the panel, that private equity was not the cause of undisciplined and unplanned growth; that the responsibility for it lay with the MFIs themselves. He also noted that the hype about microfinance being the sole magic pill for poverty alleviation was 'avoidable'. Thus, though microfinance was a key enabler for financial inclusion, multiple interventions were needed to remove poverty, including education and healthcare. All in all, it was Karnataka, and not Andhra, which was a role model for collaborative effort by MFIs, NGOs, and governments to achieve financial inclusion.

11

Return to High Growth

After weathering the Andhra storm, Ujjivan re-emerged on the high growth path by the end of 2011–12. In the four years since, right up to 2015–16, the organization has witnessed phenomenal growth and all-round improvement in its operating efficiencies. In the world of microfinance, it is not just a formidable growth engine but an increasingly efficient one too. Comparing figures at the end of FY 2012 with those of end of FY 2016, its gross loan book rose by a CAGR of 66.4 per cent to Rs 5,389 crore, and the total number of customers went up from one million to 3.3 million, that makes for a CAGR of 33.4 per cent. The total income (it is a financial company's equivalent to a general company's revenue) rose at a similar pace of 60 per cent CAGR to Rs 1,028 crore. With a net profit of Rs 177 crore, the net margin, again a regular measure of the performance of ordinary companies, works out to a highly impressive 17 per cent. Had Ujjivan been an ordinary firm, this would have been celebrated but a microfinance company, which lives by lending to the poor (remember the reaction to the profits made by MFIs in the run-up to the Andhra crisis), is not supposed to make too much profit—at least according to popular sentiment.

As impressive as growth and profitability have been, the improvement in operating efficiencies and cost control have been equally so. Cost-to-income ratio has gone down from 94.2 per cent (2011–12 was a crisis year in which the company barely broke even) to 51 per cent. This has enabled unit cost to support a much higher level of loans. Thus, operating expenses to average loan book has gone down from 13.8 per cent to 7.5 per cent. It is therefore to be expected that gross loan book per branch has gone up from Rs 2 crore to Rs 11 crore and gross loan book per employee from Rs 20 lakh to Rs 60 lakh. This improvement has been made possible by the total number of employees and branches going up at a much slower pace than total loans. Employee head count over the same period has gone up by a CAGR of 23.6 per cent and total number of branches has gone up by 56 per cent, which is, not even doubled.

As is to be expected from a well-run microfinance company, Ujjivan's gross NPAs are a negligible under 1 per cent, at 0.15 per cent. When customers repay loans with such alacrity, it is to be expected that customer retention is one of the highest in the industry at 86 per cent. This would have been higher but for the fact that Ujjivan has had to let customers go to be able to adhere to the RBI rule that a customer must not have more than two MFI loans. Not only do Ujjivan's customers want to remain with it, the MFI also has a high staff retention ratio of 82 per cent. It is therefore not surprising that it should have won a position in the top 25 best places to work (across all industries) list created by Great Place to Work (India) for five years consecutively; in 2015, it became one of the top three companies to work for, with the other two being multinationals. In 2015, it was ranked number one among microfinance companies to work for. It also became the first microfinance company to offer employees stock options, and currently, 54 per cent of all employees are covered by it.

Ujjivan has also been a great story with investors. Foreign investors who have exited over the last two years have been able to secure a return of over 20 per cent. The few individual angel investors who have remained invested in Ujjivan for 10 years now have seen the value of their investments grow by 30 times based on current market prices. The IPO, preparatory to becoming an SFB (we will look at this later), made shareholding in Ujjivan broad-based, with 41,000 individual and institutional shareholders equally distributed between both domestic and foreign categories.

One way of seeing how Ujjivan has changed over its first decade of existence is to see how the product basket it offers customers has changed. First, as a microfinance company, its bread-and-butter business remained group loans, which accounted for 88 per cent of lending. While the core loans like business and family loans have continued, a new product—agriculture and allied loans—has been added to meet the working capital and equipment cost of farming. It is available in the Rs 6,000–50,000 range and is repayable over one to two years. Another product which has been introduced is the education loan, available in the Rs 5,000–15,000 range for 12 months. There is also a loyalty loan, available for Rs 5,000–15,000, repayable over 12 months. The key changes in the overall group-loans package is interest rates coming down from 24–26.9 per cent to 22 per cent. Also, the various fees and security deposits have been done away with, and have all been replaced by a single processing fee of 1 per cent of the loan amount, excluding taxes. Importantly, the top end of the loan amounts available has gone up from Rs 10,000–12,000 to Rs 50,000 for business loan and Rs 35,000 for family loan. One aspect of all products has remained the same throughout—all interest is charged on reducing balance and not at a flat rate.

But the really big change that has come in 2015–16 is the introduction of products for the micro and small enterprise (MSE) sector. While granting the in-principle approval for SFBs, RBI mandated that MSEs be made one of their main customer segments. Ujjivan had already partially addressed the needs of this sector through its individual loan product (different from group loans) under which 110,000 borrowers, with mostly unregistered businesses, have been lent an aggregate of Rs 600 crore. Unsecured individual loans are largely given to the creamy layer of the group segment. But it needs emphasizing that though there is some overlap between the two, the MSE segment and the individual loan segment are different. Hence the product offerings and terms are different. In this scenario, Ujjivan, in 2015–16, introduced three products: the individual business and bazaar loan, available for Rs 51,000–150,000 for a

6–24 month period at an interest rate of 24 per cent, plus a 2 per cent processing fee on loan amount, excluding taxes; the Pragati Business Loan, available for Rs 51,000–100,000 for a 24–36 month period at a cost of 23 per cent and a processing fee of 1 per cent on the loan amount, excluding taxes; and an individual loyalty loan of Rs 20,000–30,000 repayable over 12 months, carrying an interest rate of 23.5 per cent and processing fee of 1 per cent of the loan amount, excluding taxes for customers who have a good business relationship, with at least 20 instalments paid.

While the foregoing requires no security, Ujjivan also introduced a secured business loan against the collateral of land and building valued at least at 150 per cent of the loan amount. This is available for a far higher amount of Rs 200,000–1,000,000 for a period of 24–84 months and carrying a lower interest rate of 20 per cent. The processing fee is 2.2 per cent of the loan amount, excluding taxes.

Another key area of emerging product offering is housing finance. This venture grew out of two realizations. One was the acute shortage of reasonable housing, particularly among the poor. The other was the finding that borrowers were using group loans to partly pay for immediate and acute housing needs. Hence, this was a largish top-up loan, so to speak, to enable borrowers to complete work on their dwellings so as to reap the full benefits from the investment made. A motivating factor was the knowledge that reasonable, livable space goes a long way in improving the quality of people's lives and helps realize the whole purpose of microfinance.

Therefore, in 2012, Ujjivan introduced an unsecured Rs 150,000 individual (that is, outside the group loan system) housing loan. Then, in 2016, a secured housing loan product was issued for a higher ticket. By end 2015–16, three home-loan products were available. An unsecured loan for Rs 51,000–150,000 for home improvement was available. It was repayable over 12–24 months and carried an interest rate of 24 per cent and 2 per cent processing fee, excluding taxes. For the same purpose, a higher secured loan of Rs 200,000–500,000 was available at 19.75 per cent interest (processing fee of 2.5 per cent) repayable over 24–84 months. Plus, a secured loan for purchase and construction was available for Rs 200,000–1,000,000 at an interest rate of 15.75 per cent and processing fee of 2.5 per cent repayable over 24–120 months.

When it started out, Ujjivan's USP was that it lent to the urban poor. But over time the rural poor also joined its clientele. Now that it has become an SFB with 25 per cent of its branches in unbanked small habitats (population of up to 10,000), rural India will figure in a much bigger way in its operations in the coming years. Consequently, a range of products for agriculture and livestock are available. An individual (not as part of a group) agricultural loan is available for Rs 31,000–80,000 repayable over 4–12 months at 24 per cent, plus a 1 per cent processing fee. This is clearly related to the cropping cycle. An individual livestock loan is available for Rs 41,000–100,000 repayable over 9–24 months at a cost of 24 per cent, plus a 1 per cent processing fee. Additionally, for the same two purposes (agriculture and livestock) two Pragati loans are available. For agriculture, the loan ticket is the same, Rs 31,000–80,000, but the repayment tenure is longer at 24 months, and the interest rate is lower at 23 per cent, plus a 1 per cent processing fees. For livestock, the ticket is higher at the minimum end, Rs 51,000–1,00,000, repayment is over a longer period of 24–36 months and the interest rate is lower at 23 per cent, plus a 1 per cent processing charge.

The rapid growth and emerging sophistication of products point to the growing importance of individual lending whose dynamic is so different from group lending, which has dominated the microfinance sector in its initial years. Through this, the aim is to take the share of the financially included (those who are better off), from less than 10 per cent to 50 per cent in five years. Such is the importance and potential of individual lending that an individual lending organization is emerging within Ujjivan. This has had significant human resource ramifications. An entirely new team has been brought in to handle this nascent category as it requires distinct skills. To this have been added members of the existing staff with special training.

The scope of human resource expansion can be gauged from the fact that the ratio between the new and old staff is 7:3. It is envisaged that most of the manpower needed for individual lending will come from outside, and will undergo a rigorous programme of training after induction. This training programme, which includes field and classroom components and uses the services of outside experts for lectures, was devised with the help of Women's World Banking. Senior project managers and technical experts have been inducted and middle-level staff who have been recruited have been sent for intensive training to specialized financial institutions in India and overseas. A referral incentive scheme and a rewards programme have been introduced to raise motivation levels within the organization and give everyone a stake in the individual loan programme.

As is the practice in Ujjivan, the individual lending product was launched after a structured effort to understand the customer' needs. Joint studies were conducted with agencies like Women's World Banking, IMRB International, and Delphi to gauge the scope and viability of products. From this has emerged the large menu of products described earlier that are geared to specific needs and cover areas like financing MSEs, meeting the needs of those in rural and agricultural operations, and funding individual requirements like housing, higher education, and medical emergencies. As a result of the explorations with specialist organizations, an independent credit methodology was introduced for individual lending. Earlier, the same credit team handled both group and individual lending, but the growing potential of individual lending necessitated the creation of separate teams. Under it, after field-based independent credit verification, proposals are sent to model sanctioning committees set up for each individual lending hub with the help of Women's World Banking.

To facilitate the credit process, the use of IT—already high in Ujjivan—has been made more extensive. Field officers are being equipped with handheld tablets to enable front office automation. This has digitized the capture and flow of customer data from the field. As a result, document turnaround time has been reduced, errors minimized, and the processing of information made more efficient. All this has enabled faster and more efficient decision-making by the sanctioning authorities. In the process, all functionaries and decision-makers have the benefit of a better MIS. 'A more digitized and automated field process will be the future face of the individual lending programme,' Ujjivan has declared.

Ujjivan is in the throes of change. The organization and the needs of its customers are growing rapidly. To facilitate this and take it along rational lines, it is looking at the lifestyle of the customer who generally comes in when her needs are quite small, then increase over time. As the organization grows and loyal customers with a good repayment record move to higher loan cycles, they are handheld to graduate from group to individual lending. As microfinance makes a concerted attack on poverty, it is individual lending which will carry the can in a big way, and Ujjivan plans to keep changing and upgrading itself to meet this challenge. Rajat Singh, head of strategy and planning, says that with increased emphasis on individual loans, it is now a separate vertical accounting for 13 per cent of business. Separate processes, people, and technology are being lined up to support that vertical. 'Individual loans will drive our next phase of growth.'

To manage rapid growth and benefit from the learnings gained from the early days, 'we have put in place a lot of strong policies and processes,' says Carol Furtado, head of human resources and service quality at Ujjivan. (Some of the following points will be covered in greater detail in a subsequent chapter.) On people, the learning has been to get people with the right profile and teams in place. Training has also been delivered at multiple levels—basic-level training, refresher training, and a lot of customized training for various activities. Internal controls have been improved. Ujjivan already had an independent credit team in place which emphasized customer selection. This has been delivered by multi-level checks to ensure independent verification with a strong field audit component.

Another key element of growing healthily has been to work out a rigorous process of selecting locations for new branches. But while pursuing high growth, a hard-earned lesson from the past has not been forgotten. An eye is kept on not letting geographical concentration get out of hand. Plus, processes have been put in place for smooth interface between field operations and the back office to handle a massive portfolio. 'As these things were followed, our portfolio was more or less intact and we were able to grow,' explains Furtado.

12

Processes and Information Technology

Ujjivan has been able to move forward on the path of high growth with stability because of several enablers. We look at them over the next three chapters. In the present one, we see how it has been able to continuously change and improve its processes to both cope with rapidly growing volumes and do business with greater efficiency and productivity, thus enabling it to lower costs. The key resource that made this possible was greater use of information technology. As process improvement and the use of IT go hand in hand, we look at the two together.

When Martin Pampilly, who had 14 years' experience in banking, first visited the Koramangala branch of Ujjivan in 2008, he felt encouraged to discover that customer relations were 'transparent'. This may have played a part in helping him make up his mind and go in for the switch. But when he joined in January 2009 as regional operations manager for the south, he took a hard look at both the front and the back end and was in for a 'shock'. Work was completely paper-based and computerization was minimal. There was no automation in branches and the regional office did the posting for transactions. Yearly and half-yearly account closings were a nightmare. This was somewhat overwhelming and he took two months to decide whether to continue. He did, and the eight-odd years that he has been with Ujjivan (and moved up to become head of operations for the entire organization) have been highly rewarding. Capturing the then-and-now picture, he recalls that then, 250 people processed 60,000–65,000 loan applications in a month; by mid-2016, the output per head had gone up by over seven times, with 165 people processing 3,00,000 loans a month.

Deepak Ayare, an IT expert with over 25 years' experience who was Ujjivan's chief information officer till 2016, joined just a few months before Pampilly, in late 2008. Then there were 85 branches, 850 staff members, and 0.15 million borrowers. (Ayare left Ujjivan on 30 November 2016.) Then, the goal was to set up 700 branches and acquire two million customers within five years. By end 2015–16, after eight years, there were three million borrowers but only 469 branches. While customer growth has more or less kept pace with earlier projections, far fewer branches are managing this enhanced workload. A part of the growth in productivity is captured in this. Growth in volume would have been even better but for the slowdown caused by the Andhra crisis and the resultant spillover. But the time was not lost. In the classical Japanese model, under which firms go in for large capital investment during periods of recession so as to be ready with the right capacity and technology for the next business upturn, 'we utilized the time to introduce new technologies to achieve automation. The productivity gains have more than justified the resources invested in technology.'

Carol Furtado, one of the earliest to join and among the senior most (head of business operations till 2016, when she became head of human resources and service quality) recalls that 'it was a centralized back office operation right from day one. The field staff would emulate the Grameen model of group lending. But efficiencies would be higher, our turnaround time would be much faster, and more volumes could be handled form the back end. All the papers would come to the back end (wherever it was physically) for data entry. Data was filled in forms at the branch level and data entry was done at the back end centralized operations. That is where we would process all the data, do the credit checks, and send out the disbursements. This gave us confidence over how to handle branches remotely. That was the base and we brought in a lot of banking processes and technologies.' Ujjivan's working was different from the way other MFIs were operating. All of them had a back end at the branch itself. Again, unlike other MFIs, the disbursements would happen at the branch level. Many MFIs took cash to the centre meetings and disbursed it there.

A key set of process changes took place over the periodicity of centre meetings, says Furtado. It was always a challenge for customers to attend weekly meetings regularly. 'But we took feedback; it was part of our DNA to take feedback from customers right from day one.' When it was realized that customers found weekly meetings difficult to attend, Ujjivan shifted to fortnightly meetings but monthly collections. Furthermore, when it was found that attendance was low at meetings when repayments were not taking place, it shifted to monthly meetings that were scheduled for the second week of the month. The feedback from all over was that borrowers were happy with the change in the number of meetings. But the load of processing the entire batch of customers was now concentrated on that meeting. There was also a lot of risk in carrying a lot of cash as seven or eight centre meetings were held in one day. There were no processes in place for customers to come and deposit the cash at the bank and not bring it to the Ujjivan branch. This led to centre meetings being spread out—and the introduction of three repayment windows—first, second, and third week. This gave customers a choice. 'We always looked at what was convenient for them. Eventually, we introduced a fourth repayment window, so all the weeks in a month had one and customers could choose whichever suited them best. Thus, we were able to bring in more efficiencies, reduce risk (not have to carry a lot of cash at one go), and made it more convenient for our staff and customers.'

Pampilly considers this decision taken in 2012 to switch to monthly repayment from weekly repayment a watershed one. This meant customer groups meeting monthly instead of weekly and the meeting supervision load of the customer relationship staff (CRS) going down by 75 per cent. It gave three additional weeks to the staff every month, raising their productivity. This, plus customers (for repayment) being distributed over the entire month, 'resulted in switching from a gas stove with one burner to four burners. The number of vouchers a cashier had to handle was reduced to a third. Each CRS could now handle 700 customers in a month, compared to 450 earlier.'

A CRS's day began with centre meetings at which attendance and repayments were recorded in loan cards and registers. Then a column was introduced in the instalment-due report to mark attendance, thus removing the need for registers, since the attendance was captured in repayment. Then, instead of posting all repayments individually, only an overdue list was prepared. This reduced the load on cashiers. Initially, there was a master group register which contained the picture and information on every borrower. Then a file was created in the IT system which contained all the information about the customer as also her scanned image. So that register was the next to go. Life has also changed for the customer. Pampilly recalls that initially the customer had to keep track of several documents—an ID card with photo, a loan card which recorded repayments, and vouchers for individual payments. Now the loan card with a photo also serves as an ID card and updating the card with repayments removes the need to issue vouchers for repayment. Essentially, one loan card does the job of three documents.

Describing the IT scenario, Ayare said when he joined, they were using client server technology restricted by LAN (local area network)—not web-based technology—with different servers based in Delhi, Kolkata, and Bengaluru. There was no centralized system. Every night, data used to get synchronized, which required the IT team tasked with doing this to sit up the whole night. At that time connectivity was neither steady nor high speed. When a connection broke, the whole work had to be repeated. They used to face different challenges at the month-end and year-end. Then, in 2010, came the new web-based technology, accessible from anywhere. The core banking vendor, Craft Silicon, came up with a web-based solution, BR.Net, which was still being used in 2016. Then Ujjivan's data centre was outsourced to IBM, Mumbai, so that it was properly managed in a secure environment.

When Pampilly became head of operations in 2011, he set three tasks for himself: make every employee feel valuable, address technology, and improve efficiency. The first step he took was to outsource the production of customer ID cards, which had become a bottleneck. The job went to Vindhya E-Infomedia, an organization which employed differently abled people. 'They produced better ID cards than we did. They have grown with us—from 10–12 people, they are now 700.' Those in Ujjivan who had been engaged in producing the ID cards were transferred to data entry. This made them feel valuable as computer operators.

At this point it is necessary to introduce Vindhya E-Infomedia, a socio-economic business process outsourcing (BPO) venture founded in 2006. It is Ujjivan's oldest BPO partner with a decade-long relationship. Vindhya seeks to have a social impact by providing employment to capable, differently able workers, who account for 60 per cent of its workforce, with the majority coming from families living below the poverty line. Vindhya first partnered with Ujjivan in handling data entry of loans and is a pioneer in servicing MFIs. Most recently, when Ujjivan started making welcome calls to all its customers in 2014, it partnered Vindhya to handle its Bengaluru call centre programme. These calls enable verifying the accuracy of important information, and understanding the service and satisfaction levels of customers. All such services are now routed through Vindhya. Pavithra Y.S. of Vindhya says, 'The association began very naturally as Ujjivan was the first MFI to centralize and set up a back office, while Vindhya is one of the largest BPOs in the MFI space.'

The latter ventured into voice processing in 2011 and has started servicing non-MFI institutions too.

The next step for Pampilly was to stop the practice of people working
in shifts, which were difficult to supervise. To end this, work volume had
to go down. This was done by outsourcing the creation of digital personal
profiles to Vindhya. The whole work reorientation was done in 10 months.
The staff who were thus freed up were moved to different functions. This
was also done keeping staff convenience in mind. Additionally, as staff was
needed for new branches, some employees were moved to branches near
their homes. After the outsourcing process stabilized in the south, it was
carried out in other regions. This was a win-win outcome as simultaneously
three things happened. Work flow was smoothened, supervisors felt happy,
and so did the staff.

Taking an overview, Furtado says loan application and customer
profile are still on paper for the group-lending customers in the field.
But a lot of the back-end processes have improved over time. 'We put
in place scanners, a workflow system, and checks with the credit bureau
when these became necessary after the Andhra crisis.' For customers for
individual loans which came in later, the data entry is done on handheld
devices by a specialized team. That has a different workflow. And now,
the group-lending staff is also being trained to get into data entry through
handheld devices. For close to two years, till 2016, these have been used
for repayment.

Scanning of documents has started around 2013 after which data
entry is done by the outsourced vendor. Then the digital file gets into
the credit queue where credit does the check. After that it goes to
operations for final processing and then goes back to the branches.
Over time Ujjivan has also reduced dependence on cash for credit
disbursement. 'Through the financial literacy programme run by
Parinaam Foundation, we started helping our customers open bank
accounts to get them to start transacting in the banks,' explains
Furtado.

Before the core banking IT system was extended to branches, the CRS collected payments at centre meetings and brought the cash to the branches. Vouchers were also prepared at the branches but were posted at the head office and then at the regional offices. Once the core banking system reached branches, the day's vouchers were posted there the very day. From April 2012, Ujjivan started closing monthly accounts the same day the month ended. Earlier there was a six-day cash float in the system. Cash was received but the overall cash position could not be immediately ascertained. Now, treasury can know the fund position every day as the books are reconciled daily.

The year 2012–13 brought about a revolution, with the introduction of a document management system and scanners at branches from where couriering documents to regional office would take more than two days. Now scanned documents get tagged on to the workflow and customer data is entered by vendors. There are as many as seven of them. With the scanned documents in the workflow, regional offices go ahead with the loan processing. The customer relationship staff is able to check the status of processing by referring to the workflow. Computerizing the workflow and dematerializing documents has led to the time it takes to process a loan application (receipt to disbursal) from 25–26 days to 6–9 days.

Going over the same process, Ayare highlighted the productivity angle. Earlier, when physical documents used to be sent to the regional office and then tracked, there were 20–25 people doing the tracking. There was a big staff at the back office to process 80,000 loans for Rs 80 crore in a month and turnaround time was 17–25 days. Then some-thing happened in north Karnataka; Ujjivan started losing customers because of time lag resulting from doing the loan processing rigorously. Some MFIs started giving loans simply by looking at the Ujjivan ID card. If a customer was from Ujjivan and she had already repaid one loan, then she was a good customer. They started giving loans within 2–3 days. So Ujjivan started losing customers and the business staff needed some help.

In response, a pilot was implemented with a few scanners at the Hubli branch in north Karnataka. A hub was created there and all the surrounding branches sent their loan applications to it. Credit would get the file, process it, and approve the loan. The data-entry operator would enter the data from the image and the loan would be disbursed. The first loan under this system was disbursed in one-and-a-half days instead of 17 days. Then the business staff wanted a solution in each branch. 'So we identified IBM FileNet as a solution and document management system and implemented it within a year. Today [in 2016] we can comfortably process over 3.5 lakh loans worth around Rs 700 crore in a month. So going from Rs 80 crores to Rs 700 crore is the technology achievement with a turnaround time of well under 10 days.'

An automated MIS allows each department, through a tracking mechanism called Web Tracker, to measure the number of loans each individual is processing and the delay that is happening. By analysing past data, you can project how many applications will be received within the next two days and plan staff deployment accordingly.

The CRS now go to group meetings with handheld devices that have the data for the meetings and dues for the day. They then post the repayments—which indicate attendance—on these devices. In the branch the cashier takes in the cash and tallies it with the repayments thus recorded. At any moment, the online system shows cash collected by the CRS and, after cross-checking by the cashier, the total cash received.

In line with this, the customer-acquisition process has also been further automated and streamlined through the introduction of a mobility solution called Artoo that can be used through handheld devices. (It has been created by an IT firm whose founder was an Ujjivan trainee, who has been able to use the domain knowledge with him and current employees.) As most loans are disbursed to existing customers who graduate to higher loan circles, Artoo uses data analysis and facilitates the process of selecting customers for new loans from existing customers. Under Artoo, the system generates a list of potential customers for individual loans as a lead to the loan officer.

He checks with the branch staff and if the customer is interested, then information is generated for checking with the credit bureau. If the response is positive the field credit officer verifies the customer information on the spot. Once this step is cleared, the branch-sanctioning committee applies its mind to the business and credit risk involved and sanctions the loan. Then the loan documents come to the regional office as part of the document management workflow for approval of disbursement. If the loan is for over Rs 1 lakh, then the fraud unit has to clear it. Thereafter, the loan is disbursed through a bank account which the customer could have opened with the help of Parinaam Foundation. A process like this automates the sanctioning of loans to good existing customers and saves a lot of manpower, which is then freed up to focus on those aspects which do not fall into the standard format and require discretionary mental application.

One of the most recent applications in the works is the rule engine. In putting it in place a process is being evolved and the software to deliver it is being implemented. Once it is fully up and running, a lot of manual work will be eliminated and productivity will be enhanced. Normally, different departments have different rules and different software to run them. Under the rule engine, you will have one software containing all the rules which you can call up. Take eligibility criteria for loans. There are company-, branch-, and profession-specific rules, as also rules governing the age of the customer and her relationship with Ujjivan. Instead of having all these rules in different software, the idea is to harmonize and centralize them. The rule engine can first throw up what a customer is entitled to.

Ayare explained how one aspect of the rule engine is already affecting credit processing (sanctioning of loans) via the document management system. The staffer handling credit has to click for each loan and then approve it. Data for the last 6–7 years shows that for 70 per cent of loans, the decision is clear. So why does someone have to actually approve this huge volume? If the software says an application passes, then it automatically does. Hence, this rule engine will save 70 per cent of manpower engaged. Only when an application fails on a rule or two does it have to go to the supervisor. Also, every rule cannot be fed into the all-embracing software. So the staffer handling credit will have to apply his mind only in cases where an application fails on one rule or another and there is a rule that has not been put into the software but has to be applied at the discretion of the staffer handling credit.

Plans for hardware mainly revolve around building in redundancies so that there are fallbacks. There will be another data centre in Mumbai and additional servers will be added to the existing, managed by IBM and Wipro. There will be a disaster-recovery site in Bengaluru managed by Wipro. The near-disaster recovery centre will be in Mumbai, also managed by Wipro. There will be three data centres which will enable a zero-data loss concept. Ujjivan will be using the Sun Solaris Super Cluster from Oracle as its main high-end server for core banking, and another blade centre server from Cisco. This entire technology will be managed by around 150 IT professionals, about half each from Ujjivan and Wipro, so the former will not have to depend on Wipro entirely for managing systems. In future, hardware, network, and branch jobs will be outsourced and most of Ujjivan's own staff will be focused on software. The current IT strength is around 60 people, including people at the branches, with 20 people in software and 40 in hardware. A network operations centre, NOC, and a security operations centre, SOC, will be managed by Wipro, monitoring risks all the time. Most of the field, sales, and service staff will have tablets, which will be used for customer acquisition, servicing, and loan management. Ayare adds, 'The IT department in Ujjivan has the lowest attrition rate. That is why we are able to grow faster.'

Now let's look at the overall picture of the software solutions being used. The loan management system for group lending is called BR.Net. On becoming an SFB (this happened in February 2017), the Finacle core banking solution is to be implemented. For customer relationship management (CRM), there is CRMNext, and for mobile solutions, I-Exceed, to be used for mobile and internet banking on tablets and smartphones—a unified mobility platform. For compliance and governance, a statistical analysis system (SAS) is used as a platform. For the corporate general ledger, there is Oracle Financial Services Software, an ERP solution, and Ramco HRMS for human resource management. Around 30 different systems will be implemented by the time the SFB will have gone live. In this transformation Ernst & Young (E&Y) is the consultant and Wipro is the systems integrator. The microfinance operations loan portfolio will be merged with the bank on commencing operations. The microfinance customers will become customers for the bank. They will be the SFB's first customers who will be serviced from the banking angle. Gradually, the bank will address the open market for fresh customers.

Ayare is proud of the fact that Ujjivan had not gone in for a bundled offer like some MFIs. 'We have invested a lot of time in selecting the best solution for each and every component of our system for a bank from what is already working in the banking industry. Technologically, we are no less than HDFC Bank or ICICI. Janalakshmi and Equitas have selected some of the components like us. We three are high on technology use. Ujjivan has had a technology focus right from the beginning and technology has helped it to grow.'

Changing processes and introducing IT are dry exercises. What links them up with the ones tasked with carrying out the changes is the human angle. When Ayare joined, he realized the major challenge was technology. He and Pampilly were given what is akin to a blank cheque by Ghosh, when he said 'go ahead and set up the technology'. What mattered also for Pampilly personally was 'having the freedom to make all the changes I wanted, particularly after coming from a banking environment in which such individual-driven changes were unknown. This raised my job satisfaction level.' He also recalls having to clear minefields and sometimes coming close to grief. One was changing the lending software Ujjivan used. 'It was problematic and the relationship with the

IT vendor was bad.' When his American boss went on leave for a month, Pampilly was able to communicate directly with the vendor and solve many of the problems. But the final finding he took to the board made its members 'furious'—the software that had been in use for one-and-a half years did not work. So he went back to the vendor, Craft Silicon, who said they could implement the new debugged version of the software in 90 days, which they did!

13

The Human Factor

A cornerstone of the idea of conscious capitalism, which Ujjivan has embraced right from the moment it was conceived, is to look after the interests of not just shareholders and investors—symbolized by Wall Street—but other stakeholders too. Important among these are its employees. Ujjivan has believed that a sustainable business is one in which workers get a chance to improve their skills, see prospects for career progression, and find some meaning in what they are doing from the social point of view, other than personal financial gain. The last is critical for a microfinance organization which cannot pay top-of-the-line compensation but in which employees can get unique satisfaction from being able to play a role in improving the lives of the poor. A conscious pursuit of such a policy has brought Ujjivan recognition almost year after year for being a leader as an employer and a preferred place to work. Following a forward-looking human resource policy has resulted in a high employee retention level of 82 per cent or more in the last three years (2014–16), higher than the industry average.

High growth over the last four years created opportunities for career progression. As new branches are opened, performers in existing operations are given the opportunity to move to the next level through the process of 'internal job promotions'. In FY 2015–16, 23 per cent of all positions were closed with internal job promotions and 53 per cent through employee and customer referrals. This is part of an ongoing policy that, in the first place, focuses on spotting performers, creating scope for on-the-job training, and then allowing an opportunity to such employees to move up. As over 80 per cent of the staff works in customer-facing positions and visiting customers is a key component of the work process, supervisors accompany them on field visit to assess their ability to deal with customers, innovate, and solve problems. A fair and transparent system of internal job postings has the key advantage of boosting staff morale.

The scope for moving up is always high in a growing organization, and to this has been added the wholly new dimension of Ujjivan turning into an SFB, that is, a bank proper. This has overnight converted the entire workforce from being microfinance employees into bank employees who figure higher in the social pecking order among industries. Phenomenal scope for career advancement while remaining in the same organization does great good to morale and organizational robustness.

Being a young business which must remain organizationally flexible, Ujjivan encourages a certain amount of role change so that career progressions are not rigidly linear. High performers identified for development programmes are sometimes allowed to take on the roles of their superiors when the latter have to be away. This enables them to prove their abilities at the next, higher, level. Plus, there is a first-level supervisor programme to enable new managers to develop leadership skills as a key component of branch management.

Mid-year and annual appraisals are conducted by the employees first self-assessing themselves and then discussing their performance with their supervisors. Talent and performance are rewarded through the annual performance bonus. An innovation in this regard is the deferred incentive scheme, which in 2014–15 covered 7 per cent of the managers. Devised to help retain them, the incentive determined is paid over two years.

Training across all levels and the training department play a key role in the management structure of Ujjivan. An induction programme, a two-part basic-level training with a gap of three months between both, is in place for new recruits. There is a customer relationship managers' training for supervisors, including branch managers, whose job is to generate revenue and engage with customers. Then there is a management development programme which includes both, an induction and a field component for those recruited from campuses. The training landscape evolves along with growth in new lines of business. A training programme has been devised for individual lending, which is the new growth area and has been designed to skill employees handling personal and housing loans. There are also specific training programmes designed for imparting particular skills like sales, sales supervision, programme management, customer care, and collection.

The organization also imparts productivity training. These are geared to improving skills in areas like sales, management, and customer communication. This training covers the field staff, sales managers (to build strong sales leadership), programme managers (for mid-level field supervisors), and customer-care representatives (acquiring the nuances of 'the customer comes first'). Going further down the specialized training road, there are functional training programmes that cover cashiers, financial analysts, those engaged in collection, and subjects like credit policy and secured home loans (this requires handling different kinds of documents establishing title). Need-based skill development covers interviewing, communication, people management, change management, advanced presentation skills, excel training, and business communication.

As the organization has grown and become more complex, a leadership development programme has been put in place which has involved selected managers spending short stints in leading institutions like IIM Ahmedabad and Harvard Business School and attending conferences and seminars. For close to a decade now, Ujjivan has been hiring management trainees from business schools. The current head of credit, head of the microfinance business, and the head of the microfinance business in the east all belong to the first batch of management trainees who joined in 2008. (Roughly 20 management trainees have been hired every year since 2008.)

The institution of management trainees, those recruited for induction directly into the management cadre, is usually a feature of large corporate houses which are seen to be at the forefront of management practices. The fact that Ujjivan, an MFI, went in for this practice very early in its life highlights the unusual amalgam that it has always been—an organization serving the bottom of the pyramid with practices typically associated with top-of-the-pyramid corporates.

Sneh Thakur, part of the management team who heads credit and belongs to the first batch of management trainees recruited in 2008, recalls, 'Very frankly, when I decided to join Ujjivan, I was not sure I made the right decision. It was an unknown entity then, never heard of or spoken about. But I got interested because it was different from banks, a totally different segment. That's what attracted me. On joining, what I loved then, and now also, is the open-door policy and transparency, and seniors more than happy to guide, advise, mentor. You are allowed to experiment. All this has made the organization special to me.'

When Thakur started off, she was in finance and Ujjivan was going in for a fourth round of equity funding. Her first big project was raising equity for the organization. 'That taught me a lot of things and I matured from being a college student to a professional, because Mr Ghosh involved me in every single discussion with every single investor, though I was then just a management trainee.' Securing this funding was one of the biggest challenges Ujjivan faced that year. Though the funding was acutely needed as Ujjivan was growing very fast, 'Mr Ghosh was very keen investors under-stand the nature of the organization. Yes, returns are a part of the deal but that was long-term. He did not want people to invest in us for a short while. He spent a long time giving them a background about this segment.'

Some of the practical training she underwent inadvertently also helped bring out her personal strengths when she was sought to be robbed at gun-point in Amsterdam during a leadership course. She realized the leadership lessons she had absorbed only when she was able to apply them during this experience. 'I decided not to part with my valuables and fight it out with the robber, and yes, I succeeded.' She lives by a few golden rules: have presence of mind, have the courage to face difficult situations and work out solutions, lead by example, and believe in yourself.

Thakur made a lateral entry and has not looked back since. Pradeep B. did not come in with an MBA label but has made good nevertheless. At 35, he is business manager for the southern region looking after the overall performance of the regional leadership team. He is also looking after housing and MSE businesses for the south. Hailing from a village in south Kanara (his father is a plantation owner) and armed with a degree in social work from Mangalore University, he wanted to engage with society and thought he would work for an NGO. He was the 64th employee to join in June 2006 and has just completed 10 years, making him one of the longest-serving employees in the firm. When he joined as part of the first recruitment exercise, he had no idea what microfinance was. His first posting was as a customer relationship manager in Bengaluru's Whitefield branch. Then, Ujjivan's head office operated out of a three-bedroom house and he would not have believed that the company would come this far.

Journeying from south Kanara to Bengaluru was a big change. He was first scared by the city's slums and thought he would not survive. He was a strict vegetarian, a Jain, and initially would not even eat vegetarian food in a non-vegetarian restaurant. But a bigger change was being posted in north Karnataka in 2008, a change that he took up reluctantly on Ghosh's encouragement. He was used to eating only brown rice, which wasn't available where he was going. Knowing this, Ghosh would have it sent to him there. 'This personal touch wedded me to the company.'

In north Karnataka he had a unique designation of branch-opening coordinator, in which capacity he opened 18 branches. 'It was a great learning experience which matured me and I started taking decisions on my own.' He was thereafter promoted to area manager and posted back in Bengaluru. In 2010 he became distribution manager and helped the organization expand in Kerala. When the 2011–12 crisis happened, he looked after a part of Tamil Nadu also. Individual lending, which was stopped during the crisis, was relaunched in 2013 when he became regional business manager. He closely worked with the Women's World Banking and visited Manila, Philippines to see the working of the CARD MRI bank there which had also started off as an MFI.

To Pradeep, who has appeared for only one interview in his life and never updated his resume, 'Ujjivan is a way of life. Company work gets first priority.' His attitude to the company was formed when he first started working at the Whitefield branch. Ghosh, who lived nearby, often dropped by and taught them by writing on the blackboard. 'He came down to our level to teach us. He would show us pictures of Grameen Bank to teach us how centre meetings should be held. "Born to Ujjivan", that is how I feel.' His ride up the corporate ladder has not been without material rewards. His yearly compensation is now Rs 20 lakh and he has just bought an SUV!

Kumdha, 45, has a charming smile. Not a corporate high-flyer, she is now a senior customer relationship staff (CRS) with a monthly salary of Rs 25,000. She joined on 5 December 2005, when Ujjivan worked out of its temporary head office in Indiranagar and the first branch had just started in Koramangala, with salary of Rs 2,000. More than maximizing her salary, she has always looked for a steady job. She has spent nearly 10 years in the Koramangala branch and declined promotions as she liked working with customers. Last year she got the 'Best CRS' award, which has made her truly happy.

When she joined, there were around 40 employees and the same number of customers, but no disbursements had taken place. The first disbursements took place on 17 January 2006, to Ramaka and Lily, and a small function was held in a corporation school in Rajendranagar. First loans were then for Rs 3,000–5,000; now it is Rs 20,000. She initially visited all homes in an area for street survey. On these visits, she gathered a group for a 'projection meeting'. At the time, there was no other MFI working in these areas. 'Customers were hesitant first as they found it strange that people would come and offer them loans, and they did not trust us.' Today customers remember how she convinced them.

Then, there was no widespread use of mobile phones and the message that loans were available was mostly spread by word of mouth. Earlier, there was a dominance of moneylenders, some of whom charged weekly 10 per cent interest. They tried to discourage people from taking Ujjivan loans by trying to sow doubts in people's minds. Now, having become much more educated about financial matters, few people go to moneylenders.

They were five sisters and one brother, Kumdha being the second daughter. When her father died, she stopped studying. By then she had completed her second Pre-University Examination (PUC). She got married late, to an automobile electrician and converted to Christianity, her husband's religion. They have two daughters, a 17-year-old who is in her second PUC, and a 13-year-old, now in the seventh standard. Whatever groups she formed had no serious trouble. When she gave a loan or recruited a customer, she would pray.

Kumdha may have refused promotions but Elizabeth Rani didn't. The manager of one of the most successful Ujjivan branches joined as a field staff. She attributes her branch's success to monitoring performance using her branch dashboard, planning, and teamwork. 'She will put many of our business school educated managers to shame,' says Ghosh. Her husband is in the catering business and one of her two sons is studying to become an engineer. She has risen in a numerically male dominated environment; only 19 per cent of Ujjivan's employees are women.

These employee profiles and their career trajectory give an idea of what it is like to work for Ujjivan. Over the years it has won numerous awards, with a majority of them focusing on its workplace environment and policies. For the last five years, Ujjivan has been ranked consistently among the top 25 companies to work for in India by the Great Place to Work Institute in collaboration with *The Economic Times*. It was ranked number one among the best companies to work for in the MFI industry in 2015. In 2016, Ujjivan was ranked the third best place to work, taking all industries together. This technically made it the first wholly Indian company, with the first two spots going to Google India and American Express India respectively, both multinationals. In employee surveys conducted as part of the selection process, Ujjivan scored over many a national and international corporate leader, not in compensation level and work environment, but job satisfaction.

One of the things that makes Ujjivan a great place to work is its pioneering role in introducing ESOP as early as 2006, when the company was still in swaddling clothes. The sixth ESOP was launched in 2015 and altogether, 54 per cent of all employees at the end of financial 2015–16 were recipients of ESOP. Importantly, ESOPs have been issued to employees across segments almost since inception. What has, of course, created a buzz is the public issue in 2016 after which the company's shares are quoting at a premium to issue price, enhancing the value of ESOP.

But at the end of the day, the question to ask is: What kind of an organization is Ujjivan and how can you benchmark it? The 2016 annual awards event for one of the regions, the east, offered an opportunity. The vast majority were young people (it is clearly a very young organization) who had either personally (best field staff) or as part of a group (best branch) won some kind of prize for the previous year's work. The distinctive aspect was that many of them had brought along their families. (This had obviously been encouraged.) And when they came up to the stage to receive their prize, the family members—either the prize-winning employee's parents or their small children—came up with them and the whole family was photographed. The children were mostly no more than toddlers and looked quite bemused, not knowing what all the tamasha was about. In one instance, an elderly lady, in a saree worn the conservative motherly way, after having some difficulty negotiating the stairs to the stage, turned around and acknowledged the audience with a namaste in a gesture of enormous simplicity and dignity.

The final impression was that the Ujjivan rank and file came from very ordinary stock, socially not very far above the hard-working poor with whom they effectively communicated and for whom, in the ultimate analysis, they worked. They were upwardly mobile even as they pulled up those who were below them. Here, they were in a carefully curated fun event, complete with vigorous dance numbers and skits performed by the employees themselves, in one of the poshest conference centres in a big city. The juxtaposition of things from two extreme ends of a spectrum— ordinary people serving even more ordinary people by using some really modern management precepts—that marked out Ujjivan, came through powerfully.

14

Risk Management

Samit Ghosh has a remarkable story to tell about the impact that Ujjivan's risk-management process has had on what it is today. Recently, while preparing to become an SFB, it got in touch with Bajaj Finance to understand how it appraised customer requests for loans to acquire consumer durables and how long it took to process each loan. This would help Ujjivan devise its own process for giving consumption loans. During the discussion the idea of measuring risk and the regions where Bajaj Finance faced poor portfolio quality naturally came up. There was mutual surprise when it was realized that these were all areas which Ujjivan had avoided owing to their poor risk profile. On realizing this, the Bajaj Finance people said that they should have had this conversation with Ujjivan earlier! 'Before we enter a state or a city we do a survey to assess the risk. We are also not present in areas found by MFIN to be troubled. Our risk-management process is outstanding,' Ghosh observes.

The bread-and-butter business of microfinance organizations is group loans given through the group-lending model. For this the customer does her own risk assessment in the sense that the group self-selects and thereby members of a group take care of each other's performance as they stand guarantee for each other. This is the reason for the success of portfolios across MFIs.

For all its handicaps MFIs have an advantage, says Alagarsamy A.P., head of audit. Slums, a negative area for banks, are target areas for MFIs. 'We have found great customer loyalty as no one else will lend to people like them. Customer loyalty explains high recovery. Unlike in banks, in MFIs, customer knowledge is high,' he adds. With high loyalty, customers do not default intentionally. But when the odd one does, the rest of the group members are not blacklisted. Repeat loans strengthen relationships.

In this chapter we will look at two aspects of Ujjivan's unique risk-management process: One, how, despite group lending being a low-risk operation even though it is not backed by collaterals, Ujjivan built an elaborate and systematic risk-management structure and process. Two, how there will be a significant change in the risk scenario for Ujjivan as it becomes an SFB and how it is reshaping its risk assessment and mitigation processes to be able to engage with it.

Ujjivan's robust risk-management framework for its operations, which it crafted early on in its existence, has evolved over the years and now covers credit, market, and operations risk. It has developed a unique process to evaluate and monitor risk at its branches (dealt with in detail later in the chapter). This includes management of internal and external factors like portfolio quality, branch supervision, staff attrition, and external events. The staff assessing local area risk help corporate and regional offices calculate risk scores for branches. Based on these, branches which are considered to be in high risk are monitored and controlled more rigorously and audited more fre-quently. This kind of monitoring of risk has helped Ujjivan steer clear of major crises afflicting the industry. It also has a comprehensive risk control and self-assessment exercise conducted by all departments from 2013–14 once every half year. From this it has built a risk register for all its departments, IT systems, and applications. There are high-risk indicators for these key risks for each department and when an indicator is breached, corrective action plans are formulated.

'Ujjivan prides itself on an independent credit department which has been there for the last eight years,' says Arunava Banerjee, chief risk officer. 'We were the trendsetters in realizing the need for this, despite risk management being taken care of by customers forming their groups. We realized this need because there are other external factors that play a role. We were also one of the first to have a credit risk function and this has evolved over a period of time. Including risk management and underwriting, we have a very large team. When you give the loan you are basically underwriting the risk. There are factors to evaluate, whether the customer is credit worthy or not, whether RBI guidelines are being followed, etc. For credit underwriting we follow a very systematic process [detailed later in the chapter]. As an MFI, emphasis was always on credit risk management as we had nothing other than the loan product.

'While we have been mindful that one of the biggest risks we carry is cash-handling on the field [detailed later in the chapter], we did not have a separate operations-risk vertical. There are various parameters that have to be used to assess operations risk. Recently we started an independent credit risk-management department and because we had framework for that, we started building up the operations-risk management framework as part of it. This is the risk we have in our people, processes, and systems and how to set up a framework whereby you actually measure and monitor these risks.'

To counter the risk emanating from choosing the wrong kind of people to handle too much cash, Ujjivan evolved an elaborate system of recruitment based on pre-verification. This was backed up by a robust customer-selection process. Thereafter came an equally elaborate process to select where a new branch can be opened. Data and analytics are being increasingly used currently to anticipate where risk can emerge and try to nip in the bud adverse developments before things precipitate. A close watch is kept on three Ps—people, processes, and premises. But there is also a reversal of a common process. Normally, when a fraud surfaces, detectives go into action, after which lessons are formulated so that future frauds can be predicted and finally dos and don'ts are put in place to prevent them from happening at all. Ujjivan's aim is to prevent frauds by using analytics to identify high-risk areas so that they are avoided. Then in the areas where it is already present, the same analytics are used to predict where frauds are likely to happen and then detective skills are engaged to nip them in the bud.

PEOPLE FRAUD

Now let us look in some detail at key learning areas over the past decade. One of them concerns people who work for Ujjivan and in this it has learnt things the hard way. Perhaps the biggest challenge that the microfinance organization has faced in its 10 years of existence is fraud relating to cash involving its own staff. Says Ghosh, 'We ran a pilot for 18 months in Bangalore to understand how to run a microfinance business in an urban environment. Basically, what we learnt was that as bankers, we did not know how to handle cash and the risks associated with transacting purely in cash.' Microfinance is a cash-intensive operation in which poor people (until, under the Jan Dhan Yojana financial-inclusion drive, everyone was encouraged to have a bank account) have traditionally done both, taken loans and made repayments, in cash. Loans are disbursed from Ujjivan branches where cash has to be maintained. Repayments are made at centre meetings from where the cash has to be brought to the branch. Cash travels to and fro between the Ujjivan branch and the bank branch.

As a result of having to handle a lot of cash at centre meetings and its own branches, with linkages with bank branches evolving very slowly, Ghosh recalls, 'we were subject to a lot of frauds, thefts, and all kinds of stuff which came with handling cash. So we had to develop all kinds of mechanisms to prevent such things, including recruitment of staff, such as background verification. There are so many people who, when they see a loose organization handling a lot of cash, jump into that and take every opportunity to really rob you.'

So the first learning was on protecting yourself against all the risks associated with handling cash and evolving a process to recruit the right kind of people who could be entrusted with the cash. Hence, a lot of challenges and risks were people-related. Ghosh adds, 'The errors we made were that in terms of process, we were very loose. There were lots of frauds; we didn't know how to do proper verification. It is very important to hire people who buy into the purpose of the organization. If they don't, then you have a lot of problems, including staff turnover. If they are not aligned, it does not work.' Furthermore, if you are a young organization without a track record, 'it is very difficult to hire competent people. You hire a lot of people who reach a level of incompetence very fast. Then, unfortunately, you have to replace them. That is a very painful exercise.' In some ways, the problem can get worse as you grow. 'When we started expanding into other regions [Ujjivan began in the south, focused around Bengaluru], we needed to hire people with the same level of conviction, honesty, and professional integrity. Quite a number of times, we found we had put in place business managers whose integrity, in the final analysis, was highly questionable and then we had to quickly take action to remove them from the organization. It also included regional heads.' He rues this key mistake made in the initial years, of 'hiring the wrong kind of people, at all levels, even though they were ex-colleagues of mine [from his banking days]'.

Premkumar G., head of vigilance and administration, says, as can perhaps be expected, frauds rose during a period of rapid expansion. (A Rs-22-lakh fraud was the largest ever.) Hence the vigilance vertical was set up. With several new systems being put in place, frauds went down. Internal fraud incidents peaked in 2011–12, which was also the peak of the first growth period for Ujjivan. The number of incidents then fell to a low in 2014–15 and again rose in 2015–16. In keeping with growth, money lost in transit peaked in 2015–16, at Rs 60 lakh.

CUSTOMER SELECTION

Now let us look at customer selection and retention. Sneh Thakur moved to credit as regional credit manager for the south in 2011 when the stress (the Andhra crisis) had kicked in. It was also the year when Ujjivan faced a crisis in some pockets—Salem and Vellore in Tamil Nadu, and Ramanagara in Karnataka. 'So we came out with different strategies to deal with our branches and customers. We introduced branch-level monitoring and mentoring by an independent function [that is, a section within the organization]. We stopped new customer acquisition in some of our branches. Repeat clients were served very selectively. We did not actually stop lending, though some were defaulters, as a lot of the issues were community- and industry-related. We made them aware of the consequences if they did not repay, and a lot of them came back and repaid after a while. We had special approval policies to cater to those customers so that the message going to all the other customers was not wrong—that we will lend again if you can pay up all your dues. So defaulters who paid up were inducted in [to the organization].'

Assessing the credit worthiness of prospective microfinance customers without much or no documentation was a major challenge. 'We figured out foremost that these people were not aware how they were being treated by moneylenders. Customers were initially also very uncertain: should we borrow or not. The key processes that evolved over time was quite a replica of the Grameen model which was introduced way back and was very successful.' At the centre of this model were women. They were more prompt as far as their credit culture and behaviour was concerned. They also knew how to utilize the money when they got a loan. At the core of this model was selecting the women by getting them to form groups from among their neighbours and friends to get a loan and then guarantee each other's repayment.

Once a group was formed, there was compulsory group training to help them understand how this whole model worked, what were the products offered, and the interest rates and the EMIs they would have to pay. Then came a group-recognition test. A branch manager would come, speak to the women, and take a look at their existing documents. The only document that they had, and till now often do, is a KYC. There would be a discussion on how they wanted to utilize the money and what kind of occupation or business they wanted to engage in so as to improve their lives. The discussion was also meant to verify that group members knew each other and the group was cohesive. 'The compulsory group training is given by the loan officer and the branch head does the group-recognition test,' explains Thakur. Thereafter, he visited the houses of the prospective borrowers to get a sense of their lifestyle, the number of dependents, how many were earning, whether family members are aware that the wife, daughter, or daughter-in-law was taking a loan, etc. The last was to ensure that repayment did not create any hassle. They were also shown a video on financial literacy, Sankalp, which discusses the ill effects of over-borrowing, multiple borrowing, and ghost lending. Then the branch manager decided whether to take the applications forward or not.

'It is more of a relationship-based lending—establish a strong connect with the customer, her family, see how they manage themselves—and is now aided by the credit bureau input' to prevent multiple lending. But this only goes part of the way as 'till date, we don't have data on the SHGs'. A woman can easily borrow from two MFIs and one SHG.

This is the core process, but over time, there have been changes. 'After the advent of the credit bureau, a key change was introducing processes to ensure that our own staff captured customer's borrowing from other institutions while having discussions [with other organizations in the area].' There have also been several small changes. Initially, there were guidelines on taking pledges, seating arrangements at group meetings, and 100 per cent attendance. There were norms on group size as well—it started out with a minimum of five members, but was reduced to two after the introduction of the credit bureau checks, which led to a 12–15 per cent rejection under the two-MFI rule, even though their credit history may be good. But once a customer repaid a loan she could come back for a repeat loan. The group size now ranges from 2 to 10. For a fresh group it is five, but can go down with subsequent cycles.

While changes in group-size rules have been triggered by regulatory changes and business requirements, attendance rules for centre meetings have been relaxed over time in response to customer feedback. Customers are busy running their small shops and trades and it is difficult for them to come to every such meeting. So compulsory attendance is now down from 100 to 50 per cent. Additionally, a family member can come and repay an instalment at a centre meeting. The compulsion to recite a pledge before every meeting and norms for seating have all been eased. Another big change was reducing the frequency of group meetings from weekly to monthly.

New processes have also been introduced. One of the biggest changes was the introduction of a branch credit policy which defined credit ceilings across society for every occupation Ujjivan wants to lend to. People were divided into three broad categories: self-employed, salaried, and job workers. Against each category, key occupations in a particular branch working area were listed and loan limits defined for them. There is a process for fixing the limits. First, there is a joint exercise by a branch and an independent credit person to identify a limit and then this is signed off by the credit department. 'We realized you cannot have the same limit for every single occupation across the country.' The branch credit policy was meant to ensure that you don't end up making a lot of loans for knitting of woolens in Salem, but that would be par for the course in Ludhiana.

SELECTING A LOCATION FOR A BRANCH

We began by citing how Ujjivan had managed to keep away from trouble-some places where there could be risk to portfolio by doing rigorous research before deciding where to open a branch. It is worth describing the exercise in some detail. Ujjivan follows a two-pronged approach (one entity puts the study together, another checks it) to assess the risk in an area before setting up a branch. First there is an area survey report by the business vertical. It identifies the city or location where the new branch is proposed and creates an initial survey report. Then there is a cross-check report by the controls function, that is, the vigilance department in conjunction with the audit department. After an analysis of these reports, the business head recommends to the chief executive about whether the location is conducive for the opening of a branch with a report on the business potential and timeline to break-even.

In the area survey a detailed study is done by experienced business staff like a programme manager or area manager to assess the area of operation, political situation, socio-economic condition, working environment, number of potential customers, their major occupations, and the prevailing source of income of a majority of the population. The source of data on potential borrowers is the population density data taken from the block development officer. This data has a ward-wise breakup of total number of households. The business-vertical executives go around these wards and speak to local people and shopkeepers to understand the main occupations and income levels. These are then put up in a table format against the block-wise details.

The area survey report also includes the experience of any existing MFI operating in that area by interacting with them. It gives details of the negative areas through communication with the local police station and also includes elements of external risk associated in that area. The PIN code report (it gives data on MFIs operating in the area and monthly disbursals by them) and rejection report from credit bureaus also provide insight into the status of the competition and credit history of the community. A risk-rating score (high/medium/low/safe) is recorded in the area survey report based on the crime assessment of that area. It is 'high risk' where cash snatching has happened earlier and police do not extend support for business operations in the area. It is 'medium risk' if there exist areas where cash snatchings have occurred but police initiated action and extended support to business. It is 'low risk' if there have been isolated instances of crime because of the presence of anti-social elements. The area is considered 'safe' if there are no records of organized crime and the possibility of any crime is low.

Besides these, the area survey and cross-check reports include information on the following: religion-wise concentration of population in specific pockets; existence of banking services; existence of courier and internet services; availability of KYC documentation and penetration of Aadhaar; other lending sources prevalent in that area; transportation connectivity; and finally, any major threats due to natural calamity, that is, if the area is prone to flood or drought.

STRUCTURED CREDIT REVIEW

We can also get an idea of the structured way in which risk is measured and tracked by looking at the credit review for the microfinance vertical in 2016. It begins with the following highlights: collection team progressing well; PAR (non-performing assets) reduction by 6 per cent. Then it outlines the following challenges: incremental overdues high on account of floods in Bihar; inappropriate overdue reasons captured; collections need to be managed in the last week of the month. In Portfolio Snapshot, it says: incremental overdues up by 20 per cent; 26 branches across eight states contributed to 59 per cent of this; (but take heart) 82 per cent of flood-affected cases collected payments in September. Overdue over three months shows a rising trend. Reasons have been given region-wise for overdue over three months. The categories, with figures, are revealing: absconding; sub-lending/benami loan; financial problem/business or job loss; medical; and last but not the least, willful defaulter. East scores the highest in willful default (566 cases) and the south the lowest (189).

The portfolio trend is given separately for group loans and individual loans. Form flow (forms reaching the back office) is also given separately for group loans and individual loans. Group-loan forms need attention in week three. Form flow for individual loans in week four needs attention across all regions. Then comes targeting—branches which need improvement. There are 20 in all, seven for group loans and 13 for individual loans. Of them, two branches—Bargarh, Odisha in the east and Thane, Maharashtra in the west—have featured in the risk review. Some specific remarks/action for branches which need improvement are worth listing: replace CRM and ABM (senior branch officials) within one month; reminder calls to all delinquent accounts; CRM exited, new CRM joined; KYC mandatory; some CRS (staff) problems in branch; sub-lending issue faced by branch for last three months; absconding and spouse death cases are high (6 per cent); and finally some good news—error rate improvement has happened. Branches which are deemed to be at high risk are monitored more closely and audited more frequently.

BRANCH RISK

An idea of how branches are tracked and measured in a structured manner can be had from the 'branch risk evaluation and parameters' for 25 September 2016. For the scoring, different weightages are given to individual parameters: credit 30 per cent; audit 20 per cent; HR 15 per cent; vigilance 15 per cent; and operations, service quality, and cash group 20 per cent. Then the weightage for each category is subdivided for each sub-category. Under credit the subdivision is as follows: credit performance score card (group loan and individual loan) 10 per cent each; group repayment 2 per cent; report of sub-lending 2 per cent; credit bureau rejection 3 per cent; number of negative customers in the last three months

2 per cent; minority concentration 1 per cent. Among other sub-categories the following stand out: under audit, branch supervision 10 per cent; under human resources, attrition 10 per cent; under vigilance, frauds in the last six months, 7.5 per cent; number of snatchings or break-ins 15 per cent; and under cash group, cash differences at the branch (number of days) 5 per cent.

The scores under each category are benchmarked against norms for high, medium, and low risk. For example, under cash difference at branch, if it is twice in the last three months, then it is high risk, if once then it is medium risk, and low risk if nil. Under branch supervision, since the last audit, if the score is less than 65 per cent then it is high risk, if 65–75 per cent then it is medium risk, and if it is above 75 per cent then it is low risk. Under reporting of sub-lending, if in the last three months it is more than 10 cases then it is high risk, if 5–10 cases then medium risk and if less than five cases then low risk. Under the all-important category of customer selection, if the last audit score is less than 65 per cent, then it is high risk; if it is 65–75 per cent, then it is medium risk; and if it is above 75 per cent then it is low risk.

Other parameters in daily branch operations which need follow-up are: incorrect NEFT, denomination discrepancy beyond five times, reconciliation of cash (joint custody), overnight idle cash in the branch, security cheques to be couriered to regional office, and so on. Under insurance-related follow-up come: death-intimation delay by more than 15 days, insurance documents pending in the branch for more than 45 days, number of write-off cases pending for more than 30 days, and recovery of outstanding loan amount after insurance settlement with nominee. Some of the audit parameters which need to be tracked under group loans are group formation, loan utilization, and documentation. Some of the audit parameters relating to branch supervision which need to be checked are portfolio management, visit by credit manager, team management, statutory display, fixed assets (make sure fixtures do not disappear), and, of course, audit compliance.

PREPARING TO BECOME AN SFB

In order to become an SFB, Ujjivan had to become compliant with the risk-management framework laid down by the Basel committee for banks across the world. The Basel II norms, as they are called, have introduced certain concepts like risk control and self-evaluation and key risk indicators (KRI) for monitoring. The RBI has asked banks to adhere to the Basel guidelines, while for measurement, they can have a format of their own. 'What will be new for Ujjivan,' says Arunava Banerjee, 'is the market risk factor, separate from the external or environmental risk.' This is more related to funding. Till now as a microfinance organization it has been relying on bank borrowing. But once it becomes a bank, those banks lending to it cannot continue to categorize these loans under their priority sector portfolio. Also, as an SFB, it will take a few years to build up a deposit base of its own. So it will have to rely on the market for both short-term and long-term funding. Banks assess each other and borrow regularly from each other for the short term, as also from RBI through repo against SLR securities. 'This will be new to us. So we will be exposed to market risk like interest rate fluctuation and its impact.'

Ujjivan is also preparing for contingencies, for which some kind of contingency funding planning will have to be done. An independent market-risk function is being built for long-term funding as it will have a stable long-term base through placement of non-convertible debentures. The overall risk in that is being managed by the risk department. 'We will have to generate reports on whether there is a mismatch between our borrowing and lending, how they are being covered, bucketing of portfolios (putting them in separate categories) which RBI has specified,' notes Banerjee.

Coming to branches, Ujjivan is trying to do an assessment of the external risk faced even by those branches which are doing well, so it is repeating annually what was done at the time of branch opening. This will be captured in the risk scorecard. 'If you are doing a granular analysis of the risk-covering portfolio, people, processes, and external factors at a branch, it helps in the overall risk management of the organization. This is a dynamic exercise on the risk situation facing Ujjivan as it is today,' says Banerjee.

But this scorecard will undergo a change as the focus will be partly on the MSME and secured lending verticals and liabilities (deposits). The first two are already a part of the scorecard as such lending is already taking place. Liability will become a part once branches start getting liability customers on a regular basis. The market risk factor will kick in and monitoring and factoring it will have to be done on a regular basis. That is what the regulator wants and Ujjivan will have to allocate capital on the basis of the market risk factor. 'That would have happened on day one of becoming a bank,' explains Banerjee. It is also taking measures to address the IT risk as a lot of investment is being made on IT and cyber security. 'There are a lot of security solutions which we are implementing as per guidelines from the RBI. This would have kicked in from day one of becoming a bank.'

Ghosh said at Ujjivan's eastern India meet: 'As a bank, risk management and compliance will be critical. As an MFI, if we lost any money it was the investors' money. But as a bank if we lose any money it will be the depositors'. We have a fiduciary responsibility towards this entrusted money. The colour of money changes the quality of risk.'

15

MFI to SFB, via IPO

Wednesday, 16 September 2015 contained the most powerful irony for Ujjivan Financial Services (to give its full name so as to emphasize its NBFC status at the time). It was a red-letter day in the life of the then nearly 10-year-old organization, yet it also signalled the beginning of the end of the organization as it had been known till then. On that day, the RBI announced the names of 10 institutions (eight of them MFIs) which had been granted 'in-principle' approval to become SFBs and Ujjivan was one of them. This was a monumental graduation and transformation of the organization which Ghosh had launched in November 2005 as an NBFC–MFI because he did not want a universal banking licence to become a good and proper commercial bank, or what the British like to call a 'high-street' bank and risk mission drift. It is because Ujjivan had delivered itself credibly as an MFI that it would graduate to the next higher level in the evolutionary ladder of banking, by becoming an SFB, and maybe, who knows, one day become a mass-market bank without any qualifying adjectives for which a transition path was outlined.

When the CEO's message went out on 15 September conveying the RBI's decision, there were spontaneous celebrations in Ujjivan's offices across the country over both the new status and prestige that the company had acquired and the hope for the predominantly young staff of rapid career progression in a new and growing outfit. Some of this found expression in social media posts. Tarak Pramanik, senior CRS, east, said he would 'look forward to the exciting journey of becoming a small finance bank'. Raj Rupala, CRM, north, promised on behalf of all that 'we will give our best in the next 18 months to become a small finance bank'. Anup Saxena, programme manager, north, and Minni Kaur, credit analyst, north, shared the same fundamental sentiment—'reaffirmed commitment to build better lives'. Himanshu Mittal, area manager, west, and Abhijeet Patil, programme manager, west, were simply 'proud to be a part of the Ujjivan family'.

What it took to become an SFB and what would be its remit mostly dovetailed with what Ujjivan was and did till then. These banks would take financial inclusion further by providing a savings vehicle within reach and easy accessibility of the poor, wherever they may be, and offer credit to all that was small and neglected in the social and economic sphere in the country—small and marginal farmers, small businesses, micro and small industries, and (here was the catch-all) other unorganized sector entities. And most significantly, these small banks would have to possess a critical enabler which would lie at the core of their viability—high technology to keep operation costs low. It is the last aspect that had been a key challenge which MFIs had to overcome as their small-ticket transactions, in the absence of technology and accompanying processes, would have otherwise added to costs, and would be ultimately passed on to the MFIs' small clients.

Central to RBI's desire to try out new things under the then governor Raghuram Rajan was the fact that not just firms, but resident (people resident in India) individuals and professionals with 10 years' experience in banking and finance could have a go in setting up SFBs. The catchment area the regulator had in mind can be gleaned from the fact that NBFCs, MFIs, and local area banks could also seek to convert themselves into SFBs. There were three specific provisions to make sure that these banks did not lose their focus. Seventy-five per cent of their lending would have to be to the priority sector, 50 per cent of the loan portfolio had to be made up of loans of not more than Rs 25 lakhs, and 25 per cent of the branches would have to be in unbanked areas.

One provision in the requirements to be fulfilled in 18 months for the selected to become SFBs was the need to restrict their foreign shareholding to the same limit as private sector banks—49 per cent. This put an immediate challenge before Ujjivan, Equitas, and Janalakshmi (all MFIs which had received in-principal approval) of bringing down their foreign shareholding, which was way above the 49 per cent. For Ujjivan, it was as high as 91 per cent. This led to the most important landmark for Ujjivan and Equitas in 2016, which was both a challenge and an achievement—seeing through an IPO of their shares to resident Indians which would make them publicly listed companies.

Before we come to the IPO story, let us take a look at the thought process that began in Ujjivan immediately after the RBI announcement to work out a transition pathway that would take Ujjivan from being an MFI to an SFB and the milestones on that pathway. Rajat Singh, head of strategy, captures the sweep of changes we will look at in detail hereafter by saying that 'to become a small finance bank almost every aspect of our business is getting disrupted'. The thought process, in fact, began immediately after Ujjivan put in the application to become an SFB, without waiting for the result. A transition team was immediately set up and Ittira Davis joined as head of transition in March 2015. From March to September, members of the national leadership team pursued bank-related research in their functional areas and compared notes at the weekly meetings of the team. A key decision was to take on E&Y as transition adviser. Then a key crossover had to be made, both in mind and substance. You could not look after what was business as usual and simultaneously plan for the new avatar of the organization, which was a full-time job. So all departmental heads who had a role in transition joined the transition team and their deputies took up their existing work.

The biggest change that would have to be planned for and achieved would be to create an entirely new business vertical that would, over time, be bigger than almost the entire existing business. Contrary to a bank which has both depositors and borrowers, MFIs have only borrowers. They lend small bits of money to the enterprising poor by mostly borrowing from banks, as only banks can accept deposits. Now Ujjivan had to acquire the liabilities side of the business, depositors, and, in a fundamental sense, be capable of taking care of people's savings. Davis, who spearheaded the entire transition process, anticipated and visualized it, noted, 'We will have to give up some of the flexibilities that NBFCs enjoy and come under the more rigorous RBI regulation for banks. In return, there will be some security (for depositors). Over five years we want to fund at least 60 per cent of our advances from our own deposits, as opposed to funding now being secured from multiple sources.' It is unique to start with a lending book which needs to be funded. The RBI has asked SFBs-in-waiting to grandfather the existing bank loans but with their own loan books continuing to grow, garnering adequate deposits would be a challenge.

To be able to attract deposits as an SFB, Ujjivan would have to take banking to the doorsteps of the truly ordinary folks living in the remotest corners of the country. One part of this exercise would be to embark on a unique branch-expansion programme which nationalized banks had undertaken only reluctantly and never entirely achieved. Fulfilling RBI's stipulation that 25 per cent of the branches had to be set up in unbanked areas would be tough as 'unbanked' meant habitations with less than 10,000 population and without a bank branch. (This branch-expansion plan had to be submitted with the licence application.) So, along with expansion, some rationalization of branches would take place as the early part of bank branch growth. It would be critical to select the right locations for the new branches. They would have to be close to existing microfinance branches which could act as hubs to support the new rural branches, as there would be a need to guide rural MFI customers to the bank branches for some new products.

An SFB would not just garner deposits, it would offer several new kinds of products. The first would be a transformed version of the MFIs' key existing product—small loans. While these would remain the bread-and-butter business, Ujjivan would also try to create a niche space by entering a mass market a couple of steps above where it is as an MFI in terms of loans. This is a market in which the distinction between 'me and my company' (for MSE owners) remains obscure. The owner runs his own business which is often not separately incorporated. As the space for micro-enterprise grows, such small business owners would need hand-holding so that they can also sell their products through large online retail platforms. Ujjivan would tie up with other industries—like Uber tying up car finance for their drivers to own their own vehicles—and have a role with anyone supporting small enterprises.

What Ujjivan needed was the database of aggregators, like Uber. Organizations having data for a customer segment become useful as that data goes beyond what a credit bureau or a rating agency can offer. The challenges associated with the new kind of loans would be to create a charge on the assets of the borrower and find a way of getting him to assign his receivables. And since the focus would be to lend more to individuals running small enterprises, key personal needs like securing funds for home improvement (adding a room or a floor) would be addressed. The challenge here would be to secure such loans even though the borrower's own title to the property may not be fool-proof. This market of the small shop or factory owner or owner-driver of a taxi is rapidly becoming mainstream, and Ujjivan would seek a foothold in it as its earlier small borrowers grow and start needing bigger loans for their micro and mini businesses. Plus, there would now be an opportunity to offer overall banking services ranging from remittances to the selling of mutual fund and insurance products.

The transition will take place with the building of new channels for service delivery to customers and building a new relationship with them. The aim will be to give SFB customers the same kind of experience that the middle class has come to expect—closer to mainstream banking than traditional microfinance. These channels will be, other than the branch,

ATMs, business correspondents, mobile telephony, and the internet. On phones, keeping in mind the nature of customers, it may be decided to have an interactive voice response (IVR) system 'to primarily tell us in which language the customer wants to speak in and then ensure someone speaks to her in that language. We need to create solutions for customers one level higher than current Ujjivan borrowers but not necessarily from day one,' said Jolly Zachariah, who supervised the rolling out of channels.

A little after joining Ujjivan, he was frustrated that the organization was taking its customers only up to a certain level and then handing them over on a platter to someone else. 'Today we can take a one-trick pony and make it more meaningful. The aim will be to keep it simple for our customers, create simple products beyond loans. In building out channels, there is first hygiene and then there is what differentiates. We want to change the nature of engagement with the customer and build a relationship that goes beyond hygiene.' A key new way of enlarging the engagement would be to focus on customers' life events—marriage, birth of child, death of spouse—'develop sensitivity towards them', essentially be more than a transaction-oriented bank.

THE IPO

While planning for life as an SFB, the most important enabler that was achieved even before that life had begun was to successfully deliver a back-to-back duo—a pre-IPO private placement and then the IPO itself. With 10 years of successful operations behind it, Ujjivan was planning to go public by early 2017. But the process was hastened when RBI's in-principle approval came with the stipulation that the SFB, like other private sector banks, would have to be majority domestic owned. Having gone in for a round of private placement early in 2015, it did not need to raise fresh capital to fund its growth as an SFB right away, but the dilution of foreign holding led to a substantial restructuring of Ujjivan's capital base.

The share of foreign-equity holding could be brought down in two ways—through either a private placement to domestic institutional investors or a public issue to domestic institutional investors, high-net-worth individuals, and, perhaps most importantly, the retail investor or the public at large. In the process, a financial institution tailored to serve those at the grassroots would be owned in good part by those at the grassroots of the investing fraternity—the small shareholder.

But bringing down its foreign holding by making a private placement did not appear promising as domestic institutional investors were shy of unlisted entities. So Ujjivan decided to go in for an IPO and roped in the services of a galaxy of leading investment bankers—Kotak Mahindra Capital, Axis Capital, ICICI Securities, and IIFL Holdings—to lead, manage, and help build the book for the issue. When the structure of the issue was finalized by the end of the year, it was made up of three parts—a pre-IPO private placement which would validate Ujjivan as an attractive investment proposition and also discover the range around which the IPO could be priced, and an IPO made up of existing shareholders giving up a part of their holding to enable an offer for sale and the issue of fresh equity.

Ujjivan began the IPO process in October 2015 by initiating work on the draft red-herring prospectus and talking to investors. It began the new year by filing the draft prospectus with SEBI in record time, less than three months from kick off compared to many taking five–six months. 'None have done this in the last few years,' says Hiren Shah, head of investor relations. The first milestone crossed was closing the pre-IPO placement with Indian institutional investors by February 2016, a month after the filing of the draft prospectus. This raised Rs 292 crore at an issue price of Rs 205 which became the benchmark price and established Ujjivan's credibility in the domestic market.

It was seen as a considerable success for three reasons. One, it represented winning over Indian institutional investors who had earlier mostly stayed away from the microfinance sector. Two, the placement took place when bank shares were being severely undermined in the market because of soaring NPAs of public sector banks. The day it received Rs 292 crore from the pre-IPO placement the market crashed by 800 points (Sensex), led mostly by bank shares. Three, the pre-IPO managed to rope in one mutual fund, Sundaram Mutual Fund (others investors were HDFC Standard Life Insurance, Sriram Standard Life Insurance, and Desai Bros), when such funds typically stay away from private placements, which have a lock-in period that they do not like. Also, the placement for Sundaram Mutual Fund came with an initial haircut of around 50 per cent as unlisted shares are valued, as per regulation, at the lower of issue price and book value. Another MFI, Equitas, while following a similar path to becoming a small bank by diluting its foreign holding, sought to adopt a similar route by seeking to make a pre-IPO placement. This did not happen and eventually it went in for an IPO twice the size of Ujjivan's. Yet another MFI, Janalakshmi, eschewed the IPO route and diluted its foreign holding entirely through private placement.

When the road show for the book-building process for the IPO began, they had to grapple with one handicap. The issue was restricted to domestic investors, usually rather conservative about valuation and pricing. It was the only IPO in several years not open to foreign investors who usually are the most aggressive in giving their valuation, on the basis of which an issue can be launched. Along with this, there were two or three challenges which investors posed to the management, according to V. Jaya Sankar, senior executive director, Kotak Investment Banking. One, the MFIs had the ability to build on the asset side, but needed to show their ability to build on the liability side—create a deposit base. It would take three to four years to complete the entire transition. The second concern was around the asset portfolio. The bulk of their lending was in the MFI category. They had not got into too much of assets in sectors like housing, auto finance, and SMEs.

The expectation of the investors, felt Jaya Shankar, was that Ujjivan would probably go through a two-to-three-year learning curve and, in the process, probably make a few mistakes here and there which would take time to rectify. There was the need to factor in these aspects. Nipun Goel, president and head, investment banking, IIFL Investment Banking, also felt that in the initial term, the financial matrix, the return on equity (ROE) and return on assets (ROA), 'could potentially dip'. A bank is bound from day one by all those appropriations, reserve requirements like cash reserve ratio (CRR) and statutory liquidity ratio (SLR). But if the management were to get it right, then in the longer term, in a four year perspective, 'the growth prospects are phenomenal'.

Ujjivan has built a very credible microfinance business in a decade by being able to control asset quality well. This is reflected in its NPA levels. Its credit processes have been very strong. They have very good underwriting practices—they assess the risks when lending to weaker sections, which requires different skills than those in mainstream retail lending. The real challenge Ujjivan will face in the medium term as an SFB will be one of transition. This will involve building a deposit base, a credible liability profile—savings bank, current account—which will require effort and take a while, as it is going to be a gradual process.

But as the road show progressed the lead managers found that, by and large, investors were convinced that the company had the necessary ingredients to become a successful SFB. 'There were three or four things that we really liked,' says Jaya Shankar. It was a play on financial inclusion and investors knew that the public sector banks had only so much ability to penetrate the unbanked or under-banked villages. If you, as an MFI, are already serving there, then you are in a much better position to take on that market. Besides, as an SFB, Ujjivan would be able to begin with an already prepared customer base of about three million of its own MFI clients. Investors also liked the fact that the successful microfinance companies were operating at pretty high ROEs, which in the case of Ujjivan, was in the high teens. Typically, no equity investor expects upwards of 12–13 per cent. This, combined with very low NPA levels, created the confidence that Ujjivan would become a successful SFB. It became clear, recalled Goel, through the IPO process that 'they are extremely committed to the cause of building a very successful institution. They don't take risks which they do not understand and they are therefore building an institution which will be here for the long term.'

According to S. Subramanian, managing director, institutional equities, Axis Capital, what impressed institutional investors about Ujjivan was that it was different from a typical Indian company. Ghosh personally had a very small percentage of holding. It was a professional company with strong backing from a set of very decent private equity investors who primarily had great hopes on both the leadership and its commitment to corporate governance. Every round of investment for Ujjivan (six) happened at a higher price. Ujjivan also had the most diversified customer base. Most MFIs catered to a small regional geographical base—Bandhan in West Bengal, Janalakshmi in Karnataka, SKS in Andhra. 'And Ujjivan did not make the mistake of going to Andhra, a very big thing. Ghosh has an ability to choose what he will and what he will not do. His background as a commercial and consumer banker has helped him understand the market. To run a business without securities and have less than 1 per cent NPAs is truly commendable. His understanding of consumers and ability to deliver to them have been phenomenal,' explains Subramanian.

A microfinance business cannot be run the way a large retail company is—in terms of a scorecard and analytics, argues Subramanian. There have to be people on the ground who meet customers, empathize with them, and collect repayment. The loan giver and collector are the same, not as in a private banking model where a loan is sanctioned on the basis of a scorecard in 30 seconds and then somebody else has to do the collection. Besides, as Subramanian noted, 'to build an institution that has been practising financial inclusion before the government talked about it and has made it commercially successful is hugely commendable. Ghosh says, the poor don't want alms, they want access to credit and by giving credit you have empowered them. What 1969 should have delivered, is now being delivered by for profit private organizations.'

'These are the intrinsic strengths,' feels Subramanian, 'which we found and were therefore willing to back Ghosh irrespective of whether he had an SFB licence or not. At the end of the day, RBI did itself proud by being able to recognize the solid work done by them [successful MFIs]. In the last six or seven years, there has not been a single mutual fund investment in a pre-IPO round. We brought in Sundaram [the financial firm]. The pre-IPO for Ujjivan created a level of confidence for Ujjivan's IPO.'

A lot of investor confidence centred on Ghosh, says Goel. He led an 'incredible management team across levels, which resonated extremely well with the investment community.' Goel first met Ghosh about two-and-a-half years ago. 'We got a very good feedback about Ghosh and the kind of organization that he had built and about 12 months ago (mid-2015) we felt that the company was very much of a critical mass and ripe from an IPO standpoint. Then we got mandated and worked very closely over the last six to eight months to deliver the IPO.'

Throughout the book-building process Ghosh had been very clear that he did not want the top valuation but the right valuation. Ghosh himself puts it thus. 'During the IPO we told investors we are building a bank. It is not an overnight thing.' A microfinance organization, built to offer financial services to the poor, was now converting to a bank. He made it clear to them that 'during the first two years our return on assets, return on equity, will dip'. A bank can never provide the kind of returns a very successful finance company can. But the risk element for both these is also different. A finance company has a higher risk and if it is well-run it provides a higher return. But a bank in general is a lower risk entity. 'We have dinned this into our investors again and again. So hopefully that will help us and we don't have to be bound by the quarterly thing.'

But Ghosh also wanted investors to make money. Jaya Shankar felt investors got comfort from the fact that Ujjivan 'had a statesman-like person in Ghosh to provide the leadership. Under him, there was also a strong, wide-ranged team empowered on business, strategy, risk management, and technology. This is the one strong differentiator for Ujjivan among the various MFIs, because it is not too dependent on one personality.' In particular, Ghosh had been very pragmatic all throughout the life of Ujjivan, careful and focused about getting the right investors who were aligned with him from a medium-to-long-term perspective. He had a very well-thought-out strategy towards developing into an SFB, understanding what the challenges were, and what it took to get there.

Putting the results of the Ujjivan IPO in a historical context, Goel observes that the focus on governance has come back in a big way, globally and in India. With foreign investment in domestic stocks being more than the institutional investment, domestic institutional investors have now realized that they had to accept this fact; the stock multiple reflects what investors believed and perceived as the governance standards in a company. 'Of late, individual investors are also becoming very discerning. Compared to seven or eight years ago, they are doing significantly more homework on investment opportunities like IPOs,' notes Goel. They are focusing on strengths and fundamentals instead of just taking a short-term view of the business. People who want to buy and hold for long don't mind paying up if they get the right mix. So HDFC trades at four times the book value not just based on its growth alone, but also on the trust and governance standards that they have set. The very high quality of governance and transparency and the resultant trust which Ujjivan had achieved was very important for long-term investors.

'For these reasons,' explains Jaya Sankar, 'Ujjivan became a very compelling investment proposition for institutional investors. That is the reason why you saw such subscription levels.' The anchor group of 17 which subscribed Rs 265 crore had names like ICICI Prudential Mutual Fund, Birla Sun Life Mutual Fund, UTI Mutual Fund, Tata Mutual Fund, Birla Sun Life Insurance, and Sundaram Mutual Fund, which 'would probably be the who's who of institutional investors'. Goel adds, 'The demand was mind-boggling and most of the large investors who matter from a domestic standpoint, participated in the IPO.'

The result of all this was that the IPO of Rs 882 crore, which was priced at Rs 210 and closed on 2 May 2016, sailed through, attracting 6.75 lakh domestic investors, being subscribed by 41 times! Ujjivan Financial

Services got listed on 10 May, opening at Rs 227, rising to a high of Rs 244 and closing at Rs 232. It reached a peak of Rs 547 in July before settling down at a little over Rs 400, that is around twice the issue price. Shah has an explanation for this: 'Four or five big investors formed a cartel and the price did not go above it. So the valuation was very attractive' for retail investors applying for the IPO. 'The subsequent rise in price was triggered by the March quarter results which came immediately after the IPO and were much better than market expectations. This brought the valuation to the right level.' Ujjivan's annual report for 2015–16 says, 'The listing of shares has started a new era for Ujjivan and all its stakeholders', not the least among them being the 40 per cent plus employees who have received ESOPs and have seen their value soar after the listing, taking their morale up with it.

The journey that Ujjivan has travelled and the hopes that have been fulfilled can be gauged from what Ghosh wrote three years ago, in a contribution in the book, *Crests & Troughs: Microfinance in India*, brought out by Axis Development Services in 2013: 'We hope that someday we will be allowed to convert to a specialized bank for financial inclusion. Right now we have a handful of largely foreign investors. We hope that one day we will have a well-diversified set of domestic investors and will be a public institution.' This is precisely what has happened!

16

Beyond Microfinance

Even though the country has a successful, functioning microfinance programme which is meant to address poverty, large sections of the population
continue to remain poor. This is because of two reasons. One, there are the
ultra-poor who are unable to successfully use the small loans that microfinance offers to raise their income levels. Two, there are several dimensions to poverty, which even a successful use of microfinance—one that
reduces income poverty—does not address. Mindful of this, Elaine Marie
Ghosh (spouse of Samit Ghosh, and a former banker herself) created
Parinaam Foundation in 2008. This was set up as a not-for-profit organization under Section 25 of the Companies Act, 1956 (read with Section 8
of the Companies Act, 2013), to deliver, in partnership with Ujjivan, the
micro-credit 'plus' programme to its customers. Led by Mrs Ghosh, who,
as executive director of the foundation worked pro bono, Parinaam set out
to offer healthcare, education, vocational training, and sustainable livelihood development support for the urban poor, and community services
to both Ujjivan's customers and BPL (below poverty line) families who
were outside the scope of traditional microfinance. Till 2015–16, over half
a million people benefited from the Ujjivan–Parinaam partnership.

On the relationship between Ujjivan and Parinaam, Samit Ghosh
explains, 'Though the foundation would primarily serve Ujjivan customers,

it was set up completely at an arm's length basis with an independent governance structure. We were very conscious of the NGO structure being frequently misused, including in the microfinance industry.'

The seed was actually sown in 2006. A few months after Ujjivan's first branch was launched in Koramangala, there was a customer meet at a government primary school in the heart of a slum. Ghosh recalls, 'I invited my wife Elaine to see what I was up to after my banking career. The little hall was jam-packed with over 200 customers all dressed to the nines! Elaine, who had dressed down in a plain cotton salwar kameez, was looking a bit out of place on the dais! After the meet as all of us men walked towards the exit, the women customers engulfed Elaine and wanted to shake her hand and have their babies blessed! This was their way of showing appreciation for the loans they had received from Ujjivan. Elaine was overwhelmed by the emotions of the women. This experience drew her, an ex-banker, into setting up the Parinaam Foundation.'

As with all initiatives of Ujjivan, the first item in its strategy was to devise programmes by undertaking research to identify the key needs of the poor. Ujjivan's organization and reach would be used to deliver these programmes, in particular a holistic healthcare one which would stretch from prevention to tertiary care. Joint efforts would be made with other like-minded organizations to strengthen the offerings, and grants and donations would be used to secure additional resources. Where no other organization was present, Parinaam would go it alone.

The first initiatives were in the fields of eye, ENT (ear, nose, and throat) and dental care and vocational training. Parinaam has been running health camps since 2006, that is, even before it was formally constituted, first in Karnataka and Tamil Nadu and thereafter in Kolkata, Pune, and Delhi. Those needing further care have been provided access to partner hospitals and helped with meeting the costs when they were unable to. It also initiated its own service-provider network in partnership with pharmacies, laboratories, and hospitals. In 2010 vocational training was started with special emphasis on developing the self-confidence of the young among the poor, and its livelihood development programme was supported by leading retail chains and garment factories to provide jobs to those trained.

A key effort of Parinaam Foundation is its financial literacy programme Diksha, launched in 2012, which is considered to be one of the most appreciated such programmes—including by RBI—in the country. Diksha seeks to teach the poor how to plan expenditure, work out budgets, appreciate the importance of savings, and, very importantly, the difference between good and bad borrowing. Over the years, till 2015–16, nearly 400,000 women have been trained and 83 per cent of them certified under the programme, which has also enabled more than 100,000 customers to open bank accounts. As a result, over 200,000 cashless loan disbursals by Ujjivan have been made possible. The programme is now being taken to children and introduced among tribals in Meghalaya.

The Diksha programme works for both the poor and not so poor. Geeta is as an ayah at an anganwadi in Pune. Her husband is a supervisor in a road construction project and their son is pursuing a degree in engineering. They are not poor by Indian standards, which is why Geeta used to spend the surplus she had on saris, cosmetics, and during festivals. The thought of saving money never crossed her mind. But once she went through the Diksha programme and obtained a certificate saying she was a 'Rupee Rani' (queen of money) her attitude changed and she began to save. She started putting aside Rs 500 per month so that she could buy her son a computer. Useful as that was, she went a step further and became a catalyst for change, without knowing the word or its meaning. At the last haldi-kumkum ceremony (a special celebration for women during Diwali), instead of spending all her money on the festivities, she took her friends to a nearby bank and got accident insurance policies for all of them, paying the premium of Rs 12 for each as a Diwali gift. In terms of the roles that Diksha uses to communicate its message, Geeta has changed from *dukhi* (sad or unfortunate) to *sukhi* (happy and contented) by learning how to be wise with money.

As part of her efforts to spread the savings habit, Geeta has bought a couple of savings boxes for the children of her relatives so that they can start saving even before growing up and not lose time, like she did. This ties up with Parinaam Foundation's efforts to take the financial literacy programme beyond women to children. In 2015, Diksha started a savings programme for children called the Chiller Programme (*chiller* in Kannada means small change). The aim is to catch them young, make them aware of the importance of saving, teach them how to handle money, and get them to start saving a little, even if by setting aside a few coins whenever possible.

The programme consists of two parts. One is a 90-minute module delivered in four parts under which, through things like role play, assignment, and discussion, children are taught the basics. The second is helping children open bank accounts. The trainer prepares a list of children who do not have an account and then interacts with a bank branch to help them open one. This is according to an RBI directive, which says children in the age group of 10 to 17 should open and independently operate savings bank accounts. In 2015–16, 30,000 children participated in the programme and 8,500 of them became richer, both materially and metaphorically, by having an account of theirs in 294 branches across 18 states.

While Diksha ties up with the government's Jan Dhan Yojana programme, a pilot toilet and sanitation programme has been launched in line with the Swachh Bharat Abhiyan. It is aimed at providing toilets to these families which do not have any. Another pilot was initiated to help Ujjivan customers buy affordable solar lamps. Working in tandem with Ujjivan, Parinaam chipped in to make the microfinance organization's low-interest education loans totally free. A scholarship fund was initiated to support those who wanted to pursue higher education.

Perhaps the most ambitious task that Parinaam has undertaken and which makes it stretch is the Urban Ultra Poor Programme launched as a pilot in a Bengaluru slum in late 2009 to cover 1,200 people in 240 families. The target was those earning less than Rs 1,000 a month, with irregular or no work and no access to any developmental credit. They do not just live in slums (officially recognized and unrecognized), they have access to few amenities, suffer from food insecurity, and are heavily in debt in the informal sector. The aim was to stand by them so that they became 'bankable', that is, be in a position to fruitfully utilize the assistance offered by microfinance organizations. Aimed at attacking generational and family poverty—by helping an entire family and not just one woman—the strategy addresses several areas: livelihood support, healthcare, childcare and education, financial literacy, and social support. This is a 12-month programme, with another 12 months of support on a needs basis. After this the women are expected to 'graduate' into microfinance customers.

Till 2014–15, altogether 22 communities have been assisted, with a total membership of 6,300. It has had an attrition rate of 27 per cent (dropouts) but among those who have continued, 83 per cent are employed and half of them have come under the ambit of microfinance. In all, 618 have 'graduated', that is pulled themselves up from being ultra-poor. But most importantly, perhaps, nearly 1,200 have been helped to secure some kind of ID, including address proof, so critical to be able to access almost any kind of public service. More than the numbers, what is important is a model has been developed and tested to pull people out of absolute poverty.

Another social initiative by Ujjivan which goes beyond microfinance is its community development programme (CDP). After Ujjivan turned profitable in 2009–10, it decided to allocate a part of its annual profit to its community development fund under its corporate social responsibility (CSR) initiative. To make it effective, the CDP is worked out bottom up. A branch forms a committee with members from staff and customers who decide on the programmes to support, which are selected on the basis of ensuring the best results to the community.

For Ujjivan, this is not entirely altruistic. The idea is to bond with the community, so that they can help one another in times of need. If there is a fire or a flood, then the branch staff helps out and when Ujjivan faces a hurdle, the community stands by it. A piece of corporate memory which has not gone away is the experience in southern Karnataka in 2009 when religious community leaders stopped repayment and the women who benefited from the loans were unable to stand by the MFIs. If these MFIs had built a space for themselves in the consciousness of the community, then maybe the story would have been different.

Ghosh is clear that if an MFI is to survive it has to have the support of the community within which it operates. 'MFIs lost their link with customers and their community so that there was no customer protest when they ran into trouble in Andhra. The future will be bleak,' he had said at that time, 'for them until they go back and rehabilitate their relationship with customer and community. They have to establish that they are there not just as moneylenders but to help them improve their lives. This perspective was lost in chasing growth.'

Ujjivan has been building bridges with the communities within which it works by undertaking social development programmes through its branches, bringing together customer, staff, and community. It began with staff helping with disaster relief when floods hit north Karnataka. They contributed a day's salary and Ujjivan matched it with a grant. Particularly successful has been the practice of allowing each branch to spend Rs 50,000 to meet local needs, which can be as simple as helping an anganwadi worker with a pressure cooker or mats for children to sit on.

Sometimes a disaster can be manmade as was the case in Ranchi, the capital of Jharkhand, where unauthorized slums were flattened by the government, rendering people homeless. Ujjivan stepped in by offering grants, rescheduling existing loans and disbursing fresh ones. Ghosh explains that 'it makes business sense to help customers in distress as, if you try to chase repayment when borrowers are distressed, they will simply run away'.

Ujjivan spent Rs 1.78 crore on CDP in 2015–16 through 382 of its branches. Altogether, 76 per cent of it went to the Swachh Bharat Abhiyan. Through it 294 government schools and 183,000 school children benefited.

Statistics come alive when you talk about real people. Arguably, the single biggest vulnerability that the country's anti-poverty effort—of which microfinance is a part—faces, is the result of a health emergency, which can push a family back into poverty, even destitution. Lakshmi of Yelahanka, on the outskirts of Bengaluru, is a veteran and model Ujjivan customer in as much as she has repaid four loans till now and is into her fifth loan cycle. She, along with her husband (they have two children), runs a 'canteen' or local eatery. Her husband, Govindappa, met with an accident two years ago and developed a severe back problem which required medical attention and surgery. The family spent more than Rs 80,000 on this, using up a good part of the loan Lakshmi had taken for the canteen business. Unfortunately, even before the family could recover from this setback, it met with another. Govindappa was diagnosed with gall bladder malfunction (gallstones) and had to stop working. Another Rs 80,000 was needed for this but the family simply had nothing left to dig into.

While one of her daughters stopped studying as her college fees could not be paid, Lakshmi herself started working in a garments factory and began defaulting on her loan. Ujjivan staffers referred her case to Parinaam, which consulted its networked hospitals and located one which could do the surgery for Rs 20,000, but even this was too high an amount for Lakshmi to afford. Parinaam chipped in with Rs 10,000, and Lakshmi somehow managed the rest. By early 2016, her husband was recuperating, ready to go back to the canteen business. Their elder daughter has resumed her studies and also applied to Parinaam for a scholarship. What worked? Neither a welfare state nor total philanthropy. It was a mix of Parinaam's continuing efforts in networking deliverers of affordable healthcare, the CSR agenda of Ujjivan which has caused Parinaam to come into being, and the philanthropy of those who donate to the foundation.

Ujjivan's CSR work, which goes beyond microfinance, has in one case resulted in a miracle. In the late 1990s, Channabasayya, a 21-year-old mentally challenged man who had just become a father, went missing. Months and years passed but he was not found by his family. After a time his wife returned to her mother's home with her young son. In 2008, some staff from a rehabilitation centre at Tirupattur in the Vellore district of Tamil Nadu found a mentally challenged man near the station and took him under their wing. With regular treatment at CMC Hospital, the man gradually became more mentally stable. Desperate to meet his family, Channabasayya wanted to go home but did not remember the address, only the district name. Recently, Ujjivan customers in Tirupattur recommended providing support to the centre which had rescued him as a CSR project. After a programme there, the centre's managing director explained about Channabasayya's situation and requested the Ujjivan staff to use their network and try and help. Pradeep B., regional business manager, collected the relevant papers and informed his colleagues in Bagalkot, seeking their help. In a remarkable coincidence, a friend of the programme manager there, Amaresh, lived next to Channabasayya's wife! The connection was made and he was reunited with his family after decades. His 24-year-old son said, 'Ujjivan is like god for us.' For this, Pradeep B. received a Service Champion award in 2015.

To get back to Parinaam, Ghosh sees it becoming very important, especially from the perspective of financial literacy. 'It is a very important element in financial inclusion which they have been delivering through the Diksha programme over the last so many years. They will have to tweak and revamp that programme under a bank [on becoming an SFB] because customers keep telling us that they want to understand what the risk elements are, how they access organized financial services, etc. They need to be educated, otherwise they will never be an ongoing user of organized financial services. They see the government subsidy coming into the bank and so they see a limited purpose. They don't have any concept beyond basic rudimentary savings or recurring savings. What are the instruments available, what are the benefits—to answer all such questions, financial literacy is a very important element.'

Ghosh then addresses a core question running through this book: How far can microfinance go in removing poverty? 'I believe, as did my wife, that financial services is only one element and you have to have multiple interventions, whether it is healthcare, children's education, providing people an occupation or skills, and addressing addictions. They are exposed to all kinds of emergencies, natural and manmade. And you have to protect them against all of these. We cannot provide everything. We are only providing what we can.'

He then addresses a related concern that crosses into academics. 'It is very difficult to isolate the impact of microfinance and say that it is because of microfinance that the improvement in a person's condition has taken place. It is a composite of a number of things. Building a village road, the mobile phone, all these have a positive impact. An identity like Aadhaar is such a huge thing for these people because earlier, they did not have anything. So many diverse elements are there which go to contribute to their well-being.'

Anyone will come to an MFI if she sees a long-term benefit from what it offers. A good measure of what an MFI can do is available from a small entrepreneur who began with a loan of Rs 15,000 and over four to five years, increased it to Rs 1 lakh and expanded the business. Or the way things have changed for somebody who has a job and takes a loan to put her children in a good school. Or a home-improvement loan that changes the quality of life. 'You can isolate these and measure the impact. But measuring the overall impact is very difficult.' In Bangladesh, where microfinance has been operating for 30–40 years, there is no dire poverty in rural areas. Today, three crops are being grown in areas which were barren earlier. And instead of bullocks ploughing fields, everyone is equipped with power tillers. 'In terms of the human development index, they have improved a lot. But have they come out of total poverty? No. What I have seen is that there has been a lot of improvement in rural Bangladesh. But in urban areas there has not been that much of an improvement, though now many work in garments factories. If you look at where they were and where they are now, their lives have changed, though maybe not to the extent of what has happened in China. But if you ask them they will say,

"It is not only because of microfinance. A lot of aid agencies have done a lot of work".

Microfinance is a financial service through which micro-loans are provided to financially excluded individuals, small businesses, and entrepreneurs. In other words, it is microcredit to borrowers who lack collaterals or any steady flow of income and credit history that can be verified. The mechanism for delivery of these loans rests on relationship-building and group guarantee. Microcredit is a subset of microfinance, a vehicle to promote economic development through financial inclusion. There essentially exist two types of impact—social and economic—on a household and on the community at large. The economic impact is felt in the household while the social impact is felt at the community level.

The need for microcredit can be varied. It includes personal exigencies (medical, sickness, death), lifecycle needs (wedding, birth, death, education, home building), and even investment opportunities (fueling the growth of existing business through investment in equipment/place of business). The impact on economic variables includes impact on income, household assets, housing, and access to food, while the impact on human capital includes education, skill, health, and empowerment. The social fabric also undergoes a change in terms of social upward mobility. Outlining the way in which Ujjivan has moved forward, Ghosh says, 'As we move forward to select areas and identify places to extend microcredit facilities, due diligence is performed in a structured approach to capture maximum information and to take informed credit decisions, maximizing the business potential subject to minimum portfolio risks.'

We began this chapter by noting that microfinance can only go so far and no more and looked at the rationale behind the creation of Parinaam. To get back to Parinaam, when Ujjivan received the 'Microfinance Organization of the Year 2011' award, the education loan interest refund programme (thereby making the loan totally free) and the financial literacy programme that run along with Parinaam received special mention. Parinaam's Urban Ultra Poor programme received international recognition in late 2013 when it was declared as the Asia-Pacific winner of the 2013 Financial Times and Citi Ingenuity Awards: Urban Ideas in Action programme. Elaine Marie Ghosh passed away shortly before the award was received. On her contribution to the Ujjivan family, her husband says, 'A lot of the values of Ujjivan originate from her.'

17

The Demonetization Trauma

16 September 2016 was a red-letter day for Ujjivan—it was one of the 10 entities which had been chosen by RBI to become small finance banks. But November turned out to be a month of both, a tremendous high and low. The high was in the middle of the month when, after completing all the paperwork, it received the final licence from RBI to become an SFB. But just a week before that, 8 November had brought about the tsunami of demonetization. Ujjivan, however, stuck to its plan and began its journey as an SFB three months later on 6 February.

The story of the intervening three months, of trauma and the determined journey down the recovery path, is worth recording in some detail for several reasons. It yielded a strategy for the future which represented a partial course correction. Plus, critically for Ujjivan, coping with demonetization validated some of its policies. Even more, critically for the country as a whole, it opened a window to the world at the bottom of the pyramid and offered an insight which was, till then, not available. This enables us to end our narrative with hope, that policy-making will improve, thus creating a better environment for those whose agenda it is to fight and eradicate poverty.

The announcement in the evening of 8 November caught everyone in Ujjivan, as in the rest of the country, by total surprise. All senior hands were on deck to make sense of the development, take stock of the situation, and outline an immediate strategy. They were huddled together past midnight, primarily engaged in creating a communication which would be passed on via WhatsApp to all Ujjivan field staff across the country so that they could get an immediate hang of demonetization and know how to handle a legion of utterly confused customers the next morning. In keeping with the national and grassroots character of the organization, which functions in 24 states, the communication was written out in nine different languages by the distribution staff, so that those at the receiving end had a ready message for the customer in a language which she understood.

As the seniors grappled with the task at hand, they became acutely conscious of a reality that had been in their subconscious all along: Ujjivan's customers dealt virtually entirely in cash and absolutely entirely when it came to repaying instalments. (The organization had made an energetic effort to help customers open bank accounts and 60 per cent of loan disbursements were being credited to these accounts. However, demonetization had the effect of these customers asking for cash disbursements because it was pointless having a balance in your bank account when there were severe restrictions on withdrawals.) The crunch was Ujjivan loans were repaid in equated monthly (not weekly) instalments which were a bit high for poor working women—Rs 1,800–2,000. These were saved up over a month and tendered mostly in Rs 500 and Rs 1,000 notes. These had suddenly ceased to be legal tender!

That very night it became clear that Ujjivan should not collect payment in demonetized notes and decided against accepting them. They also decided to not collect repayment for the next three days—the 9th, 10th, and 11th—to give customers a bit of time to sort out their cash issues. Field staff would go to centre meetings and explain the situation to customers and simultaneously explain (guided by the communication from the head office) the process of how to exchange notes at the bank. The three-day reprieve was extended to one week and customers were told that their repayment record would not be affected, but Ujjivan would accept only legal tender. This was in contrast to the decision by some other MFIs which initially accepted the demonetized notes for a few days, thus creating a bit of confusion in the minds of customers of the sector as a whole.

As the demonetization saga unfolded, the challenge Ujjivan faced over repayments settled into three parts, which happened sequentially up to a point. First came the cash crunch due to non-availability of legal tender. This was the time when there were long queues at bank branches and ATMs. As the cash crunch eased over the next few weeks, many Ujjivan borrowers faced another, more serious, crisis—loss of income. Across the country, most small businesses dealt virtually entirely in cash and were simply unable to pay their workers in legal tender. These workers, many of them migrants without bank accounts at their place of work, habitually took their wages in cash and were now fobbed off with payments in useless Rs 500 and Rs 1,000 notes. These they perforce had to exchange at places like the local kirana store at a 10–15 per cent discount. The cash crunch and resultant disruption in the supply chain forced many units to temporarily shut down, leaving their migrant workers no option but to go back home as there was no income. Finally, and this was the most invidious of all, local political and community leaders saw an opportunity in this for themselves and started mobilizing MFI customers not to repay loans, with the promise that the government would waive them.

While this was one sequence, another was the geographical spread and emergence of troubled spots for Ujjivan and other MFIs. Uttar Pradesh (UP), beginning with western UP, led the way. Maharashtra, beginning with Vidarbha, followed close on the heels; soon to be affected were also parts of Madhya Pradesh (MP) and finally Karnataka, led by the unlikeliest trouble spot, Bengaluru. There is some overlap in these two sequences but they paint a broad picture of how the situation unravelled.

The strategy that Ujjivan evolved had the following components. First, as stated above, there was a week's reprieve from repayment. Then as time went by and December arrived, the message to customers was: if you can't repay two months' dues in one go, then pay at least one month's EMI per month. Then customers were told that if they could not even pay a full instalment they could pay a part of it. The overall theme was, pay whatever you can but keep paying something so that the relationship is kept alive and on completion of one loan repayment, the customer would be considered for another. The cardinal concern conveyed to the field staff was, do not pressurize the customer as that will make her hostile and go to local leaders. Along with this, customers were called in small groups of 15–20 to Ujjivan branches and sought to be educated about the consequences of not paying at all, and the need to pay something. Simultaneously, the staff needed help as they found traditionally friendly customers becoming hostile. All this created fears about their own future and they needed reassurance on that score. So Ujjivan also organized family events for the staff of one or two branches at a time to both communicate and reassure. This helped the staff cope with stress and keep their cool when meeting customers. So the strategy to tackle demonetization was ultimately founded on the need to engage, both with customers and staff.

UTTAR PRADESH

For Ujjivan, the problem first surfaced in Moradabad, UP, recalls Manish Kumar Raj, business head, microfinance and branch banking (north and west), who had a ringside view. The area, with a political heavyweight—a Muslim MLA who was a minister in the Samajwadi Party government—had a reputation for activism. Two years previously, in nearby Amroha the suicide of a Muslim woman had become a big issue. Tension had been simmering in the area ever since. In this instance, it was first ignited with the demand for a loan waiver, and then came the RBI circular which gave financial institutions a reprieve of three months in providing for assets rendered non-performing by demonetization. This was immediately seen as paving the way for the asked-for waiver.

Within seven days, repayment dipped in all western UP branches of Ujjivan like Aligarh, Hapur, and Agra. Simultaneously, word started to go around that MFIs were collecting repayments wrongfully as the government had already waived loans. When the names of one or two local leaders appeared in the media over protests against repayment in Moradabad, leaders in other areas thought this was a way to get into the limelight and stake a claim for tickets in the coming elections. So, the issue of repayment of MFI loans became a kind of a political platform and UP became the first state to be widely affected.

Nobody had apprehended that this was likely to happen in UP and so pre-emptive action was not taken when the issue was still only at the rumour stage. 'When we realized what was happening, all of us working at MFIs took the help of the Uttar Pradesh Microfinance Association (UPMA), followed by MFIN, and then NABARD and SIDBI as well. We approached the chief secretary who referred us to the finance secretary who wrote to all the district collectors,' says Raj. A customer awareness campaign was run in the media under the UPMA banner. Local leaders first said these companies (MFIs) were shady. Then when the local administration vouched for them, the focus shifted to filing complaints with the police alleging harassment over specific instances of altercation between borrowers and MFI staff on collection visits.

As for Ujjivan, it instructed its staff not to visit customers after 6 pm and never to specifically ask for repayment but commiserate with them over their troubles and advise a return to repayment when that became possible. 'Overall, the dynamic in UP was—quick slide and then stabilization, without improvement,' says Raj. Repayment for November first dipped as low as 40 per cent, then closed for the month at 64 per cent. December repayments closed at 44.4 per cent and January, at 43 per cent. By then, however, the November recoveries had improved to 82 per cent. This is a pattern that was repeated elsewhere too. When customers resumed repayment after a gap through one EMI a month, that payment, according to established procedure, was adjusted against the oldest due, thus improving the statistics for older months even as new months began poorly.

MAHARASHTRA

The next important state to be hit by demonetization after UP was Maharashtra. In the first couple of weeks the issue uppermost there was the same as it was elsewhere—the cash challenge, customers' frustration over trying to find cash, manifesting itself in long queues at branches and ATMs. As in UP, impending elections—to municipalities in the case of Maharashtra—and the heightened political temperature they created, did their bit to add to MFIs' woes. Says Vikram Shingade, Ujjivan's regional business manager, microfinance, 'Nagar sevaks [municipal-level political workers] had a very good presence in slums and at the ground level where we also worked. They were quick to connect to the disruption caused by factory owners, mainly of textile units in the Nagpur and Amravati areas, paying wages in demonetized currency notes to our customers.' Also severely hit was Ichalkaranji, in the south of the state, with its concentration of textile mills. Solapur, in central Maharashtra was similarly affected. Borrowers who were given their wages through demonetized notes suffered doubly—first a loss of income as these notes were going at a discount, and then, the fact that they could not use the notes to repay their MFI loans.

Political elements added to the tension and confusion by distributing cash in old currency notes, a regular feature of election campaigning. They were doing this as they themselves were unclear on how to handle their own black money. When the politicians were told that MFIs were not accepting old banned currency notes, they said, 'stop repaying them'. When the Amravati guardian minister, Pravin Pote, publicly declared this, the message spread across the state, particularly the Vidarbha region. The refrain was then taken up by the Nagpur guardian minister, Chandrashekhar Buwankule. All this lent legitimacy to the rumours that the government had allowed MFI borrowers not to repay loans.

As tension reigned with MFI borrowers being unable to repay loans and also being asked not to repay, local nagar sevaks standing for municipal elections realized for the first time that microfinance was such a big industry. They rationalized this new knowledge by claiming that

MFIs were seeking to convert black money into white, hence another reason for not repaying their loans. Local politicians seeking attention before elections printed leaflets urging borrowers not to repay. They also put up big hoardings saying, don't allow MFI people to come into the village. Across the state, customers were convinced that their loans had been waived. To make things worse, a guardian minister said that if anyone comes to ask for payment, 'first beat him up and then take him to the police'. When MFIN met the Maharashtra chief minister, a message went to the guardian minister and he retracted his statement. But this happened after a gap when damage was already done.

The close link between MFIs' troubles over repayment and textile-mill owners continuing to pay wages till December in old currency notes was evident in other areas of Maharashtra like Solapur in the central region, Nashik in the west, and even areas in Mumbai, like Mankhurd. Thus, trouble was widespread across the state. Particularly troubled areas often had a well-known political party or prominent politician leading morchas against MFIs. In Solapur they were led by Praniti Shinde, the local MLA and daughter of former state home minister Sushil Kumar Shinde. In Nashik, the morchas were spearheaded by the BSP. To combat this, Ujjivan staff started distributing leaflets listing dos and don'ts (like don't believe in rumours) and also encouraged part payment.

A key initial challenge was the staff not being allowed to enter neighbourhoods and attendance at centre meetings dropping to 50 per cent. So Ujjivan staff started calling customers on phone two days in advance before a visit. In the last two hours of the working day the branch was effectively converted into a call centre. When they made a visit they went equipped with a script for standard communication. This got a good response. By early December positive statements started emerging from the chief minister. Many MFIs simultaneously took out advertisements in newspapers, explaining their stand.

As December progressed and the cash crunch eased, customer attitudes started changing. By then, those who were still holding back were mostly waiting for clarity on whether there would be a loan waiver or not. In December home visits were resumed with a particular format. The staff requested the presence of all family members so they could show them files containing positive news about microfinance and emphasized that the government had not issued any instructions, but still did not ask for repayment. This was to ensure that after the visit the entire family could discuss the issue. Customers were happy to be informed about the realities and so there was some traction. Ujjivan also started accepting cheques—even third-party ones—Paytm transfers, and online payment. These facilities were not available before demonetization. Adds Shingade, 'We were also the only MFI not to stop disbursements. When a customer in those days in the aftermath of demonetization received cash in hand of say Rs 20,000 (fresh disbursements were now done in cash), it was a very big thing and the word spread.'

When the Ujjivan staff started to meet district collectors in affected areas, they found that like local political elements, the officials were quite unclear about the role and functioning of MFIs. They asked questions like: Why do you call at borrowers' homes? Why are your interest rates so high? Hence, structured interaction with district officials began alongside those with customers. Officials were shown rate cards to establish that interest rates were not exorbitant and within the norms set by RBI. They were also informed about the process followed while visiting customers, making it clear that the purpose was to educate, not to collect payments.

The role played by local political elements can be gleaned by noting the contrast between Maharashtra and another state in the western region, Gujarat, where the atmosphere was not charged by election campaigning but driven by cash shortage. This could be seen from the experience of Ujjivan's Sabarmati Dairy branch. The dairy is linked to the local cooperative bank which pays farmers for the sale of their milk. But since cooperative banks had not been allowed to accept old notes, they were suffering from cash crunch and were hence unable to pay farmers. There, repayment initially stopped almost entirely.

KARNATAKA

In the south, as in the rest of the country, initially there was confusion in the minds of borrowers because some MFIs were accepting the demonetized currency notes. Also Equitas, till recently an MFI, now an SFB, could and did accept old notes. At Ujjivan, customers—accompanied by their husbands—came to centre meetings with old notes and argued as to why these could not be accepted. To counter misconceptions, Ujjivan formed a team in the south of senior distribution, credit, and vigilance managers which worked out an action plan. This centred on training the staff of the affected branches on the situation and the way to speak to customers and handle them. Ujjivan did not force borrowers to repay but made them aware that if they did not make even some repayment their credit bureau history would be impacted, thus affecting their chances of getting loans in the future.

Because of Bengaluru's importance (it has 22 branches and accounts for 11 per cent of Ujjivan's total portfolio) a senior manager focused on an affected branch and helped it cope with the situation. The staff faced threats in many areas they visited, so some of them were hesitant to visit customers. However, the special attention bore fruit and customers with the right disposition understood the reality and whoever could, like those with bank accounts to which their salaries were deposited, started repaying. Slowly, after a time, branch staff started going into areas, accompanied by staff from other functions like vigilance. Centre meetings again began to be held, though attendance had come down.

But even as things began to get better Karnataka was hit by aggressive third-party activity by small organizations and local politicians. As a result, initially north Karnataka districts like Belgaum, Bijapur, and Bagalkot were affected and then—most significantly and the least expected—Bengaluru. In the districts, drought was already a major issue, with 139 talukas out of 173 declared as drought affected. In 2016 there were several suicides, with inability to repay loans from cooperatives and other banks being cited as reasons. The local leaders, in whom largely uneducated borrowers have implicit faith, tried to link several issues—demonetization, no jobs, no wages, and drought—and demanded that loans be waived. By that time, the RBI directive of 60 days' provisioning relaxation came and was widely misunderstood. Even a section of the media wrote that RBI had given a 60-day loan repayment holiday. Customers were completely misguided and started bringing newspaper clippings to centre meetings and asking: 'If RBI has given this relaxation, why are you forcing us to pay?' Plus, there were some customers who simply sought to take advantage of the confusion and not repay instalments.

Pradeep B., head of MSE loans, lists three specific sets of events. Dalit leaders from Bagalkot wanted to contest the next elections and thought this a good opportunity to come before the people and fight for them. Customers from this close-knit community thus started looking at local leaders who were asking for loan waivers as heroes. In the Chikkodi taluka in Belgaum district, a lady had taken 60 ghost loans through borrowers and when repayment difficulties emerged, took advantage of the situation, organized rallies of 300–400 borrowers before the offices of the deputy commissioner and tahsildar, and sent them request letters to waive loans. This had some impact in Belgaum district.

But by far the most significant troubles in the south happened in Bengaluru, mostly in minority-dominated areas. In the area served by Ujjivan's KB Sandra branch, where around 60 per cent of customers are minorities, a few leaders spread rumours that a particular MFI was closing down. Plus, the leaders alleged that since MFIs had distributed loans with black money, the demonetization and drive against black money meant the borrowers did not have to worry about repayment. People were charged Rs 300 to Rs 400 for a form, a photocopy of a simple letter signed by them and addressed to Narendra Modi, with a copy of their loan card attached to it. This form requested a waiver as the borrower found it difficult to repay the loan. All those whose names eventually appeared in the list (of those who signed the form) would not have to repay, said the leaders.

Across Bengaluru and adjoining talukas, Muslim customers with strong community links started approaching these leaders. When MFIs initiated a public information campaign, the local leaders organized rallies and announced that microfinance loans were being waived.

There were two organizations, Praja Vimochana C (PVC) and Chandrasekar Azad Union, which distributed pamphlets and organized small rallies every alternate day. They also called on the tehsildar who organized a meeting of MFIs, customers, and the local leaders. There, MFI representatives explained what microfinance meant, under which act MFIs were working, and the fact that they were regulated by RBI. The tehsildar told MFI representatives that as customers were under genuine difficulties, they needed some time to repay.

Who were the lower level leaders actively campaigning against MFI loan repayment? They have a Congress connection in Bengaluru and a BJP connection in north Karnataka where Dalit parties are active in three districts. In Bagalkot and Bijapur, it is mainly leaders without any political affiliations. However, these parties had no direct involvement in the actual happenings.

In Bengaluru, where incomes are high, there is a concentration of MFIs and some overlending. Many customers are housemaids and gar- ment factory workers. In the first couple of months after demonetization they did not get their full salary. Many were paid a small sum for basic needs and employers directly paid for rations, which led to a cash crunch initially. Customers started first arranging for essential payments and postponing loan repayment. Also, in the initial stages of demonetization, RBI's cash supply to Bengaluru was less, as historically, the city has had a high proportion of cashless transactions. This caused Bengaluru to be worse off than other parts of Karnataka. After the cash crunch was over, the situation would have improved, but for the rallies, which had come down in the districts by early February, but not in Bengaluru. The impact of the rallies can be gauged by what happened in a branch in Chitradurga, where there was 90 per cent plus collection in November. After a big rally was held there in December, repayment dropped to 70 per cent. Industrial areas like Peenya and Yelahanka in the city told a similar tale.

Unlike in semi-urban areas in districts, in Bengaluru the branches are close to each other—one every 5 km. So rumours spread fast. Also, when paying customers on the same street find that some have not paid but appear none the worse for it, they too refrain from paying. Besides, some MFIs went in for classical window dressing—regularizing the accounts of defaulters by giving a fresh loan to repay the previous one and then leaving something in the hands of the borrower.

When these ground developments took place during the latter part of November, MFIs, through AKMI, started approaching the authorities. The MFIN president spoke to the Karnataka chief secretary who wrote to deputy commissioners (DCs) asking them to sensitize people that no loan waiver had been announced by either the government or RBI. Under the AKMI banner, MFIN officials met all the DCs and superintendents of police of affected districts and the DGP Bengaluru as protesters went so far as to attack MFI branches, Janalakshmi's KB Sandra branch being one such target. AKMI organized press conferences in affected districts like Hubli, Bijapur, Belgaum, Bagalkot, and Bengaluru.

THE EASTERN REGION

After demonetization, the eastern region led the rest of the country in repayments, not just for Ujjivan but other MFIs too. (Bandhan had done better than the rest as they could accept old currency notes, having become a bank.) In south Bengal, says Vibhas Chandra, regional business manager, microfinance and branch banking at Ujjivan, borrowers unable to repay on time had mostly been hit by the travails of small units manufacturing garments and leather goods. Their business was hurt badly because their customers, bigger businessmen mostly located in the Burra Bazaar area of Kolkata, tried to take advantage of the whole situation by paying their customers in old currency. They also gave orders for the next three-to-six months and paid in old currency notes to get rid of their stock of black money. Ujjivan's borrowers, employees of the small manufacturers, were helpless as they were paid in demonetized notes, which Ujjivan would not accept. Hence, repayment initially suffered.

Another set of customers, mostly in north Bengal, in areas served by Ujjivan branches in Malda, Raigunj, Kaliagunj, and Siliguri, was influenced by external factors—local politicians or those who had a vested interest in gaming the system. They tried to influence borrowers not to pay by spreading rumours about MFIs closing down or RBI asking customers not to repay. Customers were swayed by two factors. They believe in their local leaders and also have implicit faith in the printed word. In this case, the local leaders distributed mostly anonymous pamphlets giving wrong information, like closure of MFIs and RBI asking borrowers not to repay.

But after the initial setback, customers started to repay instalments. By February, most customers were two-to-three instalments behind, as despite wanting to pay up they were unable to garner three EMIs at one go. So the Ujjivan staff asked them to repay only one EMI to begin with, to continue the relationship, and repay the rest whenever they could. Their credit performance would not be affected and they would get further loans. But some customers who sat on the fence to see if any loan waiver came along took more time to restart payments.

The problems of cash management referred to earlier in the book have come to haunt Ujjivan along with demonetization. Initially, it could not withdraw more than Rs 50,000 from the bank in a day, whereas it needed Rs 10–12 lakhs every day to disburse loans to its customers. Hence it decided, as mentioned earlier, to hold the cash received through EMIs and disburse this to new customers. Compared to retaining Rs 1 lakh at a branch, post demonetization the cash holding had gone up to anything between Rs 10–30 lakh. To safeguard the cash Ujjivan has had to station round-the-clock armed security guards but that still wasn't enough to prevent at least a couple of heists. One took place in the Bandel branch in West Bengal, in which Rs 24 lakh were gone. In another incident in the Gandhi Maidan branch in Bihar's capital Patna, Rs 8 lakh were lost. Other than straightforward cash loss, additional costs were also being incurred—the cost of posting security, staff time spent in counting the cash retained in branches, and investment income foregone by holding idle cash overnight at branches instead of depositing it in bank accounts.

As the demonetization impact worked itself out, it became clear how socio-economic factors affected borrower behaviour. Default is more among the minorities who are at the bottom of the pyramid—'they are the poorest customers we have'—and tied to the kind of business prevalent there. These deal mostly in cash. Then there is the fact that there is more community bonding among minorities and they tend to follow the decision of their community leaders. Customers sometimes say, 'We want to pay but if we do so, we will create problems for ourselves in our community and with our leaders.' But minority customers' repayment behaviour is also not monolithic. For example, in the Northeast and a predominantly minority area of Jamshedpur like Mango, repayment is normal. This is contrary to the situation in the Baridhi area of Jamshedpur, which is also minority dominated but much poorer and hence, more vulnerable. 'To effectively serve the minority community we have to rethink our products and also maintain good relations with their local leaders,' says Chandra.

Sneh Thakur, head of credit, echoes the concern over the default rate among minority customers being on the higher side. Ujjivan has close to 13 per cent exposure. In UP, where some branches have over 40–50 per cent minority concentration, their default has had quite an impact. 'A relook at strategy, as far as minority concentration in different geographical areas is concerned, has to be done with great care as the experience is not uniform. Even in UP, post demonetization other communities have also defaulted. As an SFB, lending to customers in the priority sector will mean lending to these very customers. We have to walk a tight rope and identify the areas where credit discipline has deteriorated and minimize our exposure in those areas with time.'

In coping with demonetization, Chandra finds that some fundamental truths about the microfinance business have been re-learnt and better understood. MFIs are for-profit organizations but have a social role too. In discharging this, 'we do good but are also very vulnerable. Despite following all the rules we are asked by the local administrations to explain why customers are complaining. Three or four of our staff are constantly being summoned by various officials—DM, DSP, BDO, SP—and have to keep reiterating that whatever we are doing is legal and we as businesses have been licenced by RBI.' MFIs keep having to fight against a lack of understanding among people about their role. 'Officials often treat us like a chit-fund company like Saradha or Sahara [which is under a cloud] and are suspicious of us as they cannot categorize us as either a bank or an insurance company.'

The demonetization crisis has inevitably brought to mind the previous big crisis faced by the industry, in Andhra Pradesh. As Chandra notes, 'We have found yet again that if you stand by your customers, they stand by you. We have data on every customer and what challenge she faces and are giving them time accordingly. This is helping them repay and our repayment rate is better than that of many of our competitors.' Just as there was a shakeout in the industry after the Andhra crisis, there is likely to be another after the demonetization crisis is over. Earlier, customers had little choice. Now, there are more MFIs to choose from, and what's more, a borrower cannot take loans from more than two MFIs. So for an MFI or micro-lender (an SFB is one), the quality of customer service will be very important.

But there is also virgin territory to be tapped. Our conversation took place at the opening of a new Ujjivan branch in an unbanked area near Kolkata proper. There are seven–eight bank branches on the way (this is a de facto urban area categorized as rural) to a point of about 4 km before this branch. Then after the Ujjivan branch, there is no bank branch for 7 km on an important artery that takes people to Rajarhat. People in the area travel at least 4 km to withdraw money from an ATM. But Ujjivan is going deep into rural areas also, as in Habra, where it is opening four rural branches in unbanked areas, two of them near the Bangladesh border. There, in a radius of 13 km, there is no ATM, forget about a branch. There, people are travelling 20 km to withdraw money from a bank branch. The uneven spread of banking explains some of the trauma that MFIs have faced in the aftermath of demonetization.

One of the greatest gains from demonetization for Ujjivan is validation of the rigorous manner in which it decides which geographies to operate in. In West Bengal, Shantipur in Howrah district has been affected by demonetization. Ujjivan had rolled back its branch there three years ago. In Howrah district overall, Ujjivan had, in recent years, maintained a limited presence with five branches, when others MFIs had multiple that number of branches. But even the limited presence was subsequently reduced. Four branches were rolled back and customers transferred to nearby branches. In Jharkhand, Ujjivan has surveyed, but not opened branches in Godda, Daltongunj, Palamu, and Giridhi. In the last it had even taken up premises. Similarly, in Bihar, areas surveyed but avoided are Arrah, Buxar, Sewan, Chhapra, and Sheohar. Post demonetization, it is clear that it was good not to have gone into these areas. This underlines the greatest gain for Ujjivan from the Andhra crisis, having suffered low-impact damages since it was not present in that state.

FINANCIAL IMPACT

To cope with the external shock caused by demonetization to the microfinance sector, Ujjivan has had to change its provisioning norms. Thakur describes the norms existing till demonetization came as 'fairly conservative'. While relaxing these Ujjivan will ensure that it will be 'extra cautious compared to the rest of the industry'. Normally, Ujjivan starts providing for an NPA on the eighth day of it becoming overdue. 'While we will continue with these norms for AUM [assets under management] that were in place prior to November 2016, the portfolio affected due to demonetization will attract differential provisioning considering the 90-day leeway RBI has given on sub-standard asset classification of these assets.' Adoption of existing norms as is would be uncalled for because the customer, apart from those who are politically motivated, is genuinely impacted. 'The idea is to provide sufficiently so that in the states where we are currently [in early 2017] facing problems, we will be sufficiently covered to absorb the losses. We had to take a stance midway and revise our norms accordingly for both group and individual loans. All accounts which were overdue prior to 1 November have been downgraded as per our existing policy.' With the new asset classification, Ujjivan will provide for adequately to cover losses that may come up, if at all, across impacted places. 'With the asset differentiation, Ujjivan will continue to be profitable but not as per its budget or plan.'

Demonetization took a toll on Ujjivan's business during FY 2016–17. 'Overall, we have done 25 per cent less business than what we would have,' says Rajat Kumar Singh, head of strategy and planning. Earlier, it was looking at its assets (loans) growing at 30–35 per cent year on year. Demonetization took that number to 18 per cent. November to March saw a marginal fall in the loan portfolios.

Bad debts increased over the period. Ujjivan's gross non-performing assets (GNPA) as the financial year ended, stood at 3.8 per cent. 'In micro-finance, generally there is negligible GNPA. Hence we have adopted fairly aggressive provisioning norms. In December, Ujjivan was the only MFI to indicate that there could be losses. There will be some losses, more than what we have projected, but it won't be detrimental, won't pull us down. Our profits will be impacted. Maybe they will not be as robust as what we had expected earlier in the year but they will be better than last year.' In the event, net profit rose by 17.5 per cent in 2016–17, compared to more than doubling in the previous year.

Other than affecting financials for one year, demonetization would have a longer-term impact too. It gave a boost to digitization. Adds Singh, 'Given the customer segment that we are in, against the earlier plan to go in for digitization in the second year onwards as an SFB, we have to prioritize this as there is a lot of awareness and the government is spending a lot of money to make customers aware of the benefits of going digital. So from financial 2018 we will move to the UPI [Unified Payment Interface] App, Bharat Bill Payment System, and such systems which will help us go digital faster.' Ujjivan will also be able to offer its customers all the services that other e-wallet companies do, like phone and DTH recharge, electricity payment, school fees, and travel-related payment.

Secondly, in a more fundamental way, Ujjivan would have to carefully review its overall microfinance business. It would have to avoid all the geographies with poor credit histories post demonetization. 'We also have to review the impact of demonetization on customer psyche in a permanent way. We are in the process of redesigning the whole microfinance operation,' says Singh. Microfinance strategy will go through a significant change in product, geography, and channels like the use of mobile phones and ATMs. In this Ujjivan will be helped by the fact that it has now become a bank, and is therefore not bound by a lot of RBI regulation for microfinance and has the ability to give customers more. The housing business would remain more or less the same. 'With all the sops the government was giving, chances are that our business in affordable housing will be better.' It is the MSME business which could suffer temporarily because of the turmoil that demonetization had created. To sum up: the long-term impact on housing and liabilities (bank customer deposits) is likely to be positive, and on microfinance and MSE business it could be neutral (significant strategy change is on the way). 'Maybe for one or two quarters we have to go slow, look back, and reflect. The long-term cost to Ujjivan will be, perhaps, two- to three-quarters lost.'

LESSONS FROM DEMONETIZATION

Demonetization has set before MFIs two kinds of lessons. One is it has highlighted an unlearnt lesson from the past. Industry veteran Mahajan points out that for the sake of growth at a very fast pace, some MFIs have been lending recklessly. The default that has taken place in pockets and areas was not just because of demonetization, but also because people were over-leveraged. Then when the shock of demonetization came, they just tipped over. Unfortunately, despite the fact that this kind of a situation was also there in Andhra Pradesh, some of the players did not absorb the lesson. Echoing Mahajan, Ghosh says, 'There will always be one or two players who will ruin the market. Aggressive, excessive lending continues, mainly by lending without proper assessment and giving very large loans which are beyond the capacity of typical MFI borrowers to repay.'

Pointing to a new insight gleaned from demonetization, Ghosh adds, 'We have to be sympathetic towards our customer and our interaction and contact with her has to be continuous. We have to make sure we don't aggravate the situation.' A single-minded pursuit of a '99 per cent repayment track record, come hell or high water, is only going to lead to mass default'. This is something that MFIs have had to learn the hard way, because earlier, they did not have much experience of mass defaults. Now that they are wiser, they have to change their strategy and cannot continue with doing business the way it was done in the past.

As for the industry as a whole, the condition of small MFIs will be troubled. After the loss inflicted by demonetization, they will have to recapitalize themselves but, seeing their vulnerability, banks and institutions will be very careful about lending to them in the future. This will prevent them from rebuilding their businesses.

It is not just smaller MFIs which will be affected but also the MFI business in areas where there is a large concentration of small businesses. This has been highlighted from the experience of parts of UP and Maharashtra, which have faced serious problems. Western UP, for example, is economically more vibrant but dominated by small businesses—manufacturing cricket bats, brassware, locks, leather goods. As Ghosh sees it, 'something like demonetization impacts the unorganized sector the most. Mr [Narendra] Modi realized that employment for the masses who come in from the countryside is provided by the micro and small businesses. The government had taken such good measures like MUDRA (Micro Units Development and Refinance Agency Bank), to promote these sectors, but unfortunately, demonetization impacted them the worst and consequently set back the whole process of providing gainful employment and livelihood through MSME businesses. I think that will have a long-term negative impact.'

18

Light at Tunnel's End

Despite the trauma of demonetization, Ujjivan stuck to its agenda and transformed itself into the Ujjivan Small Finance Bank on 6 February 2017. It was half a step forward for Ghosh who, in 2005, wanted to start a bank to serve the financially excluded masses but in the absence of a banking licence had to settle for setting up an NBFC—Ujjivan Financial Services. Now, by becoming an SFB it would be able to offer the entire range of banking services to its customers but would also have to live by certain restrictions. The other half step that remained ahead for Ghosh and the Ujjivan team was to use the provision in the SFB licence which held open the option to convert into a full-fledged mass-market bank in five years.

The mood at the inauguration ceremony in Bengaluru was celebratory—not so much 'we shall overcome' as 'we have overcome'. It was marked by the presence of the global founder of microfinance, Muhammad Yunus—who had started on the journey 40 years ago and set up Grameen Bank in Bangladesh—and two other occurrences. One was the screening of a film, *Paiso Ki ABCD*, which carried forward Ujjivan's distinctive work in financial literacy. It wove the tale of a mithai shop owner Murli who is hit by a burglary in his house which makes him lose over Rs 30,000 cash. This, because he refused to go to a bank as, he firmly held, they didn't treat people like him with respect. Eventually, he is won over by his wife's sister who introduces the couple to the new style of banking that organizations like Ujjivan bring and happily embraces the banking experience.

The second and cerebral part of the inauguration was a discussion by several leaders of microfinance who looked forward to identify the opportunities and challenges that lay ahead for MFIs and SFBs. They also looked back to learn lessons from the journey of microfinance so far and fleshed out the type of regulation needed to make microfinance grow and prosper. These made up a key takeaway—an intellectual roadmap for the sector.

The phrase 'financial inclusion' was not in the RBI's lexicon till 2004–5 but the drive for it was there all along, recalled B. Mahapatra, former executive director of RBI. Nationalizing the Imperial Bank of India to create State Bank of India, major nationalization of banks in 1969, experimenting with regional rural banks in 1976, cooperative banks, and later, local area banks, all point to the different permutations and combinations which were tried out. But RBI knew that 'something was missing'. At the same time, there were the MFIs, very young in the field, and NBFCs doing quite well. They could be more informal, nimble-footed, flexible, and close to the ground.

There were several reports that talked about a small bank, a regional bank which could cater to the needs of local people and bring about financial inclusion. As MFIs were working only on the credit side, the idea of a small bank offering the whole gamut of banking services was thought of. When Raghuram Rajan became governor and Nachiket Mor a director on RBI's central board, the idea of creating a 'differentiated' bank—a term not present in Indian banking law but created by RBI—came up. The aim was to create a player to cater to a niche market out of the existing law itself. To make credit more affordable, RBI would allow the new banks to accept deposits and thus reduce their cost of funds. As many of the MFIs were already pan-Indian, they would not be geographically restricted 'but confined to lending to small people and in small doses'. The idea was to simultaneously strengthen them by giving them opportunities on the liabilities side and bringing them under RBI regulation so that they could command the respect that a bank did. Eight of the 10 SFB licences went to MFIs, so that by doing more of what they were already doing, they could deliver a critical mass.

But what this recent innovative burst could not undo was RBI's long-term regulatory stance, which microfinance pioneer Mahajan had much to find fault with. 'The regulator is 20 years behind. Regulation is always behind practice and the regulator needs to learn; being two years behind is fine but not 20. Everything that is cutting edge about the regulator like National Payments Corporation of India (NPCI) has moved out of it. What is left behind is people who are risk-averse, innovation-averse, and standing in the way.' He recalled that the business correspondents' regulation was first drafted in 2006 but was still extant today. 'For 10 years, RBI had stalled each one of them [clauses] paragraph by paragraph till it finally arrived at the 2016 regulation.' His point was that 'if the regulator also becomes modern, digital, learning, and everything we relate the IT world to, then we can control those epidemics (in the microfinance sector) of overborrowing and overlending. If we can do algorithmic stock trading, why can't we do algorithmic regulation? The RBI knew for two years that overlending was taking place in Andhra but did nothing.'

Muhammad Yunus added his voice to the need for the right type of regulation in the future for microfinance to grow and prosper by observing that 'we call it bank, the Grameen Bank, but we don't do everything that other banks do.' He drew the analogy of American and European football. 'Both are called football but are so different. If you wanted to hire a referee from American football to manage European football, it will be a disaster.' Microcredit and microcredit banks call themselves banks but are so different from regular banks. 'I try to make fun of it by saying, when we needed rules for Grameen Bank we looked at how banks did it and then did the opposite. Till today Grameen Bank does not have a single branch in any city or town in Bangladesh after 40 years. When they said you need to be regulated, I said definitely but we need a microfinance regulatory authority. It took us a long time to convince the government but Bangladesh has a separate microfinance regulatory authority. The governor is the same but everything else is different. If you keep it under the same regulatory authority, sooner or later you will become the same as everybody else. This is what we do not want to be.'

Mahajan seconded this, adding, 'We need a different law, regulatory framework for institutions that work with the hitherto excluded. You cannot use the same Banking Regulation Act, 1949 (without amending it) and the RBI Act, 1934 to run a new generation of institutions and to meet today's challenges in 2017. We need a regulatory revolution first before a digital revolution can make a difference.'

Mahapatra held his ground by pointing out how RBI had innovated while having to work within constraints: 'The very idea of a differentiated bank, despite there being nothing in the law, is a reality today. This is a regulatory innovation in the sense that the same law which enables RBI to give licence to a (regular or universal) bank also licences Ujjivan Small Finance Bank. What RBI has done without going in for a new law or amendment to an existing law is to give a banking licence under section 22 with one hand and taken away with the other hand in terms of licencing conditions—you can do this this this, you cannot do this this this.' Pointing out a reality, he added, 'If you went for a new law or (tried to) amend the existing law, it would have taken ages and the small finance bank would never have been born today.'

When Mahajan pointed to the need for the regulator to learn from the world of information technology, he was referring to the brave new world of opportunity for microfinance that Sharad Sharma, a fellow of iSPIRT, the advocacy group for the software products industry, had outlined. When Aadhaar was on the cusp of hitting the magic number of enrolling a million people every day in 2013, the conversation was: now what? This led to taking on the challenge—'What if we can fix payments'. The concept was that just as one can send a mail to a person by knowing only his email address without knowing where his server is, could you do that for payments? 'There was a belief that here in India we could make this happen.' He attributed its current absence to the incumbent system used elsewhere in the west by credit card players who were not very strong in this domain and so prevented this from happening. 'I am happy to tell you that earlier last year (2016) the Unified Payments System, run by NPCI, came into play. By using Bhim or other apps, all you need to know is my payment address to send me money without having to know which bank I am with. I can send you money and you will receive it in the same way. This system does not exist anywhere else in the world. It is a uniquely Indian system and it is mostly free. It is also not so outlandish. If the exponential growth since then continues, then by April [he was speaking in February] we will have more people transacting using the wallet-Unified Payments Interface than using the debit card system which has been around for 25 years.'

Pointing to the significance of this innovation, Sharma said, 'The reason why this matters is because it enables something called flow-based lending. This lets the mithai shop owner in the financial literacy film shown earlier, demonstrate to Ujjivan (on the basis of his digital payments data)—look this was my earning through last week, and the week before, and the week before. You may not want to take a long-term bet on me but give me a one-week loan without a collateral as you can predict what my earnings will be next week.'

Ujjivan is now in a position to give that loan without a collateral by looking at the last two–three weeks' data. Added Sharma, 'As a bank if you can see that in the first week of the loan his earning was similar to what it was in the week before, then you can now rotate that loan for another week and yet another week. Now giving a loan in this way is entirely possible on the phone and it will cost you only Rs 4 to process that loan.' For that mithai shop owner Murli, using electronic 'know your customer' (EKYC) to establish his identity does not cost much money. Reliance Jio has shown that it works, with 97.2 per cent of their first-time KYC requests succeeding. Murli can also sign the loan agreement on the phone itself. Now 11 per cent of the rental agreements in Bengaluru are signed using a system called eSign (online electronic signature service). 'India will eventually be the largest user of eSign in the world because it is only in India that you do not need anything other than a mobile phone to eSign a document in a way that is the same as your wet signature. So now, Murli can actually process a loan just as easily on the phone as you saw in the film with bank-account opening. By reducing the tenure you can make him eligible for a collateral-free loan in a way that was not possible earlier. So we think this system will power an increase in flow-based lending.'

How big will that be? Sharma said that as a result of discussions within the government, RBI, and iSPIRT, the target for 2017 has been fixed at 100 million using UPI. The target being discussed for flow-based lending in the next 18 months is Rs 80,000 crore. India is starved for credit among micro-entrepreneurs and small businessmen and there wasn't a system available up till now to deliver credit to them in a way that is not only cheap but is also very accountability focused. If a person does not return that loan his credit rating will be affected and his ability to raise capital impaired. 'We think we will create a society which will be very different from the one today because you will see alternative lending, digital lending, change in a radical fashion small businessmen and micro entrepreneurs. That is the world coming up in the future. People who have the highest default rate have so far secured the lowest interest rate. We gave 70 years to the regulators to solve this problem. All we are saying is, give technologists seven years to find a solution. Because ultimately it is an information asymmetry problem which will get solved not only in India but in other parts of the world as well.'

Rajiv Lall, MD and CEO of IDFC Bank, which along with Bandhan, had earlier secured a universal banking licence, underlined the thought process by adding: 'Nandan [Nilekani] says India is a country which will be data rich before it will be "rich" rich. So the democratization of savings and lending will rely on data generated by millions of people who are included into the transactional system. That data is going to be the currency instead of forms and collaterals.'

Underlining the enormity of change that was being foreseen, Mahajan said: 'This is not a linear progression but a phase shift. The microfinance sector, which started in the 1990s, has even today not touched a USD 10 billion outstanding mark. It was about to get there but then demonetization happened and it has fallen. This, in a nation where the financial sector has touched a trillion dollars. So just 1 per cent of the total outstanding has reached the poor after all this effort. This is after Professor Yunus proved to the whole world 40 years ago that the poor are credit worthy and 20 years after it was proved to the world that institutions which lent to the poor were equity worthy.'

Digitization will greatly help. 'But if we look at the film,' added Mahajan, 'if Murli's wife was not able to get that loan of Rs 4,000 from her sister, the kids would have been pulled out of school. When the Indira Gandhi Institute of Development Research did a study three years after the Andhra crisis, they found that the per capita expenditure of Andhra's poor had come down by 19 per cent; of that 17 per cent was on food and 43 per cent on education. Microfinance is a way of enabling the poor to get out of the poverty trap and digitization is a way of greatly reducing the transaction cost and significantly reducing the risk, particularly if you seamlessly link with the credit bureau and also build the financial history.'

It was left to Mary Ellen Iskenderian, president and CEO of Women's World Banking, to outline the concerns that remained while taking justifiable pride in what had been achieved. 'The Aadhaar system has eliminated the issue of identification which plagues so many emerging markets.' But there are concerns. The initial reason for expanding the remit of the microfinance bank was to allow savings deposits. But, 'who are the savers in households? They are, by and large, women. One of the concerns we at Women's World Banking have when we look at financial inclusion is, how are men and women going to be able to share this extraordinary opportunity equally? We saw an enormous increase in account penetration in India during 2011–14, to 53 per cent. But unfortunately, we also saw the gap between men and women in financial inclusion increase—from 17 per cent to 20 per cent, precisely because women did not have access to the technology. The gap between Aadhaar registration and mobile phone ownership largely comprises women. It is not just a lack of access but also understanding and awareness of how to use that technology to its best purposes.'

To have an idea of what needs to be done, Professor Yunus sought to put microfinance in a historical context. The first issue is: 'Financial services is the oxygen of the economy. The mass of the people cannot breathe that oxygen. Economically they are dead. It is not about democratization, it is about survival. Our whole discussion and policy making should be addressing this issue. The second issue which worries me in recent years is wealth concentration. All the wealth of the world is concentrated in a few hands and we are hearing about this year after year. My question is, who makes it happen? Is it that they are bad people? It is the system that we have created which takes all the oxygen to them. That's where the role of financial institutions comes in—carrying all the oxygen to a few people. So it is not simply creating some microcredit at the bottom, it is total reorganization of the system so that it does not become a one-way process where everything goes to the top. We have to redesign the whole financial structure itself which is completely destructive, harmful, dangerous. Today, it is a ticking time bomb. If we don't do that then all our society, economics will fall apart. The third point I wish to make is the ownership of the whole thing that we do and this is one we have done [in Grameen Bank] right from the beginning, making the borrowers the owners of the bank so that it does not go outside, stays completely inside. All the controversies came because someone is taking away our money.'

The truly radical idea to emerge from the whole discussion, outlined by Mahajan and Yunus, looked at what shape microfinance would take in the future. Mahajan bemoaned the fact that 'the microfinance world is still stuck with the one product that Professor Yunus designed 40 years ago. The world of microfinance needs micro-equity, micro-insurance, far more than it needs microcredit. My belief is digitization will make a great breakthrough in those two areas. On overborrowing and very quickly to sub-prime, those two can also be much more carefully monitored through digital means.'

Yunus sought to anticipate the issues lying ahead of microfinance by noting a key one facing the sector in Bangladesh where, in 40 years, it is now in its second generation and so 'we have to look at the young ones coming out in the families of Grameen borrowers'. There, an attempt is on to completely redesign the system, 'saying, don't look for jobs, jobs is an obsolete idea, this is just to destroy yourself. A job kills your creative power. So be a job creator rather than a job seeker.' So Grameen Bank is helping create 'social business funds, offer them equity. You come up with a business idea and we will put our equity into it. You make it successful, return our money, and you are on. We point out, with the Grameen Bank educational loan, you went to school, you went to college, you have a good education, and you are looking for jobs, and sitting there, as there are no jobs in the country. I say, that's the first mistake you did, you went to college. You shouldn't have done it. You should have done what your mother did. Your illiterate mother did a smarter thing than you did. The smart illiterate mother took a 30–40-dollar loan and went into business. That's what she did in the last 20–30 years and she has grown on that. And now you are telling me that you have to wait for someone to give you a job. If your illiterate mother can be an entrepreneur, why can't you? Shame on you. Why don't you go back to your mother and learn from her how to be an entrepreneur? Entrepreneurship is the future for you. So, we are expanding into giving equity to some young people with business ideas. Whether that is the right path or the wrong path, it is for you to judge but my point is, we have to pay attention to the new generation coming up within the families of microfinance recipients. It is a mission-driven thing, it is not where you make money. You solve the problem that you see right now, otherwise it will kill us all.'

To give a focus to the diverse ideas shared, Ghosh brought together three strands of thought: the specific path before Ujjivan, the lesson learnt from demonetization, and the radical thought outlined by Mahajan and

Yunus. 'As a small finance bank we will journey in unchartered waters. We have done a lot of research using a lot of technology but it will still be hit and miss as we go along and do not know if we will succeed. Our objective at the end of five years is that RBI also permits us to apply for a universal bank licence. It is not that we want to be another HDFC Bank or Yes Bank. What we really like to do and where we still see a huge gap is in mass-market banking. I hope that after five years we become a leading mass-market bank in India. That's our vision.'

Then Ghosh tied up the lesson learnt from demonetization with the radical thoughts of Mahajan and Yunus, which have the potential to change the very basic model of microfinance. For it to deliver, it has to shift from providing just debt in the form of working capital to equity too. He put it all in a financial framework by explaining to this writer that to support entrepreneurship, it is necessary to provide entrepreneurs with not just debt, like working capital. 'There has to be a system by which long-term debt capital is also provided to them (microfinance customers) to an extent, as for any business. After demonetization, we MFIs are continuing to try to get back the loan we have given, but if we had provided them long-term debt then that would have been a shock absorber for them and supported them through this period. And if they lost some equity we would have also had to take a haircut. If a portion of the financing is in long-term debt then the pressure of repaying it is not there and customers can cope with such external shocks, partly by skipping dividend.' That is the new horizon ahead.

Index

About the Author

Subir Roy went to Calcutta Boys' School and read Economics at Presidency College, Kolkata, India. He has spent four decades in journalism at senior positions in leading Indian publications. His key interests are public policy, information technology, affordable healthcare, and urban issues. He loves to travel, particularly to the north Indian hills, is a self-confessed foodie, and was a keen amateur photographer until digital photography became ubiquitous. He is the author of *Made in India: A Study of Emerging Competitiveness* (2005).